GHOSTS
IN THE
MACHINE

GHOSTS
IN THE
MACHINE

Women and Cultural Policy in
Canada and Australia

Garamond Press

Acknowledgements

Many friends and colleagues in Australia have made my encounters with their country rewarding and enjoyable. I would especially like to thank Annette Van den Bosch and all our collaborators, Hart Cohen at the University of West Sydney, Kathe Boehringer at Macquarie University, and Paulette Montaigne, Canadian High Commission, Canberra. Thanks also to Garamond Press and to Rick McCormack of the Simon Fraser University School of Communication for technical assistance.

Alison Beale, Vancouver, November 1997

To my co-editor, Alison Beale, for her friendship, research and liaison while on two Fellowship visits to Australia; to Garamond Press editor Aida Edemariam for her precise editing and helpful suggestions; to the Australian contributors, Patricia Gilliard, Deborah Stevenson, Elizabeth Gertsakis and Jenni Barret for their friendship and professionalism throughout the process of preparing this book.

Annette Van Den Bosch, Melbourne, December 1997

Printed and bound in Canada

Garamond Press Ltd.
67 Mowat Ave., Ste. 144
Toronto, Ontario
M6K 3E3

ISBN 0-920059-29-5

Canadian Cataloguing in Publication Data

Main entry under title:

Ghosts in the machine: women and cultural policy in Canada and Australia

Includes bibliographical references.
ISBN 0-920059-29-5

1. Feminism and the arts - Canada. 2. Feminism and the arts - Australia. 3. Canada - Cultural policy. 4. Australia - Cultural policy. I. Beale, Alison C. M. II. Van Den Bosch, Annette.

NX180.F4G46 1998   700'.82   C97-932732-6

Distributed in Australia by:

St Clair Press Pty. Ltd.
P.O. Box 287, Rozelle,
NSW 2039

Contents

Contributors

Jennifer Barrett teaches in the Department of Art History, University of Western Sydney, Nepean. She is currently researching visuality, public space, democracy, and the public sphere. She has worked as an arts consultant/researcher in the area of cultural policy, in arts advocacy organizations in New South Wales, and in local government.

Alison Beale is an Associate Professor in the School of Communication at Simon Fraser University, Vancouver, and has also taught film and communication at the Université du Québec à Montréal. Her current teaching and research focus on the history of ideas in communication, and on Canadian and comparative cultural policies. Alison is a past president of the Canadian Communication Association and has served on the boards of cultural organizations and comunications journals. Alison held visiting fellowships at the University of Western Sydney (1993) and Macquarie University (1995). She is currently researching the representation of the public interest in European Union cultural and communication policies.

Monika Kin Gagnon is a Vancouver-based writer and curator. She has published on art, culture and feminism since 1984 in numerous Canadian publications, is a co-founder of *border/lines* and Public Access artists and writers' collectives, and is the former editor of Parallelogramme. She has been the Director of Artspeak Gallery, and was co-curator of *Rx: Let's Play Doctor*, *Racing Through Space*, and *topographies: aspects of B.C. art*. She is currently at Simon Fraser University's School of Communication writing her doctorate on representations of race in children's culture.

Annette Van Den Bosch is an art historian with a PhD in Fine arts from the University of Sydney. She is the director of graduate programs in arts administration at the national Centre for Australian Studies, Monash University, Clayton, Victoria. Her previous appointments were at the Australian Film, Television and Radio School, Sydney, and in art schools, and she has been a member of boards and comittees of the Australia Council and the Schools Commission. In 1994 and 1996 she was a Visiting Scholar in the Graduate Program in Arts Administration at Columbia University in New York. Her research and publications are on the art market, arts policy and sponsorship in Australia and the United States.

Elizabeth Gertsakis is an Australian artist, curator and author. Exhibitions of her photographic installations include *An Innocent Reading for Origin* (1987), *A Glamorous Private History* (1989), *Sentimental City* (1993), *Beyond Missolonghi* (1994), *Metal to Flesh* (1995) *and Idealism and Deformity* (1997). She is widely represented in Australian public galleries, is participating in the 1998 Adelaide Biennial and is participating in an international exhibition on Republicanism that will be touring the United Kingdom, South Africa, Canada and Australia.

Barbara Godard is an Associate Professor of English, French, Social and Political Thought, and Women's Studies at York University, Toronto. She has published widely on Canadian and Quebec writers and on feminist and literary theory. She is the recipient of the Gabrielle Roy Prize of the Association for Canadian and Quebec Literatures (1988) and the Award of Merit of the Association of Canadian Studies (1995) for her translations and critical writings. She is a founding co-editor of the feminist literary theory periodical *Tessera*, and is editor of numerous works, most recently (with Coomi Vevaina) *Intersexions: Issues of Race and Gender in Canadian Women's Writing* (1995).

Patricia Gillard is Head of the Department of Communication Studies at the Royal Melbourne Institute of Technology University, Melbourne, and Director of the Telecommunications Needs Research Group. In 1994, as a member of the Broadband Services Expert Group, she advised the Prime Minister on Australia's broadband futures, later working on new technology policy with the Office of the Status of Women. She was three years in the position of Head of Research and Development for ABC Television and is currently a Director of the Melbourne Community Television Consortium (Channel 31) and a Member of the Museums Board of Victoria.

Andrea Hull is the Director of the Victoria College of the Arts, Australia's premier arts training institution. She is also a Board member of the Australia-Korea Foundation, Melbourne Theatre Company and the Premier's Council for the Arts, a trustee of the Victoria Arts Centre, a Director of the National Academy of Music and the Chair of the Victorian Arts Tourism Industry Council. From 1988-94 she was the CEO of the Department of the Arts for the State of Western Australia. From 1979 to 1988 she held three directorial positions at the Australia Council: the foundation Director of Strategic Development, which located the arts onto national social and economic agendas; the foundation Director of Policy and Research where she initiated seminal work that substantiated the case for the arts and artists; and the Director of the Communty Arts Board.

Brenda Longfellow is an Associate Professor and the Film Program Coordinator at Atkinson College, York University, Toronto. She has written extensively on Canadian and Quebec feminist cinema in *Cine Tracts*, *CineAction,* and *The Canadian Journal of Film Studies*. She is an award-winning film director, including the documentaries Our Marilyn (1987) and Balkan Journey (1996). She is currently at work on a film biography of the poet Gwendolyn MacEwen.

Andra McCartney has a long-standing research interest in issues of gender, arts and technology. From 1987-92, she established and directed the Science and Technology Careers Workshop at Trent University, Ontario, a residential conference for female high school students. Her Master's thesis in Music (York University, 1994) explores the words and work of fourteen Canadian women composers of electroacoustic music. Her PhD dissertation on Vancouver composer Hildgard Westerkamp will explore themes of identity and epistemology in soundscape composition. Andra is also a sound artist, currently working on a cycle of tone poems that integrate vocal and environmental sounds. Andra also writes music for dance and multimedia performance, and co-hosts a community radio program (CIUT 89.5 Toronto) on soundscape and radio art.

Deborah Stevenson has a PhD in Sociology and is Lecturer in arts and cultural policy in the School of Leisure and Tourism Studies at the University of Technology, Sydney, where she is also the director of the postgraduate Arts Management Program. Dr Stevenson has worked as a cultural planning consultant for local government and been involved actively in local cultural policy development. She has published a number of scholarly articles on cultural and urban policy matters, and her most recent book is *Agendas in Place: Cultural Planning for Cities and Regions.* She is currently writing a book for the University of Queensland Press on arts and cultural policy in Australia since 1983.

Australian and Canadian Cultural Policies: A Feminist Perspective

Annette Van Den Bosch and Alison Beale

Introduction

Since 1990 there have been many productive exchanges between Australia and Canada in the fields of cultural studies and communications.[1] When the idea of our collaboration first came about we were captivated by the similar-but-different situations, issues and analyses shared by Canada and Australia in the sphere of cultural policy, which is our common ground as a communication researcher and a specialist in art history and art markets. For us as for other researchers, superficial cultural resemblances, parallel histories, and familiar legal and constitutional systems soon gave way to the realisation that in fact so much is different and so much needs to be explained in detail. The mirrors that Australia and Canada hold up for each other are also magnifying glasses.

In our explorations of our work we found that we were interested in comparing a number of facets of cultural production and cultural policy in Canada and Australia, from specific cultural forms and their recent development, to the policy process itself. As feminists we had paid close attention to the participation of women in cultural production, in policy, and in research. As we discussed these areas we identified a source of frustration in feminist cultural theory preoccupied with questions of gender and representation, in which policy occasionally appeared as hegemonic discourse but was not subjected to analysis and intervention.[2] On the other hand, in the early 90s both mainstream liberal and neo-marxist cultural policy analysis in Australia and Canada showed remarkably little feminist influence. It was dominated by agendas of national cultural preservation, or by questioning these agendas, and by managing changes in technologies and in cultural markets.[3] To a lesser extent it was concerned with multiculturalism, racism, aboriginal peoples, and community arts. The specifically gender-related concerns of the 1970s came a distant third. Among feminists the representation of women in the media, and the employment of women as cultural producers, critics, and administrators had, rightly, become recognized as more complex, problematic, and inadequate goals than some had originally believed. Nonetheless we felt that dissatisfaction with institutional feminism was only part of the reason why feminist perspectives, which had multiplied during the 1970s and 80s, remained marginal to the agendas and critiques of cultural policy as they were developing in our two nations.

In the 1990s the re-structuring of cultural and social programs in the disappearing welfare state poses special challenges for women and for social minorities. With a focus on the international market as the preferred source of revenue, those cultural industries identified as viable exports, such as feature films, television programs, recorded music, cd-roms and other multi-media technologies receive the greatest outright support from government. Other forms of cultural production, such as craft, the fine and performing arts and community arts, are construed as part of the feminine welfare state sector, as opposed to the export earning, technologised world of the masculine "bottom line".

Ghosts in the Machine, our title, refers to a gender perspective on the economic rationalism and state neo-corporatism that dominate cultural policy in capitalist democracies such as Australia and Canada. What this book has come to represent for us as a project is a twofold approach to cultural policy from a feminist perspective. We want to begin to document the knowledge that different women possess about the politics of culture and by so doing expand the normally very narrow parameters of policy analysis and intervention. The women who have written for this volume have worked as artists, for arts and community-based organizations, and in government, the universities, and broadcasting. Most of us have worked in more than one of these spheres.

Secondly, we offer an attempt to understand the position of women's knowledge of and interest in cultural policy within the conjuncture of global economic change through which our two countries are passing. This period has marked and parallel impacts upon our national cultural policies. We believe that a feminist critique and intervention in cultural policy is an important check on dominant methodology and epistemology and that it provides, in the current context of cultural policy as an instrument in national participation in global and regional markets (ASEAN, APEC, NAFTA), one of the few consistent means of exposing the gendered and undemocratic nature and impact of such policies. What began as part of a movement to establish direct contact between postcolonial English-speaking countries in the field of cultural studies (which was previously dominated by American and British scholars) and to learn something about each other's experience, has come to make even greater sense as we trace the parallels of our national cultural strategies in the context of global economic restructuring.

Cutural Policy from the 60s to the 80s

Canada and Australia are similiar in their colonial heritage, forms of government, recent patterns of immigration, social policies and cultural administration.[4] In the post World War II period Canada has influenced Australian arts and film policies, as well as policies regarding indigenous peoples and multiculturalism. While both countries have grappled with the cultural domination of the United States and Europe, Canada's proximity to the United States has intensified struggles to protect its airwaves and cultural industries. National self-definition has been a key mandate for cultural policy in both countries, and historically, cultural policy has defined issues of cultural representation as *national* issues. But of course representations are determined by forces which are more local, more international, and more problematic (in gender terms, among others) than the official story often suggests. Two of our contributors open up the privileging of "nature" in Canadian and Australian nationalist discourse to critical feminist review. Elizabeth Gertsakis' photo-text plays with concepts of women as a colonial sight/site in Australia. Brenda Longfellow's chapter deals with the contrast between a nationalist account of thematic cohesion in Canadian films, especially in their representation of space, and the actual films of Canadian and Quebec women film-makers. As Longfellow observes, "Feminists working in areas as diverse as postcolonial theory and Eastern European feminism have pointed out how the female body is assigned an absolutely central position within the symbolic regimes of nationalist discourses..."

The politics of representation also need to be looked at alongside questions of employment and economic equity. In both countries current employment and audience profiles in the arts and media show a high participation rate for women as practitioners, administrators and audiences but poor financial rewards, subsidies and sponsorship compared to men.[5] Professional\amateur and metropolitan\community distinctions also correlate to gender. These distinctions are explored in Annette Van Den Bosch's chapter on Australian women artists' careers. Similarly, access to advanced arts and media technologies, and the unequal valuation of knowledge possessed by female and male arts workers, teachers and administrators reflect the ways in which skills are distributed and ranked along gendered lines. Andra McCartney examines this issue in her chapter on Canadian women composers of electroacoustic music.

In the 1960s national cultural development and self-definition were dominant themes in both countries. The centralisation and nationalisation of cultural policy in Australia was formalised in legislation introduced in 1967 by Prime Minister John Gorton. This legislation established the Australian Council for the Arts (later the Australia Council), the Australian Film and Television School, and in 1969 a Creative Development Fund and a Film Investment Fund to revitalise the film and televison industries. Andrea Hull reviews this history in her chapter on the development of public arts funding in Australia.

In Canada in the 1960s there was a parallel expansion in these areas through existing institutions such as the Canadian Broadcasting Corporation and its francophone counterpart Radio Canada, the National Film Board, national and regional museums and galleries, and the Canadian Film Development Corporation (1967). Pressure to create support and protection for Canadian book and periodical publishers, supported by a Royal Commission in Ontario, began to have some effect in Canadian policies by the early 1970s. The Province of Quebec established a Department of Cultural Affairs in 1961, establishing a mandate for that Province in fostering French-language culture in North America, and leading to the establishment of institutions and programs in the following years that mirrored their federal counterparts.[6]

The flowering of cultural expression in both countries in this period was at least as strongly affected by immigration, improving economies, the discovery and marketing of aboriginal arts, and a prevailing spirit of modernism. However, the new or expanded institutions supported by government gave employment and opportunity to creative artists in experimental programs, and the commissions and tenured jobs of artists contributed to the growth of the arts in both countries.

In the late 1960s and 70s, both Canada and Australia underwent political change as a result of the women's movement, multiculturalism and aboriginal rights campaigns, and anti-racism intiatives. In Australia, especially, the Vietnam War was a watershed for the development of a new politics. Aspects of this new politics became institutionalised, for example, in the creation of Studio D, the Women's Studio, at the National Film Board of Canada, and, in both countries, through Royal commissions and government departments concerned with women's rights, and the beginnings of publicly-funded aboriginal broadcasting. The politicization of culture as a result of social movements in the late 1960s represented the beginnings of a move away from Euro-centric and centralised cultural models, a direction in cultural politics that has gained force over the last twenty-five years. As a result of state intervention new identities were reflected for the first time in broadcasting, film and publishing as well as the fine and performing arts. In Canada provinces, notably Quebec, and some municipalities, such as Toronto, expanded their involvement in cultural affairs. Youth, women, immigrants and aboriginal people were targeted for participatory film, broadcasting and community art projects. In Australia the Community Arts Board went into partnership with shires and municipalities to develop local initiatives, and multiculturalism and recognition of aboriginal culture began to be promoted in mainstream institutions.[7]

The recession of the early 1970s had two effects on cultural policies. First, there was a drop-off in the financing of some of these new programs and institutions. The budget of the Canada Council, for example, declined in the late seventies, and cultural agencies were moved from the Department of the Secretary of State to the Department of Communication, where they became secondary considerations to broadcasting and telecommunications.[8] In Australia, the controversial dismissal of the Labor Government by the Governor-General in 1975 also led to a decline in regional and progressive iniatives under the succeeding Liberal regime. By the late 1970s governments in both countries were affected by ideological shifts which emphasized the market as the the most rational and effective method of the *distribution* of goods and regulation of industries.

In the late 1970s and into the 1980s the cultural industries model became dominant.[9] Arts and media producers, professional organizations and lobby groups were drawn into collaboration with this model and began to use its economic research protocols in order to establish an economic rationale for support for the arts. A example of this strategy in Australia is *The Individual Artists Inquiry* (1983)[10] , which demonstrated the poor returns for artists and the income discrepancies among arts practitioners. The National Association of Visual Artists, NAVA Australia, formed in 1986 as a professional and advocacy group established the first national data base of artists. The major national arts lobby in Canada, The Canadian Conference of the Arts, and provincial and major city arts organizations have published many similar studies. The 1980s was a period in which many organizations found themselves caught between competing agendas of equity in employment and fairer media representation of the population, and economic rationalism in the form of "professional" management and fundraising to replace lost public revenue.

From the Massey Report to Creative Nation

A Canadian Royal Commission Report of 1951 and an Australian Commonwealth Cultural Policy manifesto of 1994 mark the beginning, and perhaps the end, of an era in modernist cultural policies designed for national development and intended to define and defend the relation between culture and the state. Public investment in communication technologies is privileged in both documents. In the Massey Report and succeeding Canadian cultural policy reviews the "problem of geography" in creating a united and socially coherent country can only be overcome by public investment in these distributive technologies. In Australia, forty-some years later, the rationale in *Creative Nation* for investment in communication technology has shifted to securing the place of Australia within regional and global markets.

The findings of the 1951 *Massey-Lévesque Royal Commission on the Arts, Letters and Sciences* (Massey Report) led eventually to the establishment of the Canada Council in 1956 (since 1997 the Canada Council for the Arts), and helped reinforce and expand national programs for university research, broadcasting, and national museums and heritage. Analysis of this landmark report has occupied a central place in English-Canadian critical research on Canadian cultural policy of the last five years.[11] The report is the culmination of a colonial legacy of British paternalism, the Mathew Arnold - inflected "liberal humanist nationalism,"[12] which was supposed to civilize Canadians through education, broadcasting and the arts supported by public funding. It also left its mark in the cultural protectionism of Canadian broadcasting and arts policies; it articulated the "market failure" argument for state intervention; it defended the philosophy of cultural development; and it upheld the principle of the bilingual structures of Canadian state-funded broadcasting and arts institutions.

Centralisation and a preference for national institutions over local and regional arts practice are problematic aspects of the Massey legacy. In broadcasting, for example, the development of a national public broadcasting system has not affected the long-term profitability and expansion of private broadcasting, and this has in turn imposed a commercial imperative on CBC television which competes with private sector media for advertising revenue. The two solitudes of the public broadcaster's language-based networks (CBC and Radio Canada) form part of the impermeable barrier between Quebec and the rest of Canada. Most significantly, the public broadcaster has operated as centralised state broadcaster - excluding from the outset forms of community or local control.[13] Its recent critics have concentrated on the Report's European cultural chauvinism and anti-American Adorno-like take on popular recordings, film, and television of the period.[14] Far less attention has been paid to the fact that a more politicised and practice-oriented community model for publicly-funded arts programs was promoted by artists, unions and community organizations in the late 1940s but failed to garner the support of influential curators and arts patrons at the time of the Commission. Today this is not only a road not taken, it is a road erased from the collective memory. [15]

In historic perspective the relationship of Canadian women to cultural policies follows a pattern which is similar to the Australian experience, although the timing of certain developments is different. Class, ethnic origin, race and language have played a related part in the extent to which women have been restricted in earning income and recognition from their cultural work, from working in cultural institutions as curators, producers and managers, and from achieving influence in the making of cultural policy. If the cultural industries, especially the public sector, are somewhat more accessible to female employment since the employment equity struggles of the 1970s, a few high-profile women do not make up for what may be fairly described as a low-wage ghetto for women. Women's greatest success-measured in terms of participation, and (to make a value judgement) cultural significance, has been as creative artists, as volunteer and underpaid labour, and as audiences. Unfortunately these contributions, despite the current rhetoric of consumer sovereignty in the case of the (majority female) arts audience, do not translate into economic benefits and decision-making power.

The major lobbies for women in Canada are the National Action Committee on the Status of Women (NAC), a comprehensive organization initially founded in 1972 to monitor the results of the Royal Commission on the Status of Women of 1971, and a parallel organization in Quebec, the Fédération des Femmes du Québec (FFQ). The Canadian Advisory Council on the Status of Women (CACSW), established in 1973 as an advisor to government departments became an important commissioner and publisher of research on a wide range of issues. Through the 1970s and early 80s these organizations influenced legislation on the representation, employment and training of women in the arts and media, as well as on taxation, workplace regulation and other social legislation affecting the cultural sector.

Between 1987 and 1993-4 NAC suffered the loss of about 70 per cent of its federal funding, as the Conservatives cut the Women's Program of the Department of the Secretary of State. In 1995 CACSW was eliminated in the Liberal federal budget.[15] Certainly these cuts illustrate a confidence in government that these programs and agencies could be eliminated and downsized with limited political damage. But to put these changes and their reception in context one also has to look at the drastically decreased budgets of the CBC/Radio Canada, NFB, Canada Council, national research councils, and parallel organizations in most provinces and most significantly, the changes to social welfare measures that have been linked to the "deficit reduction" budgets of all levels of government. For government, one beneficial effect of the early cutbacks to women's organizations was to reduce a source of vocal criticism of the general cuts and of the implications for all Canadians of the North American Free Trade Agreement. In her chapter Barbara Godard looks at the gender issues in the relationship between government "restructuring" of cultural institutions and programs and cuts to social spending generally, with special emphasis on Ontario, Canada's most populous province.

During the 1980s and to the present day, institutionalised feminism (for example in the universities and in the national women's organizations) has been the site of debates and reorganization related to the under- and misrepresentation of ethnic minorities, lesbians, and especially, women of colour. These struggles within and around women's organizations took place at the same time as changes related to race and Canada's multiculturalism policy. Canadian citizenship has historically differentiated among citizens depending upon their origins, including their "race." When the concept of multiculturalism was first articulated in the 1960s it did not include any mention of race. To some critics, irrespective of the strategic opportunities it may have brought the Euro-Canadian cultural minorities who fought to have it introduced, official multiculturalism therefore masked and marginalised race, and perpetuated the racism of Canadian society. The revised 1988 Multiculturalism Act, while it continues to enshrine multiculturalism within the framework of official Canadian bilingualism, in other words as clearly subordinate to it, has shifted the emphasis from cultural maintenance and social integration to recognizing the fact of racial inequality, and promoting equality measures.[16]

There have been some changes in the last ten years in the leadership and composition of women's organizations, and some response from cultural organisations and government bodies to demands for better representation of people of colour. Simply to list such changes can often obscure the labour that goes into debating and achieving cultural shifts, and can imply some sort of closure to such processes. In contrast, Monika Gagnon's chapter reconstructs in detail the *work* that is required to create spaces within institutions and within cultural practice, and to transform institutions and cultural practices so that representation (of people, of their cultural expression) moves away from, to use a term appropriate here, the tokenistic. This work and struggle, like domestic labour, is usually hidden from view in official policy forums. The campaign to have some of the anti-racist events Gagnon looks at funded by government, the events themselves, their media reception, and her own open-ended analysis of them constitute breaks with the packaged politics of culture that too often characterize policy debate, and certainly policy analysis.

While the legacy of the Massey Comission continues to be

debated in Canada, that is, whether it represents the last of the old or the birth of the new, and whether many of the policies and institutions that developed subsequently would not have developed anyway, there can be no doubt as to the direction that cultural policies have taken over the last thirty years. It says a great deal about similarities between Canada and Australia that their cultural policies treat geography as a problem to be solved through technology. Although in the Australian case the uniqueness of its natural environment and its island status have also been read as forms of protection for a nascent, hybrid culture, the same problems of linking a geographically scattered population, and, in the 1990s, linking the island to Asia and the world, have led to an updated version of technological nationalism in cultural policy.

Technological Nationalism: The Australia of Creative Nation

Cultural policies have become neocolonial and neocorporatist through a process of shifting the definitions of both audience and market outside national boundaries. What distinguishes cultural policy now is its reliance on international rather than national consumption. The impact of the worldwide financial crisis of the late 1980s on Australia was to intensify government pressure toward a market orientation for cultural industries. In the political economy of 1997 and beyond, cultural producers and audiences will be obliged to respond to the collaboration of the state and market.

Creative Nation (1994)[17] was the first comprehensive Australian cultural policy statement. It was a product of the Ministry of Communications and the Arts, and embodied the influence of former Labor Prime Minister Paul Keating himself, as much as the Australia Council. The policy strategy included a budget of $A252 million (to be spent between 1994-1998), which was, however, a small part of the $1 billion annual budget for Communications and the Arts. The policy and its administrative model tied the arts to distribution technologies more clearly than ever before. The assumption was that the new technologies and the markets that they open up, in Australia and abroad, will finance Australian cultural development. The reality is that between 1987 and 1994 there was a 21 per cent decline in creative producers' incomes from both government and private sources.[18] Creative producers were also affected by the introduction of new technologies, such as cd-rom, and will be most affected as digitalised broadband services influence the economics of production and distribution.

The new policy agenda was also characterized by a significant move away from the principles of arms-length funding, and by the detachment of cultural funding from direct ministerial control. A separate Major Organizations Board (MOB) was established to fund the national flagship companies such as Opera Australia, the Australian Ballet and the Sydney Symphony Orchestra. The former peer review processes of the Australia Council Arts Boards allowed practitioners to, in effect, make policy while participating in the selection process for grants. New procedures have restricted this input from creative producers. The Australia Council, under a new Chair, Hilary McPhee, was given a broader brief by the federal government to develop the marketing of Australian culture and to encourage more private sector sponsorship of the arts. In a related move the Australian Foundation was created on the model of the U.S. National Endowment for the Arts (NEA) to promote cultural development through community and business partnership. Its establishment was a direct response to criticism of the Australia Council that it was captive of its clients. Similiar criticism was used by the New Right in the United States in its attacks on the NEA, and the results proved similiar for Australia Council. There was a cutback of 12 per cent for the Council in the 1996 budget under the new Liberal government, and a reduction in the Council's support for programs for women, aboriginal Australians and people of non-English speaking backgrounds.

The Broadband Services Expert Group (BSEG) Reports [19] and *Creative Nation* attempted to position Australia in domestic and international markets as having a unique approach to technology. The commodity that was being constructed and marketed was a new form of Australian nationalism, in which the creation of Australian software and multimedia products, and cd-rom access in schools were to be the key to market success overseas and to the next stage in the "modernisation" of Australia. The blending of new technologies and nationalism once again leaves untouched the problematic patriarchal character of both nationalism and of technology. The assumption that technology is neutral masks the ideologies of gender that structure representation and reception even, or especially, in new media. Patricia Gillard, as the only woman "expert" on the BSEG panel provide evidence in her chapter that even when women are members of policy inquiries and commissions they are discouraged from arguing from a gender perspective.

There are in fact no significant differences between the two major parties, Labor and Liberal, in terms of cultural policies, and Liberal policies following on from Labor's *Creative Nation* are no less patriarchal, only more transparently so. It is claimed by the current government that the new identity of Australians is a hybrid, inclusive of differences. However, apart from the separate status of Aboriginal Australians, there is in fact only one sanctioned identity. The invocation of 'broad community support' by the Liberal government in its policy statements collapses differences among audiences, marginalises dissent, and reduces the complex concept of the public discussed by Jennifer Barrett in relation to Community Arts, into an exclusive and homogeneized model of the "community" and of the Australian citizen.

Implicit in the 1980s model of cultural industries was a perception of culture as part of the leisure industry. The split between work and leisure, and public and private, has been part of the traditional gendering of social and cultural life. *Creative Nation* was an administrative and marketing document, not a critical analysis of Australian culture, and it shifted the concept of culture from a way of life to a commodified product. Furthermore, in *Creative Nation* a privileged cultural sector has clearly been conceptually shifted further into the masculine domain of paid work and profits through an emphasis on new technologies and multi-media dissemination. The financial, regulatory and technological implications of multi-media therefore extend far beyond the sector itself. If governments are going to conceive of culture as closely aligned with "masculine" models for the design and implementation of the new technologies, a process which is evident in Patricia Gillard's analysis of BSEG's consulting procedures, this will further disempower women.

The influence of artists themselves on *Creative Nation* has been slight. Only one of the main policy platforms of the National Association of Visual Artists, (NAVA), was endorsed by *Creative Nation*; the establishment of a copyright protection agency for visual artists, VI$COPY, with funds of $1 million a year provided to establish a copyright collection agency. Luckily, one group of artists who will benefit most from copyright protection are Aboriginal and Torres Strait Islanders, as ownership of and responsibility for imagery is inherited through kinship systems. It remains to be seen how effective copyright legislation will be abroad, especially in some Asian countries where pirating flourishes.

While indigenous culture has received some recognition, women's cultural production within indigenous communities has not received comparable attention, especially in the marketing of indigenous art forms as markers of national culture. Emily Kngwarreye was awarded an Australian Creative Fellowship for her painting, but women's ceremonial culture that takes place outside the museum and art market definitions of culture is treated with suspicion and, sometimes, contempt.[20]

Feminist cultural historians have identified the ways in which the representation of culture has been gendered through hierarchies of genre and categories of amateur and professional. Women's culture in Australia continues to be denied in the maintainance of traditional disciplinary distinctions. The existence of a women's material culture is barely acknowledged at heritage sites and museums, at the level of community and in the public culture. And, women's material culture is not represented in the growth of science and transport museums, such as the Australian Maritime Museum in Sydney, in which discourses of technology and development dominate. The extensive use of multimedia in museums in the next decade will favour wealthy institutions and exacerbate inequalities between museums and other heritage sites. Already, the increased corporate sponsorship of major museums and the social functions associated with this funding has established a private audience for corporate sponsored functions in public institutions, and has resulted in an over-emphasis on the blockbuster exhibition. This emphasis, too, is unlikely to reflect women's culture.[21]

Current policies in Canada and Australia emphasize the preservation of national cultural industries and the development of production capacity in new technologies. As the cornerstones of cultural policy, these policies neglect questions of access to education and training and the already severe gender imbalances in the labour force and among users of high technologies. Arts Training Australia has undertaken yet another analysis of the labour force characteristics of visual arts and craftspersons[22] at a time when there are widespread concerns about changes in education and training in the visual arts. In schools the emphasis on performance testing has downgraded specialist art subjects within the national curriculum. In technical and further education, the competency-based industrial training models used are not appropriate to the visual arts. The incorporation of art schools into universities in the 1980s has raised new questions of gender equity in funding related to research grants. There have been extensive reductions in craft studies courses and in visual arts teacher-training places. Many women have been employed in arts education rather than figuring as artists, and educational jobs are now rapidly being lost. The technological approach, which may or may not succeed as an economic strategy in the context of global markets, has placed more emphasis on design and computer-generated imagery than traditional fine arts and craft skills, including the craft skills of Aboriginal and ethnic minority women. Current policies may prove to be a step backwards even from the limited equity agendas which had been allowed to enter the arena of cultural education.

Cultural Policy Research

This review of policy directions related to *Creative Nation* shows how extensively the agenda of technological nationalism affects policies on a range of cultural issues, and suggests how widespread the gendered implications of these policies can be.

To what extent does policy research in Australia respond to gender issues? Like the competing agendas for cultural diversity and administrative efficiency that characterized the 1980s current academic cultural policy research operates along lines characterized by a division between critical work and work oriented to administration. As one Australian cultural bureaucrat has commented,

> Critical research of cultural policy has in my view been less influential in policy development...the target audience in the end seems to be the academic or student. I'm not convinced that influencing the practitioner, bureaucrat or politician has been the primary objective.[23]

Much current policy research in Australia concerns the analysis of data on specific aspects of the cultural industries: for example, audience research for galleries and museums, market research for film funding and production, BSEG research on the provision of multi-media infrastructure, and studies for the film industry and the Australian Broadcasting Corporation (ABC). In the split between academy and bureaucracy, gender and social issues intrinsic to cultural policy are included in Cultural Studies, and other academic discourses, but are not heard or admitted to the forums of policy formation. It is important to identify some of the ways in which women's issues are separated from other policy debates in film and media, education and social policy, in order to refocus gender questions for cultural policy.

Patricia Gillard shows in her chapter how women as audiences were not adequately addressed in the BSEG Reports. Julie James Bailey has argued that despite the impact of "second wave" feminism in the 1970s on such institutions as the Australian Film, Television, and Radio School, women have been more successful in employment in academic film and media education than in the film industry itself. A lack of concern about gender issues in the mainstream industry and a lack of interest in this sector, other than in terms of its productions, on the part of feminist film and media theorists affect the production of research that could be useful to women's concerns about employment and representations.[24]

The conservative social agendas of the 1990s have displaced the politics of representation, and in its place, in Australia under the Liberal-National Party coalition federal government there are a set of taxation and social welfare measures designed to allow mothers to remain at home, and to force young adult students to remain dependent on their families. The new social policies will reinforce the stereotypes that have persisted in the media. The National Working Party on the Portrayal of Women in the Media[25] found that in 1993, the status of women in the media had not substantially changed since 1988 when a large content analysis research project was undertaken.[26] Content analyses such as these studies may be more useful in drafting policy for media regulators than critique. They may enable greater emphasis on involving women in policy processes, especially where they are the predominant audience or consumer for particular media.

New applied research models can also be helpful to women's interests at the local level. Cultural planning processes for local government have developed from the relationships between local planning, arts bureaucracies at the federal and state level and, the employment of community arts officers in local government. In many cases they have been constrained by limited definitions of culture, the entrenched organisational practices of local government and the territoriality and conflicting agendas of those involved in traditional arts and cultural practice. Deborah Stevenson, a member of the City of Newcastle Cultural Review Commission, argues in her chapter that the first step toward the attainment of integrated cultural planning is to move from external research and formulation of cultural policies, and the separation of "culture" from other areas of municipal concern, to cultural planning processes that involve political representatives and citizens and eventually create a cultural ecology model for the community in which cultural impacts are considered in relation to all aspects of local development.

Conclusion

If policy was a temptation that required some negotiation in Australian Cultural Studies,[27] it has been not so much a temptation as a familiar environment for Canadian researchers in communications and cultural studies, for whom policy research, both critical and administrative has been part of the foundation of these fields. Each starting position has its blindspots, but in both cases one of these is gender.

The level of sophistication of academic cultural policy study in both countries is high, and it now includes numerous reflections on the state of the art. A recent Canadian book reviewing the cultural industries[28] manages to bridge the gap between administrative and critical research, and includes evaluations of the successes and failures of sectoral policies, combined with an original overview of the achievement of Canadian cultural policy generally. It concludes with an assessment of the challenges to policy researchers in the present context in which the relationship of the state to publics and markets is undergoing transformation. Much research in the area is equally ambitious if not always as successful. The highly self-conscious way in which participation in cultural policy study seemed suddenly to be debated in Australia in late 80s and early 90s [29] reveals not so much awkwardness and genuine hesitation, as an extremely articulate manifesto which was the product of years of reflection and work in the field by a number of individuals finally entering a concerted phase of publication.

Yet, as Alison Beale argues, the absence of a gender perspective in most of this work has several implications. It leaves researchers and policy makers without a means of linking topics such as female audiences, practitioners, cultural bureaucrats, the representations of women, education and training, the development and implementation of technology, and other topics, to studies of the *general direction* of policy. Research that does not include a gender perspective will also be unable to benefit from the research methods and protocols for researchers dealing with individuals and communities developed in feminist research over the last twenty-five years. It will be less likely to value the personal statement and the creative production as legitimate forms of policy research and intervention. By overlooking the ways in which "culture" is gendered it may miss out on an important way of understanding its treatment in public policy, especially in the current economic climate. And finally, the interested and value-laden nature of feminist research, its multiple points of analysis and its varied strategies re-cast the question for academics and policy-makers of whether, or how, and in whose interest policy research should be done.

These are some of the reasons why we have put this book together. We have tried to respond to some of the lacks that we perceived in the field, and we have also had the good fortune to discover that many of our colleagues on both sides of the Pacific shared these concerns and were already addressing them in their work. As editors we thank our contributors for collectively surpassing our expectations and transforming our ideas, and hope that this book contributes to opening up cultural policy to a broader range of interventions from all those to whom it matters.

Notes

1. The first annual conference of the Australian Cultural Studies Association, Sydney, 1990, and the conference "Post-Colonial Formations" at Griffith University, Brisbane, in 1993 were attended by many Canadians and were key moments in developing these relationships. Articles of mutual interest on policy topics have been published in journals such as *Media Information Australia*, *Meanjin*, *Continuum*, *The Canadian Journal of Communication* and *The Australian Journal of Canadian Studies*, by the Institute for Cultural Policy Studies at Griffith (now the Australian Key Centre for Cultural and Media Policy), and in conference proceedings.

2. The influential theoretical work of Ien Ang on media audiences (for example in *Desperately Seeking the Audience,* London: Routledge, 1991) is one such example. Ang's resistance to administrative research of audiences (ratings) parallels her theorized resistance of audiences themselves to the monolithic construction of the audience that television seeks to impose. Elizabeth Jacka argues that Ang casts the audience as actually powerless, while representing it as the opposite, and that she makes a calculated refusal to deal rigorously with the methods of social science used in policy research. Elizabeth Jacka, "Researching Audiences: A dialogue between cultural studies and social science," *Media Information Australia*, no.73, Aug.1994,45-51. See also Stuart Cunningham,"Cultural Studies from the viewpoint of cultural policy," in Graeme Turner (ed.) *Nation, Culture Text,* (London: Routledge,1993):131-132.

3. See Stuart Cunningham, *Framing Culture: Criticism and Policy in Australia*, Sydney, Allen and Unwin, 1992, and Stuart McFadyen et al, *Cultural Development in an Open Economy, Canadian Journal of Communication* v.19,no.3/4, 1994.

4. A thoughtful comparison of current Australian and Canadian social policies and

politics related to globalisation is John Wiseman," National Social Policy in an Age of Global Power: Lessons from Canada and Australia," in *Remaking Canadian Social Policy: Social Security in the Late 1990s*, ed. Jane Pulkingham and Gordon Ternowetsky, (Halifax, N.S.: Fernwood Publishing, 1996):114-129.

5. See notes to chapters by Annette Van Den Bosch and Barbara Godard, and *The Arts: Some Australian Data*, (Sydney: Australia Council, 4th Edition 1992); *Cultural Trends in Australia No.1: A Statistical Overview*, (Canberra: The Australian Bureau of Statistics, 1994); "Cultural labour force results," Canadian Conference of the Arts Bulletins Page, July 21, 1995. http://www.ffa.ucalgary.ca/cca/bulletin/july21.htm; and Decima Research/Les Consultants Cultur'inc, *Canadian Arts Consumer Profile, 1990-1991: Findings* (Ottawa: Communications Canada, 1992). The authors thank Catherine Matysiak for additional research on Canadian cultural statistics.

6. George Woodcock, *Strange Bedfellows: The State and the Arts in Canada*, Vancouver: Douglas and McIntyre, 1985, pp.94-95.

7.Gay Hawkins: *From Nimbin to Mardi Gras: Constructing Community Arts*, (Sydney: Allen and Unwin, 1993). See also the review of this book in Rachel Fensham,"(Post) Community Arts?," *Continuum*, v.8, no.2, 1994, 188-195, and Hawkins, "Writing on the Edge of History: Documenting Cultural Institutions," *Media Information Australia*, no.73, August 1994, 35-39. For a review of multiculturalism related to Australian arts policy see Annette Blonski, *Arts for a Multicultural Australia 1973-1991: An Account of Australia Council Policies*, (Sydney: The Australia Council, 1992).

8. Woodcock, 1985, 118-119.

9. The rise and effects of this model are discussed in Alison Beale,"Subjects, Citizens and Consumers: changing concepts of citizenship in Canadian cutural policy," in *Alternative Frontiers: Voices from the Mountain West*, ed. Allen Seager et al, (Montreal:Association for Canadian Studies, 1997): 51-65.

10. David Throsby, *The Artist in Australia Today: Report of the Individual Artists Inquiry*,(Sydney: The Australia Council, 1983). The key Canadian policy document setting out the cultural industries model is *Vital Links: Canadian Cultural Industries*, (Ottawa: Ministry of Supply and Services, 1987).

11. Paul Litt, *The Muses,the Masses and the Massey Commission*, (Toronto:University of Toronto Press, 1992); Kevin Dowler,"The Cultural Industries Policy Apparatus," in Michael Dorland (ed.) *The Cultural Industries in Canada: Problems, Policies and Prospects*,(Toronto: James Lorimer and Company, 1996):328-346; Alison Beale, "Harold Innis and Canadian Cultural Policy in the 1940s," *Continuum* v.7,no.1, 1993:75-90.

12. Litt, 1992, 104-122.

13. Marc Raboy, *Missed Opportunities: The Story of Canada's Broadcasting Policy* (Montreal: McGill-Queen's University Press, 1990).

14. Litt, 1992, 38-55.

15. Dot Tuer, "The Art of Nation Building: Constructing a 'Cultural Identity for Post-War Canada," *Parallelogramme*, v.17,n.4,1992.

16.Heather McIvor, *Women and Politics in Canada*, (Peterborough: Broadview Press,1996):328-330.

17. Christina Gabriel,"One or the Other? 'Race,' Gender and the Limits of Official Multiculturalism," in Janine Brodie (ed.) *Women and Canadian Public Policy*, (Toronto: Harcourt Brace, 1996): 182.

18. *Creative Nation: Commonwealth Cultural Policy*,(Canberra: Ministry of Communications and the Arts, October 1994)

19. David Throsby and Beverley Thompson, *But What Do You Do For A Living?: A New Economic Study of Australian Artists*,(Sydney: Australia Council, 1994)

20. Broadband Services Expert Group (BSEG),*Networking Australia's Future: Interim Report* and *Final Report* (Canberra: 1994)

21. Ngarrye women in the State of Victoria objected to development proposed for Hindmarsh Island on the basis of the presence of sacred ceremonial sites. The confidentiality of their testimony was broken, and their claims and government treatment of their testimony were reviewed in State and National Commissions of Inquiry in 1995.

22. Annette Van Den Bosch,"Art Audiences and Art Funding: Some Contemporary Relationships Between Art and Business in Australia," in Martorella, R. (ed.) *Art and Business: An International Perspective on Sponsorship* (Westport, Conn: Praeger, 1996)

23. Arts Training Australia, *Mapping the Visual Arts and Crafts*, (Sydney: Department of Employment, Education and Training,1995).

24. Cathy Santamaria, "Contract Research: The Bureaucracy-Researcher Relationship," *Media Information Australia*, no.73, August 1994,9.

25. E.Cox and S.Laura, *What Do I Wear in a Hurricane: Women in Australian Film, Television, Radio and Video Industries*, (Sydney: Australian Film Comission and National Working Party on the Portrayal of Women in the Media, 1992):69.

26. *Women and Media*, (Canberra: Department of the Prime Minister and Cabinet and Office of the Status of Women, 1993)

27. Saulwick Weller and Associates, *Sex Role Portrayal of Women in Advertisements*,(Canberra: Office of the Status of Women, 1987), and Sally Hartnett and Associates, *The Portrayal of Women in Advertisements*,(Canberra: Office of the Status of Women, 1988)

28.Colin Mercer, "Cultural Policy: Research and the Governmental Imperative," *Media Information Australia*, no.74, August 1994, 16-22.

29. Michael Dorland (ed.) , 1996.

30. Stuart Cunningham, 1992; Tony Bennett,"Culture, Theory and Policy," *Media Information Australia*, no.53, August 1989, 9-12; and Tim Rowse, "Cultural Policy and Social Theory," *Media Information Australia*, no.53, August 1989, 13-22.

Inside the Machine: The Development of Cultural Policy by Federal, State and Local Government in Australia

Andrea Hull

"The arts in Australia have too long continued to arise out of and reflect the Western European tradition from which they derived and have been too little influenced by the environment, dreams, prejudices, interests and values which are peculiarly Australian. I believe that this failure to be influenced by and reflect our own especial way of life has been part of the reason why the arts have been regarded as suspect by so many of our people, many of whom still see them as alien, an expression of snobbery and of privilege, or simply as 'strictly for the birds.'" [1]

Thirty Years Ago [2]

Up until thirty years ago hundreds of artists left Australia often because they felt they were not valued. Towards the late 1960s Liberal Prime Ministers Harold Holt and John Gorton had begun, with the active advice of H.C. (Nugget) Coombs, first chairman of the Australia Council, to accept that the federal government had a critically important role to play in supporting the arts. In 1967, a fledgling Australian Council for the Arts, focusing on the performing arts, was created.

Before 1967 the six state governments built glorious public citadels in the classical tradition to house each state's material culture. The heritage collections these libraries, galleries and museums contained were seen as precious objects and displayed, rather than interpreted as elements in a specific value–laden narrative. Local governments supported libraries and facilities such as schools of art and mechanics institutes, in which local arts councils, country women associations and music and dance teachers could encourage the arts. Local governments also began to plan and build cultural palaces for the performing and visual arts.

Artists were rarely involved in decision making about the arts. "For artists themselves, it was thought, while often personally charming, were notoriously irresponsible, hopeless with money, totally self-centred, and probably immoral. They were certainly incapable of reading a balance sheet...." [3] The Australian Elizabethan Theatre Trust established the first national performing arts companies and training schools in drama and ballet. Together with the Arts Council movement it spearheaded activities and provided school children and country residents with a steady stream of cultural product from the cities. "The Perth and Adelaide festivals provided the marooned island peoples with international culture. Our TV and cinema was dominated by Hollywood and Pinewood." [4] Crafts were seen as the domain of women's leisure time and therefore marginalized. Aboriginal culture was not supported or valued. A significant exception was the artist Albert Namitjira who painted watercolours and oils in a manner familiar to a European sensibility and who for a time was courted by art connoisseurs.

Australians were the inheritors of a cultural tradition that was often of little relevance or use to them. At the same time, there was a great deal of unacknowledged and unknown cultural activity in Australia's past. John Berger has written: "A people or a class which is cut off from its own past is far less free to choose and to act as a people or class, than one that has been able to situate itself in history." [5]

Both Aboriginal and non-Aboriginal Australians were severed from their culture in two ways, first by the time and manner of

European settlement, and secondly, by the development of a dominating national culture that could relate only to white, predominantly Anglo-Saxon men (and probably its relevance was becoming more and more distant even to them). This official culture ignored Aboriginal culture and the approximately 30 per cent of Australia's population that had an immediate personal or family interest in a language other than English. More than 250 Aboriginal languages, and between four and five hundred Aboriginal dialects existed, while over a hundred other languages and dialects were used in Australia by 140 ethnic groups and yet Australia remained an ostensibly monocultural and monolingual society. This was reflected in the official policy of assimilation for Aboriginal people and for the large number of European immigrants to Australia in the postwar years. In consequence, there were few opportunities for contributions to be made to the publicly accessible cultural life of the country by non-English-speakers.

Cultural Transformation: The Early 1970s

In the 1990s we acknowledge that Australian artists and writers have made their mark on fellow Australians and on an international market. Our visual artists and our crafts people are forging fresh images and creating new markets for their work. They have stimulated burgeoning corporate art collections, trade union commissions, programs for art in public places, and art prizes just as they have contributed to a general public education which has led to outstanding crowds at exhibitions. Our performing artists, dancers, musicians, circus performers, comedians and actors, have developed a distinctive performing style which is exuberant, witty, and confident. Australian films are screened throughout the world, actively facilitated by the Australian Film Commission's marketing program. Much of this work reflects a profound change in our perception of traditional and contemporary Aboriginal arts and of our multicultural realities.

How have these changes happened? What role has government played at all three levels – federal, state, and local? What role did artists and arts advocacy groups play? What were the social and economic contexts within which the shifts occurred?

In the late 1960s and early 1970s "new issues and new social movements were undercutting the hegemony of a complacent conservatism."[6] In 1972, a Federal Labour Government was elected for the first time in a generation. The postwar baby boomers overwhelmingly voted in a Labour Government under the charismatic leadership of Gough Whitlam. Significantly, many artists also engaged in political activity at this point, and formed "Artists for Whitlam" committees in some states. The Labour Party established arts policy committees which emphasized the need for government support for individual artists, and greater access to, and participation in, the arts. They also challenged the prevailing guidelines which directed a large share of the funds available towards the major opera and ballet companies.

Whitlam's vision included a massive expansion of the federal government's support for the arts, film, and cultural life. The budget doubled in 1973. Australia Council Chairman, Nugget Coombs, observed that for those involved in the arts, the situation after December 1972 had "all the hallmarks of a cargo cult whose ship had actually arrived."[7] Whitlam opted for two independent statutory bodies, the Australian Film Commission and the Australia Council, which would advise the government at arm's length on film and arts policy and allocate funds. The new Australia Council consisted of seven art-form-based boards music, theatre, visual arts, literature, film and television, aboriginal arts and crafts overseen by a council, and met for the first time in February 1973. The nature and art-form bias of the boards was the subject of concentrated lobbying by artists who wished to have more say in their destiny rather than politicians and bureaucrats solely determining structure and processes. In 1975 the Film and Television Board transferred to the Australian Film Commission and in 1978 the Community Arts Board was created.

The decision to use peer group assessment that is, the appointment of artists as decision makers on art-form boards was most significant, and championed by both artists and government supporters. Nugget Coombs described it as "Guild Socialism or participatory democracy" and believed that "the principle was entitled to a realistic test, the outcome of which I thought would be of considerable significance for social theory." [8] This model has led to "the most extraordinary efflorescence of the arts ever seen in this country.[9]

But the model of arm's length funding and peer group assessment, visionary and effective as it was, still caused problems to politicians, Canberra bureaucrats, and the ever-volatile arts community, who still did not see that a supply and demand ratio simply meant some got money and a vastly greater percentage did not. Through the 1970s and 1980s there were approximately a dozen different inquiries into the Australia Council or public funding/administration of the arts. Perhaps the most conceptually challenging review was the 1976 Industries Assistance Commission inquiry into the performing arts chaired by Richard Boyer. At the time both the economic rationalist nature and industry/economics language of the inquiry and the subsequent report caused widespread angst amongst artists.

Despite some misgivings, by the early 1980s the notion of an arts industry had become part of the rhetoric of arts administrators and advocates. Supporters of the arts had traditionally relied on arguments based on ideas of public good or quality of life. But in an era of economic rationalism a new statistical paradigm was forged to substantiate the case for the arts. In 1982 The Australia Council established a Policy and Planning Division which provided it with a proactive and coordinated research and policy development program.

Following lobbying from the arts industry and the Australia Council, the Bureau of Census and Statistics redesigned occupational and industrial classification systems and has allowed for the capture of more accurate census information. The central intergovernmental body for cultural policy discussion, the Cultural Ministers' Council (CMC) agreed to make a statistical project a priority. The Australia Council commenced a range of statistical and analytical projects to define and describe the scope, size, and relativities of the arts industry. The results of the ground breaking inquiry into the individual artist were published as *The Artist in Australia Today*. The statistics generated by all these projects were used by the Australia Council in submissions to relevant federal government inquiries: for example, the Australian Broadcasting Tribunal's inquiry into cable and subscription television, the Department of the Attorney-General's inquiries into audio-visual copyright and moral rights and performers protection, the Commonwealth Department of Education Review of Australian Studies in Tertiary Education, and the Commonwealth Taxation Summit. The Bureau of Statistics also agreed to create a dedicated unit for the culture and leisure industries.

Artists and arts workers became adept at using the resultant substantiated quotes: (the arts industry is) "bigger than beer"; "more people go to a performance than football"; and "more people play a musical instrument than play tennis." These statistics and clever visual imagery formed the basis for an advocacy campaign known as National Arts Week for three consecutive years (1987-1990).

Another seminal inquiry occurred in 1985/86 in a period of funding and staff cuts to the Australia Council. The Commonwealth House of Representatives Standing Committee on Expenditure, under the chairmanship of Leo McLeay, inquired into Commonwealth assistance for the arts. The report was entitled *Patronage, Power and the Muse*, and prompted concerns that the needs and roles of the artist had been overlooked and that it recommended too much power be handed to the Canberra duopoly of ministers and public servants. Despite this many of the recommendations had been implemented by 1995. The Canberra department responsible for the arts has assumed a major coordinating role, a national cultural policy has been developed and the Australia Council's prime responsibility is defined as being to the public, not to the artist.

The most obvious function of the Australia Council's art-form boards (renamed funds in 1996) is to establish criteria and priorities, and then to respond accordingly to applications and to distribute money. But the real work of the funds has always been in the strategic analysis of each art form examining its strengths and weaknesses, its audiences, and its reflection of international influences. Applications for grants provide considerable material for these analyses but so too do the art form practitioners who bring expertise and objectivity to the process.

Effective policymaking must reflect practice as well as new visions. In the twenty-four years of the life of the Australia Council, over a thousand Australian artists have participated in decision making on Australia Council boards and committees.

For instance, artists in the crafts agitated for the separate creation of a Crafts Board in 1973; artists, community activists, and others argued for a separate Community Arts Board in 1978; artists and others urged the Council and its boards to embrace arts activities that better reflected our pluralities. The fact that artists have participated directly in the development and destiny of their art-forms and have not been victims to a patronizing and paternal mode of decision making has had a major impact on the vitality and confidence of Australian artists.

The Federal/State Nexus

Devolution of funds and responsibilities from the Australia Council's art-form boards to state arts ministries has been discussed for over two decades. In 1980 a report prepared for the Federal and State Arts Ministers Conference recommended an approach that defined spheres of influence and understanding. No satisfactory agreement has ever been reached by federal and state governments. Both federal and state arts bureaucracies fund major organizations and projects. Individual artists in the states generally prefer the safety and relative objectivity of a national body to more parochial state-based decision making. However, when grant decisions do not reflect a per capita state equity, there are always complaints. Furthermore, the Australia Council's fixed refusal to fund state opera companies and festivals, plus its perceived bias towards the Sydney/Canberra/ Melbourne triangle, has long been a source of irritation for the distant states.

The most recent attempt to clarify responsibilities was the cultural framework agreed upon at the Cultural Ministers' Council (CMC) in 1990. The CMC has become an increasingly important forum for federal and state cultural ministers, particularly with the strategic role now played by state governments. In the early 1970s, the South Australian Government, under Premier Don Dunstan, pioneered a form of state patronage which has been taken up in turn by other states; Victoria, Western Australia, and then Tasmania, New South Wales, and most recently Queensland. By the late 1980s all states had consolidated their arts and cultural responsibilities in portfolios that included libraries, museums, galleries, film, visual arts, and sometimes heritage. Each state now has a ministry for the arts based on the European ministry of culture model and which reports directly to the minister. The states are not only responsible for supporting and encouraging cultural diversity but must also take into account the manifold needs of people living throughout the state, no matter what their educational, social, financial, or geographic status. State governments have also embarked on major new capital works programs for the arts in the form of performing arts complexes, new art galleries, and restored buildings for local arts activities.

By the early 1990s a shift was discernible. The arts portfolios attracted increased political patronage whereby state premiers either became minister for the arts or allocated the responsibility to a senior colleague and therefore increased the status of the arts and ultimately resources available. The arts community was involved in policy reviews and a modified peer assessment process whereby their recommendations went to the minister. These developments, together with the establishment of major industry assistance and development programs, meant that state cultural ministries were more in tune with their own arts community than they had been in previous decades. The state ministries can now ensure an integration of the arts agenda into wider economic and social state agendas and are certainly more responsive to initiative and innovation.

The state-based clients of libraries, museums, and art galleries are probably satisfied, although major issues such as whether to charge for admission, whose collections are housed and owned, whose value systems are espoused, and the need for extended labels and other interpretative devices, are still subjects of debate. Film and arts grants programs, on the other hand, do not contain enough monies to satisfy expectations. Even though processes are largely transparent and include public advertising and peer review, grants programs have the capacity to generate all the emotions that are attached to rejection. At the state level these are more intense and volatile.

In order to complement grant programs, considerable attention is paid to the development of strategies to integrate the arts into statewide government agendas, and to establish links with the private sector. These approaches are designed to yield long-term support for the arts and culture industries, which will hopefully lead to more employment opportunities for artists, increased investment in the arts industry, and greater access to the arts. In 1989 Western Australia initiated a strategy to integrate the arts and culture agenda with the social and economic agendas. This decision led to rewarding new partnerships. For example, the state's economic strategy utilized the skills of artists and designers in the primary product and export-driven economic sectors. A public art scheme involved the Building Management Authority, the Department of Transport and the Health and Education Departments in partnerships that saw the commissioning of site-specific art works. The Lotteries Commission allocated over $5 million to community development programs that used cultural activities as their medium. A Health Promotion Foundation allocated over $1.5 million per annum to cultural activities as an accepted, legitimate way of reaching targeted audiences with a health message.

The evolution of an international cultural development strategy placed the cultural assets of the state on trade and political agendas. Relationships with Southeast Asian neighbours were nurtured through cultural projects such as ARX (Artists regional exchange in the Asia/Pacific region) and the exchange of artists-in-residence, such as choreographers and gamelan orchestra masters. Well designed imagery and the use of Western Australian arts products, for example local tableware and textiles at formal functions and Western Australian performers as entertainers enhanced the state's profile and displayed its cultural values and assets. The state also recognized designers, artists, and natural products through a protocol gifts commissioning program and the outfitting of government offices.[10]

This integrated approach to cultural development was echoed by the Victorian Government in its cultural policy statement

Arts 21, by the Federal Government's Creative Nation and most recently by the Queensland Government's 1995 Building Local, Going Global cultural policy statement.

Local government

Of all three tiers of government, local government is closer to the ground, and the policy segmentation that occurs at the federal and state levels is often dissolved at the local level. Tourism, heritage, historical, demographic and ethnographic factors are all part of a local agenda. Artists work alongside architects, planners, and developers to create new streetscapes and new towns, and to renovate old spaces for new uses. Local consultation is essential and often community participation is encouraged. Federal and state arts and other government departments provide funds for such activities.

In the mid-1970s local councils began to enter the cultural arena in a strategic way with the first pilot appointment of community arts officers in Melbourne and Sydney. This pilot scheme, supported by the Australia Council's Community Arts Board and by the state governments, was so successful with local governments that it spawned a major network of community cultural development officers (and community arts officers) throughout Australia; these officers now facilitate, support, and plan all relevant cultural activities and facilities.

Local government spends $463 million annually on arts, cultural, and related activities. The issues directing local government expenditure in this area have largely been defined by relative geographic distances from the cultural capital. At a community level it has often been women who have nurtured, shaped, and invested in community cultural life. Many community projects have drawn on oral memories and history. Valuing the ancient and Aboriginal past of a community has helped to create greater understanding, and valuing the industrial past has given new insights into the lives of immigrants. All projects can provide opportunities for mixing age groups, genders, and ethnographic groups, thus creating new social relationships and a more vibrant community.

The rural town of Narrogin in Western Australia, the inner suburb of Prospect in South Australia, the outer suburbs of

Broadmeadows in Victoria, and Logan City in Queensland are examples of award-winning communities that have used the arts to create relevant stories in murals, banners, theatre works, books, and streetscapes. Major city councils have now created significant cultural management teams. For example Brisbane City Council's Cultural Services Section has regional community arts officers and extensive artists-in-residence projects in communities. [11]

The Arts as Corporate Identity.

The cultural industries are acknowledged as a significant force in the country's economy. The most recent edition of The Australia Council publication, *The Arts: Some Australian Data*, showed:

> Total spending by all Australian Household on arts and entertainment was $8.8 billion in 1993/94.[12]

> Average household expenditure in this area increased by $5.72 per week between 1988/9 and 1993/4.[13]

> The estimated total value of supply of goods and services to the Australian economy from the arts and cultural industry in 1993/4 was $4.8 billion.[14]

> The 1991 census showed over 50,000 people were employed directly in the industry[15] and over 148,000 in the wider industry.[16]

All of this has been possible because governments at federal and then increasingly at state and local level have supported artistic activity which reflects voter's expectations and aspirations. The combined federal, state, and local government outlay on cultural facilities, services, broadcasting, and film production in 1992/3 was $2,540 million. Total spending by all governments on cultural and arts activity was $153 per head of population ($71 by Commonwealth, $56 by state/territory, $26 by local government.) This amounted to 1.5% of Commonwealth own-purpose general government outlays, and 1.7% of state/territory outlays. [17] In addition to this allocation, partnerships have been developed across the three tiers of government, within government departments, and between government and the private sector. In the past two decades government cultural policy has focused on support for the creation and production of our cultural product. The third element that is currently and finally being attended to is the distribution of our product more effectively throughout this vast land.

The political effect of the profound cultural transformation that has occurred over the last twenty-five years culminated in the critical role played by arts and cultural issues in the 1993 federal election. The Labour Party won the election and acknowledged the pivotal role played by the arts in its achievement. The Liberal Party acknowledged that their defeat was partly due to their underestimation of the significance of the arts as an election issue. Both parties have increased the stakes since. The Liberal Party published its first cultural policy statement, *The Cultural Frontier* in 1994 and the new Labour Government published the first ever national cultural policy statement *Creative* Nation in 1994. They are remarkably similar.

Cultural policy is a protean concept. Culture is the sum total of what we have added to the natural world, and a policy is a general plan of action and practices. Viablecultural policies must embrace what we do, and not simply focus on what we ought to do. Most young people, for example, pursue cultural activities that do not feature in the cultural lexicon of middle-aged policy writers. Rather than looking for ways to lure them into concert halls in dinner suits, cultural policies should consider ways to improve the training and employment of young musicians and the playing of Australian music on airwaves. One of the virtues of the three published cultural policy statements *Creative Nation*, *Arts 21*, and *Building Local Going Global* is that contextual issues such as these are broached.[18]

Federal and state arts ministers and representatives of local government, meet annually as the Cultural Ministers Council (CMC) to discuss a cultural agenda formulated by their departmental heads. These include cultural statistics, heritage collections, libraries, arts touring, film and television, orchestras, international cultural diplomacy, taxation, copyright and moral rights legislation, advocacy issues like the cultural dimension of the General Agreement on Trade and Tariffs (GATT), and arts and education.

Some of the successful outcomes of the CMC have included a major statistical profile of the cultural industries; a strategy for the documentation, conservation and distribution of the nation's heritage collection; new federally funded performing arts programs such as Playing Australia (a fund to support national touring of the performing arts); visual arts programs such as Visions Australia (a fund to support national touring of visual art exhibitions) and a festivals funding program. The Cultural Ministers Council is a consensus forum and traditional political party lines and federal and state rivalries are assumed to be put aside in the bigger interest of the arts and cultural agenda. But the reality is that the agendas and topics are well massaged in advance by the bureaucrats and real debate is rare.

After years of lobbying by arts industry advocacy groups the federal government amalgamated its communication, and arts portfolios in 1993 and formed one department. At the federal level, the department coordinates statutory authorities like the Australian National Gallery, the National Museum of Australia, the Australia Council, the Australian National Maritime Museum, the National Library of Australia, the National Film and Sound Archives, the Australian Film Commission, and the Australian Film, Television, and Radio School. It directly assists Artbank, the Public Lending Rights Scheme, the Australian Film Finance Corporation Proprietary Limited, the Australian Children's Television Foundation, the Australian Ballet School, the National Institute of Dramatic Art, and the Australian Opera. It administers tax-related schemes such as the Taxation Incentives for the Arts Scheme, the Tax Register of Cultural Organizations, and the certification of films for tax concessions.

This consolidation of cultural functions at the federal departmental level has been seen as being at the expense of the status and functions of the Australia Council, which in the 1970s occupied a pre-eminent role in federal cultural matters. This ascendancy of the Federal Department of Communications and the Arts has become most apparent in the cultural policy statement *Creative Nation*.

Women as Artists and Administrators

At federal and state level, affirmative action policies and programs are in place and all government departments are equal opportunity employers. During the 1970s the women's movement, the women and arts movement (fuelled by a visit from American visual arts writer and feminist Lucy Lippard in 1974), the 1975 International Year of Women, the employment of women in middle and senior management positions, and the establishment of senior women's advisory committees to prime ministers and premiers all had their impact on government arts and cultural activities. Women began to infiltrate male-dominated boards and committees. Projects specifically supporting women artists, and arts projects for women were funded; the women's art register was founded; women's theatre groups and circuses began performing women's work; and anthologies of Australian women poets and writers were published. Significantly, those traditional women's domains, the crafts and community arts, were authorized at government level.

Despite predictions that amateurism, welfare, and therapy art would invade the hallowed halls of artistic excellence, both crafts and community arts were accorded board status by the Australia Council in 1973 and 1978 respectively. For the crafts the impact was spectacular. In a short time, our potters (e.g., Marea Gazzard, Joan Campbell, and Janet Mansfield), our jewelers (e.g., Darani Lewers and Felicity Peters), and our textile artists (e.g., Mona Hessing and Kay Lawrence), have ensured that the old debate about the artistic legitimacy of the crafts has been transcended. Their work, drawing materials and inspiration from this ancient land, has in fact been artistically significant. Very appropriately, it is well represented in the new Parliament House in Canberra. In a way, the crafts offered fresh fields for women which were untrammelled by the male hegemony that still holds sway in the fine arts. Women were also leaders in community arts as organizers, artists, and community arts officers. The Art and Working Life Program, located within workplaces and supported by the Trade Union movement, supported women artists, who in turn produced posters for campaigns against sexual harassment, racial discrimination, and sloppy safety measures. Women artists also helped the union movement recover its history through the design and making of banners and murals. As writers, dancers, poets, crafts workers, and musicians, women have also contributed to an emerging understanding of the richness of Australia's cultural diversity.

A number of specific activities addressed gender issues. The first was the Women and Arts Festival and Research Project, initiated by the New South Wales government, which took place in 1982.[19] The second was the Australia Council's Women and Arts Project.[20] A strategy for action was devised and its proposals for improvement included child-care facilities, a training inquiry, exercise of leverage on funded arts organizations and direct action by the Council which included a three-part program to train and educate women and the arts community. Firstly, chairing and negotiating skills workshops were conducted in all states for hundreds of women arts workers. The workshop was conducted back to back with an arts-related conference, during which all sessions were chaired by (newly trained) women. This program still impacts on the conduct of arts forums. The second training project was a financial planning workshop for women, while the third was equal employment opportunity workshops for arts managers. The aim was to assist the managers in the implementation of equal opportunity principles through employment practices and selection of work and artists. These projects were conducted in collaboration with, and often extended by, state arts departments.

The Women and Arts project was enhanced by the legislative base chosen by the Australian Government to advance affirmative action, equal employment opportunities, and other anti-discrimination tactics. This decision was based on the view that behavioural change would precede attitudinal change and that behavioural change, for Australians, would only occur through a legislated medium.[21]

Women are now represented as chief executive officers and chairpersons in government cultural bureaucracies and arts organizations. Three state arts departments have women CEOs, the chairs of the Australia Council, the Australian Film, Television, and Radio School, and the Australian Film Commission are women, as is the CEO of the Australian National Gallery and state opera, dance, and theatre companies have women as general managers. Aboriginal women are also prominent as artists and arts leaders.

Conclusion

The concept of cultural rights espoused in *Creative Nation* is that all people, despite their geographic, financial, educational, social, or linguistic background, are entitled to contribute actively to the cultural life of the country and to participate in it.

Governments now plan, regulate, subsidize, and intervene in a whole smorgasbord of cultural industries and activities. Until *Creative Nation*, this cultural planning was done in a piecemeal way, for example, we have tough defamation and censorship laws yet visual artists still do not have legislative protection of their moral rights. Aboriginal artists and aesthetics are valued and celebrated yet appropriation of Aboriginal imagery has only recently been challenged in law.

In my view, the existence of a national cultural policy has to do with the need to define, reassert, refine, or project a national identity, often following a period of imperialism or oppression brought on by outside economic, military, political, and latterly by cultural forces. In Australia's case cultural policy statements come precisely at a time when our younger generation are wearing baseball hats, eating at McDonalds, and playing basketball; when the Australian government has aligned with the French government and challenged the U.S. determination to include audio-visual industries in the GATT (general agreement on tariffs and trade) free trade rounds; when, with the centenary of federation occurring in 2000, there is a widespread view that constitutional links to Britain need to be reappraised, and when, as a consequence, there is an increasingly strong republican movement.

The cultural policy statements all position the arts and cultural life of Australia in an industry framework and link them with major technological and multimedia developments as part of an enhanced distribution strategy. The arts are also intertwined with tourism, marketing, public diplomacy, and other

economic strategies. These visions, as articulated in the published cultural policy statements, have caused some disquiet
amongst those who fear that the arts structured as industry and
focused on commercial opportunity will kill off vigorous experi-
mentation. But cultural policy statements are a pause in print.
None of them lose sight of the pivot around which a cultural life
revolves, which is the wellspring of artistic activities that are
authentic for and attractive to a home audience and hence,
hopefully attractive because of their difference to the outsider.

An effective cultural policy operates within the context of a
people's history and stories; their geographic, demographic,
and ethnographic certainties; their educational activities and
facilities; and the nature of their voluntary and community
activity. People make a cultural life. As J.H. Simpson writes,
"cultural policy is effective when it enables the average man or
woman to validate the uniqueness of her/his personality in a
society which threatens constantly to thrust her/him into anonymity, facelessness and unimportance." [22] Ultimately, national,
state, and local approaches to cultural policy have been and must
continue to be effective in this way.

Notes

1. H. C. Coombs, first chairman of the Australia Council, speech 1969, UNESCO
Seminar on the Performing Arts, Australian National University, Canberra, 1969.
2. This article is about some of the issues that have informed the development of
cultural policy in the three tiers of government in Australia. The period explored
is 1970 to 1995, which coincides with my own involvement in cultural policy within
Australia, since I occupied senior positions in the Australia Council from 1974 to
1988 and was then the CEO of the State Ministry for the Arts in Western Australia
from 1988 to 1995. The article draws primarily upon my own memory, supple-
mented by my own papers and by other references, and thus makes no pretence
to reflect the whole story. Rather it is the perspective of one who was inside the
machine at the time and therefore cognizant of the forces that were driving
policymaking and change.
3. Philip Parsons (ed.), *Shooting the Pianist: The Role of Government in the Arts*
(Sydney: Currency Press, 1987) p.12.
4. Andrea Hull, "A Preamble to the Cultural Framework", (paper presented at the
Cultural Ministers Council, 1990 Rotarua, New Zealand). The Perth Festival began
in 1953 as an initiative of the University of Western Australia and the Adelaide Festival

was initiated in 1960. Both were designed to bring the best of the international arts to Australia. At the time, there was little Australian product on television, apart from sports coverage and games shows.

5. John Berger, *Ways of Seeing*, (London: Harmondsworth, Penguin), 1972. p.33. Based on the BBC television series.

6. B. Head and J. Walters (eds.), *Intellectual Movements and Australian Society*, (Melbourne: Oxford University Press, 1988). Also quoted in L. J. Hume, *Another Look at the Cultural Cringe*, (The Centre for Independent Studies Limited, 1993)

7. H. C. Coombs, *Trial Balance* (Melbourne: McMillan, 1981), p.252.

8. Ibid; p.254.

9. Philip Parsons, *Shooting the Pianist*, p.12.

10. Western Australian Department for the Arts publications Annual Reports (Perth 1989, 1990, 1991, 1992, and 1993); Artsline (Perth 1994); International Cultural Development Committee Brochure (Perth 1992); Submission to the State Economic Strategy (Perth 1990/199); Business Plan (Perth 1994); Western Australian Government Publications; WA Advantage (Perth 1991) Economic Strategy; Social Advantage (Perth 1992); Into Asia (Perth 1992); Also, Andrea Hull, "Towards Integration Through Partnerships: Western Australia's Cultural Policy" , *Aesthetex: Australian Journal of Arts Management V4, no. 2* (Winter 1992).

11. Brisbane City Council, Cultural Services Update (Brisbane, 1995).

12. The Australia Council's Compendium of Arts Statistics, *The Arts: Some Australian Data, Fifth Edition*, (Sydney, July 1996) p.4.

13. Ibid; p.6.

14. Ibid; p.32. One way of establishing the size of an industry is to measure the total value of goods and services which it supplies to the general economy. The value of the total supply of goods and services to the Australian economy of the narrowly defined arts industry groups (radio and television station services; film industry; museum and art gallery services; live theatre, music etc; creative artistic services) was approximately $4,793 million in 1993-94. The following list compares the total value of these arts and related industry groups with a selection of other Australian Bureau of Statistics groups:

Industry description	1989-90 $ million	1993-94 $ million
Cosmetics and toilet preparations	683	731
Footwear	1,185	1,267
Refrigerators, household appliances	3,091	3,304
Beer and other alcoholic beverages	3,472	3,711
Sport and recreation services	3,740	3,998
Clothing	4,335	4,634
Petroleum and coal products	10,444	11,164
Arts industry groups (as above)	4,484	4,793

15. Ibid; p.36.

16. Ibid; p.40. The wider arts industry includes: Publishing; Publishing and printing; Music stores; Architectural services; Advertising services; Libraries; Mu-

seums and art galleries; Entertainment (undefined); Motion picture production; Motion picture film hiring; Motion picture theatres; Radio stations; Television stations; Live theatre, orchestras, etc; Creative arts (artists, writers, etc); Parks and zoological gardens; Photography services.

17. Ibid; p.78.

18. Department of Communication and the Arts, *Creative Nation: Commonwealth Cultural Policy*, (Canberra, 1994); State Government of Victoria, *Arts 21: The Victorian Government's Strategy for the Arts, into the Twenty First Century* (Melbourne, 1994); Queensland Government, *Building Local Going Global: Cultural Statement* (Brisbane, 1995).

19. Australia Council, *Women in the Arts* (Sydney 1983). A study of the obstacles women artists and arts workers encounter. The study was conducted between 1982 and 1983 by the Research Advisory Group of the Women and Arts Project, New South Wales.

20. Australia Council publications: *Women in the Arts: A Strategy for Action* (Sydney, 1985); *Women in the Arts Project Report* (Sydney 1986).

21. Conversation in 1983 with Dr. Peter Wilenski, chairman of the Public Service Commission (1983-87) and an outstanding public sector administrator and reformer.

22. As quoted in Andrea Hull, "A Place in Time - The Community Arts Movement in Ten Years Time" keynote address to the National Community Arts Conference Melbourne May 1980.

Feminist Speculations on Value: Culture in an Age of Downsizing

Barbara Godard

Money is only one sytem of value,

Money does not define the value of art.

—Barbara Sternberg [1]

To protect culture and intellectual liberty in practice would mean... loss of publicity and poverty. But those, as we have seen, are women's familiar teachers... Since all the fruits of professional culture - such as directorships of art galleries and museums, professorships and lectureships and editorships - are still beyond their reach, they should be able to take a more purely disinterested view of culture than their *brothers...*

—Virginia Woolf [2]

Is there a crisis in the arts? [3]   Am I writing a "lament for a nation"? Or scratching graffiti in a prophecy of doom? Moving between these genres, I shall analyze the changing discourses on culture in Canada.

The sense of crisis along with this oscillation between melancholy and foreboding has been instilled by a succession of newspaper headlines announcing changes in the funding of the arts. Each day brings a new bulletin: "CBC Under the Knife"; "Budget Cuts to Grants Will Force Shutdowns, Book Publishers Say"; "Metro Cuts Arts Grants by $345,000"; "Arts Voices Petition PM to Rescue Harbourfront"; "Telefilm Shuts Foreign Offices"; "Tory Cuts to Ontario Film Development Corporation 'Disastrous'"; "Grant-slashing Reshapes Lists." [4] This litany of cutbacks to cultural agencies has come in the wake of the budget announced by the federal government in March 1995. After the election of a Conservative government in Ontario in June 1995, such headlines appeared at a dizzying rhythm encompassing every phase of communal existence from education to transportation and public safety. In this trend of government "downsizing," public culture is vanishing.

In Ontario especially, such amputations of public policies and institutions have been made tyrannically by cabinet fiat at lighting speed with no consultation or public debate. Increased feminization of poverty was the effect of decisions immediately after the election to cut back welfare payments and to strike down the Employment Equity Act. Some 130 feminist groups, signatories of the Ontario Women's Declaration on December 6, 1995, demanded that the new government "cease its policies of discriminatory cutbacks" so that the "hard-won legal, economic, social and political gains women have achieved" could be maintained. They also protested against the "deep cuts for funding for the arts and culture," stressing a connection between women and the arts in this social realignment. [5]

Although women constitute 49.73 per cent of all visual artists in Canada, according to the 1991 census, their art practice is no more visible in commercial galleries today than it was in 1970 and has been erased from historical documentation in art galleries. [6] Artists are among the poorest members of Ontario society having an average income of $14-15,000 for most arts occupations, with visual artists at $8,800 well below the provincial average. Women artists' earnings are even lower, averaging only 63 per cent of what men earn. [7] How can artists expect to be spared in what is increasingly evident as class warfare waged with new tactics and ferocity between haves and have nots? The vulnerable are being scapegoated for problems in the economic system as the wrath of the middle-class in an age of downward mobility is vented on the marginalized and the poor. Indeed, it is precisely their poverty which makes artists targets of a rhetoric of marketplace success in which exchange is the only criterion of value. Through a process of separation and abstraction money is posited as a commodity exchangeable for itself. In a developed system of exchange, as Marx argued, "the ties of personal dependence, of distinction, of education ... are ripped up ... and individuals are *seen* as independent."[8] Knowledge, art, health - nothing can be allowed to interfere with the bottom line! Myths of massive government indebtedness and metaphors of "good housekeeping" attempt to legitimize cutbacks as economic necessity while concealing the recent changes in government policy which have produced these new patterns of public debt.[9] The advantaged are also intervening in discursive practices with a new inflection of the term "interest group" to delegitimize collective struggles for equality and stifle public debate on what is a radical restructuring of economic and social policies underway in Canada.

Political struggle is organized through signs with the mass media being one of the institutional sites for this discursive contestation. "Public interest" is one semantic configuration currently undergoing resignification. A column in the *Financial Post* by Michael Walker, head of the right-wing Fraser Institute, titled "Disarming Special Interests is Key to Re-engineering Ontario Economy" exposed the neo-conservative strategy.[10] Neither business groups nor bond-rating agencies, both of which have vested interests in government policy, are considered "special interests" by Walker. No concern is expressed over the $4.8 million in government support of the Canadian Chamber of Commerce in 1994 in addition to the tax-exempt status of its membership dues. A grant of $250,000. to the National Action Committee on the Status of Women, however, generated protest.[11] The Canada Council has been a favourite target for attacks by conservative groups such as the National Citizens' Coalition which denounces culture as just an expensive "special interest" the overburdened taxpayer should be spared.[12] The label's effect in diminishing the force of claims to "public interest," to a "civil society" or a collective project of society, must be understood as a strategy in a discursive struggle around "interest" to position one group as speaking subject while relegating all others to silence. This "naturalizes" a shift in relations within the social contract to consolidate the power of rich white men.

The sense of impending doom was heightened in August 1995 when Statistics Canada released figures on Government expenditures on culture which registered a steady decline since 1989. A cut in 1993/4 of 1 per cent by all three levels of government followed four years where, dropping 5.2 per cent, cultural spending had lost ground to inflation.[13] The federal government led the way with cuts of $2.8 billion (a decrease of 1.8 per cent), followed by provincial governments with cuts of $1.9 billion (a decrease of 1.8 per cent). Within these global figures, the cuts were distributed differently so that spending on broadcasting remained at 53 per cent of the total federal cultural budget, while expenditures on other areas including film and video, book and periodical publishing, and sound recording, were down by 9 per cent. Simultaneously, grants to artists and cultural institutions dropped more than 7 per cent. In Ontario, the drop in provincial cultural funding was 7 per cent, second highest among the provinces, bringing Ontario's per capita spending to fifty-five dollars, well below the national average. A further cut of $5.1 million to the Canada Council in the March 1996 federal budget belied the pronouncement in the Throne Speech that "Culture is at the core of our identity as Canadians" and has the government's firm support. The staggering 28 per cent cut to the Ontario Arts Council in two steps in July and October 1995 – down $12 million for 1996-7 from the year before – was merely a prelude. With a third cut of $5 million or 16.5 per cent, the council's budget has been slashed by more than 40 per cent in two years, to $25 million from $43 million.

It is not my purpose to analyze cutback data but to isolate some of the episodes in a narrative that is fostering my unease. Both its repetitiveness and its generalization are disconcerting, for incident after incident involves the same two actors: state financiers and artists in fixed positions of subject and object. These tales signify a break, a shift in financial commitment that will transform culture in Canada. Of what magnitude? With what shifts in participation? What is being lost? Might a prompt response yet turn a plot of tragedy into one of comedy - of diversity, of sublation at a higher level? Questions concerning the relationship of the signifiers "nation," "culture," and "state" are never addressed explicitly. What would be the implications of a rupture in their alliance? Whose "culture" is at stake here? Women's culture? What "nation"? Among the many contradictions in the discourses of "culture" and "nation" regarding government policies of support to the arts, the artist's role since the nineteenth century has always been vexed: is s/he a covert legislator, a civilizer, or a visionary, a dissident? In this ambiguity of the artist's social role, the reaccentuation of "interest" around claims to the "public good" finds fertile terrain. Rather than reading the current situation like a futurologue within a rhetoric of crisis, as the news media would invite, I shall engage in a genealogical exercize with the tangle of discourses from the past. I want to insist on the perennial nature of this "crisis."

Within the persistent contradictions in arts policy in Canada there is nonetheless in the present conjuncture a change intimated in Susan Walker's 1994 year-end summary of the arts: "Ask not what your government can do *for* you, but what your government is doing *to* you."[14] The shift in prepositions signals a transformation in the role of the state in fostering a public concept of the common good, manifest in the establishment of arts councils. Under the aegis of "procedural liberalism," which has been reshaping the Canadian state since the passage of the Charter of Rights and Freedoms in 1982, individual rights have been privileged.[15] Walker's title signals an additional shift: "Professional arts nags had work cut out for them." "Arts nags" (descriptive or pejorative?) are organizations mediating relations between artists and the state. In this case, she was referring to the Ontario Arts Network, disappointed about the Canada Council's hastily planned consultation tour in December 1994 over proposed changes in the Council's policy. With little notice to formulate their positions, artists and their organizations had none of their customary input into these policy decisions. However, Michel Dupuy, Minister of Canadian Heritage, not Roch

Carrier, Director of the Canada Council, was named by the OAN as the "Most Disappointing Man of the Year."

Nonetheless, the artists' criticism of Carrier highlights a difference from earlier times when the Canada Council carried out "Soundings" with the arts communities in order to have grassroots feedback so as to perform more effectively its role as artists' advocate with the federal government. Indeed, in another period of stress for the Council on its twentieth anniversary in 1977, when planned cuts following upon inflation, separation from the Social Sciences and Humanities Research Council, and the possibility of Quebec independence curtailed the scope of Council action and promised a "new society with a social contract radically different from that on which the Council was founded,"[16] Mavor Moore (its first Chair from the arts community) set up a "task force" with members of the Advisory Arts Panel of Council. They formulated policies and initiatives for the renewal of the Canada Council's mandate to "energize" or "seed" artistic activity. This proactive stance was articulated in the twenty recommendations in *The Future of the Canada Council*. A report with a difference, its introduction took the form of a concrete poem. Artists themselves formed the 1812 Committee, a common front against government cutbacks. By documenting the economic and political importance of the arts, this committee made the arts an election issue in 1979 with political parties developing position statements on cultural funding. A subsequent conference of federal and provincial ministers of culture, the first such intergovernmental meeting, attempted to establish more coherent relations between the cultural policies of different levels of government. This scrutiny in turn resulted in the establishment in 1981 of the Federal Cultural Policy Review Committee (Applebaum-Hébert) whose report generated many counter-arguments in texts published during the eighties by the Canadian Conference of the Arts, though little legislative action.

Presently, artists' support for the Council is lukewarm, squeezing it more tightly in its ambiguous "arms-length" position between arts communities and government. With per-capita spending on the Council at $3.40, the lowest in eight years, and anticipated cuts of 5 per cent over the next four years pending the results of the Liberal government's programme review, the Canada Council's panic in its hurried consultation is not surprising. Frustrated in their scramble for funding, however, artists have become suspicious of the Council they must placate, particularly since the Council's discourse increasingly echoes the rhetoric of the marketplace.[17] In the "consultation workbook" sent to artists, the absence of previously central statements on historical context and policy principles for public funding of the arts was disquieting in light of the Canada Council's critical negotiating role with government. Such anxiety was justified by the decision subsequently taken by the Council after the 1995 federal budget to cut back funding to arts service organizations (such as the Writers' Union and the Literary Translators' Association) which formulate principles and open a discursive space for the arts in the public forum.

***

What may be forgotten, in the current dissatisfaction with the Canada Council, is how it has radically transformed the situation of the arts in Canada over the last forty years in nearly every dimension, from the diversification of art forms to the dispersion of venues and the proliferation of languages. Particularly notable has been its redrawing of the boundaries between professional and amateur so that the independently wealthy are no longer the only artists. Many more women are included, myself among them. Remembering forces me to recognize how my own intellectual formation has been shaped by Canadian cultural policy. I have long taken for granted the possibilities these policies opened for intellectual and artistic training and practice which have constituted the habitus making materially possible who I am. Without these policies, there would be little Canadian literature, film, painting, theatre for me to teach and translate. So many more opportunities have been available to me (and to other women) than to my mother's generation because of the period of unprecedented cultural activity in Canada which followed the establishment of the Canada Council in 1957.[18]

Encouraged by both the political rhetoric of the period and the financial support of the Canada Council with its awards for graduate work, and grants-in-aid of translation, as well as its institutional infrastructural aid such as university libraries and grants in support of publishers and periodicals, I have been able to earn a living within the literary institution. Moreover, my pleasure in the rich diversity of theatrical performances, music concerts, art shows and films written and performed by Canadians every night at some eighty-six galleries and sixty-three performing arts facilities in Toronto in the 1990s is limited only by the difficulty of making a choice among them.[19]

How different this is from the 1950s! I remember them as one long dull wait for something, anything, to happen. The dark ages. Indeed, as the Massey Report notes, at the beginning of the decade, there were only twenty-five bookstores across Canada selling books exclusively. Today there are 180 in Toronto alone.[20] For those of us stage-struck at an early age by the Toronto Children's Players, there were only a few productions each year at Hart House and the Crest Theatre to sustain our passion. "Spring Thaw," an annual revue of the New Play Society, and the Stratford Festival enlivened the spring. The National Ballet performed for a couple of weeks a year while the Toronto Symphony Orchestra had monthly concerts during the winter. Chamber music could be heard on Sunday afternoons in the sculpture court at the Art Gallery. For contemporary Canadian art by local artists, one could go to Eaton's College Street store which housed the only commercial gallery in Toronto. For a long time I thought of myself in the fifties and early sixties as a chrysalis wrapped within my parents' constricted world. Research has shown me that my horizons were, relatively speaking, broad. This *was* the Toronto arts scene! I'd even attended poetry readings by Margaret Atwood and Gwendolyn MacEwen at the Bohemian Embassy in the House of Hamburg.[21]

When the Ontario Arts Council was established in 1963 its first move was to assume responsibility for a number of these organizations previously funded on an ad hoc basis by the Community Programs Branch of the Ministry of Education, along with the Canadian Opera Company, the National Theatre School, the Shaw Festival, Toronto Workshop Productions, and the National Youth Orchestra. The OAC also funded some orchestras in smaller cities, the periodicals *Canadian Art* and *Evidence* ("bright, anarchistic"), and amateur organizations such as the Potters Guild and the Dominion Drama Festival. These grants, fifty-seven in all, accounted for its initial $300,000 allocation.[22] Thirty years later, the OAC's funds have been disbursed to 888 art organizations and 1800 individual artists, involving 389 communities. Some forty large institutions, including many of those receiving funds in 1963, obtained funding of a hundred thousand dollars or more each.[23] Evident in the relatively high number of organizations to individuals in these statistics is the continuation of the OAC's initial commitment to "organizations that will use any profits they make to continue and extend their programs year after year."[24] Stability and longer seasons were considered crucial to artistic excellence and were achieved through the maintenance of professional companies who would otherwise lose their artists to higher paying and more artistically challenging companies in the UK and the US. "Ontario can ill-afford to lose any of these professional organizations," proclaims the first annual report of the OAC.[25] Noting a considerable "growth in the amateur arts in Ontario as part of a surge towards the arts in Canada and the United States generally,"[26] the OAC's policies supported amateur arts and art education to develop involved and discriminating audiences and improve artistic standards and production values. This, it was felt, would enable greater professionalism in the arts. The emphasis on organization and performance advantaged certain arts over others, as well as perpetuating the consumption rather than production-driven model of cultural policy in Canada. Democratization of the arts through education for personal development was thus paradoxically linked to elitism in producing occasions for the perfection of specialized skills.

The explosion in the number of professional artists (double the growth rate of the total work force in the last twenty years)[27] is a sign of the phenomenal success of the arts councils – and of a limitation. Yes, there are today many and varied venues for art: the CBC is no longer the only steady employer for actors and musicians. Yes, the standards of training of artists and production values of performances have increased enormously, as artists have moved through the ranks of the small professional companies to the stages of the large commercial theatres: a Mirvishization more than a nationalization of theatre! However, though the existence of the arts councils has legitimated participation in the arts, authorized the profession "artist," it has not significantly changed the economic status of artists who remain mostly part-time professionals. Artists today don't have million dollar contracts like baseball stars. Most still have salaried jobs in addition to their status as self-employed artists. The type of job may have changed since the fifties to part-time or occasional work which allows them to feed their passion yet keep it the central focus in their lives.

There are also major distinctions between the arts in respect to funding, with the three performing arts, dance, theatre and music, receiving 42 per cent of grants in Toronto in 1988, museums and galleries another 40 per cent, with writing, film and the visual arts sharing the rest in decreasing proportion.[28] This discrepancy results from the self-employment of the last named group. Labour intensive, art becomes increasingly expensive in an age of mechanization. Yet salaries (time) are more flexible expenses than rents or materials (goods) and make weaker claims to support. Artists are still subsidizing the rest of the community by making art or performing for relatively low pay. The ripple effects benefit administrators and landlords who command "market" wages. Significantly, government contributions to sports through funds or lands for stadiums like the Skydome in Toronto are not considered "special" handouts, as are grants to artists, though many of the latter, such as the OAC's Artist-in-the-Schools Program, are in fact payment for services rendered.

The myth that artists are a privileged elite has become a form of oppression, Heather Robertson suggests, a means of segregation which, like reserves for the First Nations, works to keep them "powerless and poor" and, consequently, less creative.[29] Robertson's response to this impoverishment has been to challenge the arts councils' bureaucracy, drawing attention to the inverse pyramid of benefit from grants which subsidize the art collector's speculation. The administrator alone has the permanent job. This situation might be overcome, Robertson suggests, by more direct government subsidy of the artist, without the intermediary arms-length councils. Government would be more accountable to the public than a bureaucracy and the criterion for grants would reflect more a "national interest" rather than an administrator's taste. However, the history of the Canada Council suggests that a move to democratize does not automatically nationalize. Greater funding which came with the introduction of government appropriations in 1965 produced closer scrutiny and parliamentary interference in the censorship of grants on moral and political grounds.[30]

Moreover, the current system of subsidy might be seen as productive in a different way: it constitutes a cultural community, both the artistic community producing a cultural discourse and the informed and involved audience to sustain the intensification of arts activity since the fifties. This collective politicized discourse of artists has been the major site for articulation of cultural policy subsequently developed by governments. It is the availability of such an audience to support Canadian artists which has enabled them not only to pursue careers in Canada but to produce original works responsive to the contingent, the local. With changes in the economic basis of art came changes in its production. No longer dependent on the market place of the metropole, artists could create more freely for a Canadian public. The explosion of creative work by choreographers, composers, poets, painters, filmmakers, photographers, in the last thirty years has transformed the arts scene, made it a place of creative innovation rather than colonial repetition.

Why, then, my melancholia if the artist is still impoverished? What is this thing I don't know how to lose, or for whose loss I have found no valid compensation and so remain a prisoner of affect, of anxiety in being?[31] Am I carrying the heavy burden Virginia Woolf laid on the "daughters of educated men" to protect "culture and intellectual liberty"? It is easier for them to question established values than for their brothers, she suggests, since women are "immune ... from certain compulsions" and "able to take a more purely disinterested view of culture" because of their habit of "poverty" and the fact that all the plums of the arts institutions-- "directorships of art galleries and museums, professorships and lectureships, and editorships"-- are not accessible to them. [32] Are women and culture always to be linked only through poverty?

There are many complex issues of aesthetic value and social mission I shall not explicitly address. I offer no general account of the relation between the distribution of cultural capital and the accumulation of productive capital. Only scattered speculations on the question of value, aesthetic and cultural. Unwilling to invoke the grand humanistic narratives of discovery and emancipation, or the grand nationalistic narratives of communal celebration and glorification by way of explanation for my pursuit of this obscure object of desire, though enlightenment (intellectual awakening) and a sense of belonging to a project of community have clearly been significant for me, I am left with the feel of Ontario red cedar to my touch and a sense of wonder.

Moments of being?[33] I hesitate to use Woolf's Modernist discourse of aesthetic transcendence, yet I am haunted by something like beauty, a moment that makes the familiar strange and transforms my relations to my surroundings. Barbara Hepworth's sculptures exhibited at the Art Gallery of Ontario in 1995 induced one such moment. The artist's concentration on her material made light radiate from a variety of woods and stones. The pathos of gesture in their positioning.[34] How hug a stone? The vitality and beauty of the trampled earth made manifest. I tread lightly in awe. Ekphrasis? Or acknowledgement of Hepworth's skilled hand? I remember the redness of cedar and a pen knife in my own hand, the sensation of wood coming alive against my skin in a process of transformation. This is not the enjoyment of money in a rhetoric of calculation. Could I account for beauty within an ethics of concern? On what terms can I make claims for such an event?

Despite many contradictions in its formulation, an enlarged space for such moments of beauty was made within a social contract that forged a new alliance between nationalism and the welfare state after the shock of the Depression and WWII rocked European humanism. Now, forty years after that shock and the establishment of the Canada Council, another change is underway in an era of continentalist Free Trade. What seems fast vanishing is the sense of *romanitas*, of law and tradition as the basis of civilized society, which has distinguished a Canadian ideal of collective from the American ideal of individual rights.[35] There is no place for beauty as a common good to be protected by the state within the individualistic, neutral discourse of procedural liberalism which (mis)represents its production of inequality through symmetrizing the operation of exchange value.

***

The shift in metaphors of cultural intervention in Ontario Arts Council reports over thirty years provides some measure of the change. In its inaugural year, 1963-64, the OAC report details its particular scope of action and sets out its mandate in a therapeutic or juridical metaphor of balanced growth: the state will guard against the "deformity" of "one-sided development" by "strengthening and deepening in the minds of our people a richer and fuller appreciation of the quality, character and majesty of intellectual and cultural pursuits." While knowledge of the Arts is considered a good in and of itself – "a noble, vital, permanent element of human life and happiness" – it is also a necessary complement to specialization that would impede "real progress" which is the development of "all the faculties belonging to our nature." Variety or diversity is important. Classical ideals of harmony and balance are joined to humanist values of self-knowledge. Especially, however, this knowledge is required to counteract materialism: "If a great increase of wealth takes place and, with that increase of wealth, a powerful stimulus to the invention of mere luxury, that, if it stands alone, is not and never can be progress."[36] Here, in their clearest formulation, are the lofty cultural values of idealism associated with "literature" in Canada at the end of the nineteenth century.

Significantly, the words "arts" and "culture" are used interchangeably in the terms of abstraction and absolute of the nineteenth century. Divorced from skills or processes they became synonyms, according to Raymond Williams, for "a whole way of life, material, intellectual, and spiritual." Separating certain moral and intellectual activities from the "driven impetus" of a new kind of society, then functioning as court of appeal or "mitigating and rallying alternative" to this society, arts and culture are a complex response to both industry and democracy.[37] Artists had to face the resulting contradictions in their role. Were they Shelley's "unacknowledged legislators of the world," society's guides or seers, mediators between humans and nature? Or were they rather radical interpreters of a superior reality, misunderstood and scorned by society whose vulgarity they, in turn, despised? Civilizing? Or disrupting? Both the artist's social responsibilities and the aestheticism of art for art's sake are upheld in the opening statement by the Chair of the OAC, J. Keiller Mackay. The contradictions in perspective are manifest too between the Executive Director's sense of his mission to develop a "Peace Corps of the arts" which will send professionals touring the province "to train and inspire the amateurs"[38] (the arts as welfare work in a cultural backwater or colonial state of underdevelopment) and the report's utopian vision of the results of this initiative where "the present renaissance going on in the arts would blossom into a truly Golden Age" (aesthetic idealism).[39] Significantly, this will happen only if adequate funds are available (realism). Arnoldian sweetness and light will come into being with the help of, not against, Philistinism. [40]

With no tradition of cultural philanthropy in Canada, the Ontario Arts Council envisaged itself not as public patron, but as broker or matchmaker. As the report notes, in the absence of "fantastically wealthy foundations that give fifty million dollars annually to the arts in the US," Ontario is going to have to rely more on "business and industry for help."[41] The OAC conceives itself as a "catalyst,"[42] convening meetings of businessmen and industrialists in order to induce them to place the arts higher in their priorities for corporate donations, neglected in favour of educational and medical projects. So, the OAC would make a "strong plea to them for the artistic spirit of man," as has the

Chairman with his tropes of knowledge and health.[43]

The arts have a special role, then, but not in opposition to the market place. So too, the elitism of the discourse of artistic excellence is moderated by democratization through photographs of amateurs: the cover of the Report features a small boy painting while, the caption tells us, his parents are taking classes at the Hockley Valley Summer School. A gently corrective, paternalistic tone figures the connection of the OAC to the government through the Ministry of Education, whose Community Programs Branch it expanded. Training, working for the future, is emphasized, in an atmosphere of exposure to the "best that is thought and known." This, it is felt, would stimulate a dormant capacity to appreciate the eternal.

The linking of the arts to education underlines the persistent force of the idealist epistemology, reigning in Canadian education (particularly in university level literary studies) since the 1880s, on the formulation of theories and policies of culture to exert a civilizing influence. As Henry Hubert has argued, such an idealist emphasis on literature and poetics over rhetoric, has been related to a suspicion of democracy that values free speech, and to a disdain for seeking economic advantage.[44] Contradictions abound, however. The OAC's emphasis on creativity and imagination reflects both a reformist democratic zeal and a belief in the advent of a leisure society: it is a model for developing audience taste through the practice of the arts as much as through attending arts events that attain European and American standards of artistic excellence. Proactive in educating citizens, the report is also proactive in wooing business support. Not surprisingly, perhaps. Roy MacSkimming notes ironically (?) that the Council began as "A Gleam in Robarts' (and Gelber's) Eye," as a collaboration between the minister of education turned premier and Arthur Gelber, a businessman, active on the board of the National Ballet and president of the Canadian Conference of the Arts.[45] With other directors tired of getting money for such organizations under the table, he convinced the new premier to institute public funding for the arts on a stable basis through an arms-length institution. This partnership of business and education established culture in a third and autonomous space as a complete way of life, as evident in the report's rhetoric. Reactive rather than proactive to artists' creating, the institution has been an enabling body rather than a producing one for individual artists whose names are listed in the report only in the activities of the Art Institute of Ontario, which purchased some works for its touring artmobile. This is a tendency which has been perpetuated in the OACs unique modality of awarding grants to individuals only on the third person recommendation of OAC funded organizations.

The OAC report for 1992-93 is a much briefer document, although it covers a much greater number of divisions and grants. In it the space allotted to culture has narrowed in the very act of multiplication. "Culture" and "art" no longer figure as an idealized abstraction or a distinct way of life. The arts are considered a business: culture is neither singular nor isomorphic with nation and state, despite the populist address of the report to "Ontarians." Technology, linking the arts and industry, will lead the way in the unification of the many cultures of Ontario in a social morphing. The Chair's opening remarks offer no general pronouncements on the value of the arts, but zero in on economics. With a minimal budget, the OAC has "promoted" and "invested" in activities that have "improved the quality of life everywhere." There follows a rapid enumeration of the many activities of the council introduced with active verbs, "promoted," "fostered," "encouraged," "funded," supported by statistics to demonstrate the number of citizens involved – for example, 700,000 students are in education programmes providing an "appreciation" of the arts.[46] Emphasized is the excellence of investment in the arts in a competition for scarce resources. Good is measured only in terms of the cost/benefit ratio of the balance sheet. Comparative statistics are provided to show that public funds spent on the arts ($4.38) are much lower on a per capita basis than those spent on health ($1,681) or education ($614). Culture is highly profitable: there is "a real return on the modest sums allocated to artistic creation."[47]

The language of creativity and imagination introduced fleetingly in this phrase is notably absent from most of this "Message from the Chair." "Innovative" is linked to the cross-disciplinary projects and new technologies supported by the Venture Fund. Mixing is the crucial trope in this document. In most cases, "art" is presented in a list that denies it any special status or sphere, and it is almost always figured in relation to institutions. OAC collaborated with "artists, art and professional organizations, municipalities, school boards and 100,000 volunteers and art lovers."[48] Citizens showed their "attachment to the arts" as consumers not creators. They "purchased theatre and concert tickets, books, magazines, pictures and handicrafts, visiting museums and art galleries, attending festivals, registering their children for courses or local artistic activities, and listening to radio or television programs which owe their existence to artistic creation."[49]

Broadly inclusive though it is, this is not an anthropological view of culture as the everyday practices of a distinct group of people. Rather, it is a populist view of culture as recreation or leisure that includes forms of mass culture and communication, of passive consumption as well as of active production. The OAC is no longer a "catalyst" in a process of transformation, but a facilitator or distributor of "services," responsive to needs and the market. Distinctions between "high" and "low" culture are deliberately blurred in an effort to demonstrate the mass involvement of Ontario citizens in cultural activities. The concept of culture as absolute is replaced with the concept of universality as a touchstone of value. Numerical inclusivity works as proof to establish the importance of the arts' claims on the public purse in comparison to the claims of health and education which were preferred social values linked in the 1963-4 report.

The wellbeing and development offered as the effect of the arts is no longer the classical balance of different spheres, but economic progress alone: "For very little money, the arts play a vigorous role in stimulating local economies and creating employment."[50] Neither leisure nor detachment from industry will be promoted by education in the arts. In fact, rather than a "frill, a time-filler between science and math classes," any experience in the arts is touted as "one of the best ways to develop the skills necessary in a high-tech society that values problem solving."[51] Education and the arts no longer develop the whole person, but offer training in specific technologies. In this, art is claimed to have a leading edge over science or business. Similarly, while a rhetoric of service characterizes the function of the OAC as handmaid to the arts, the organization privileges administrative functions and the artist only indirectly; for example, a grant to the Small Theatre Administrative Facility in order to remedy a perceived weakness in administrative infrastructure. Better business practice for theatre, apparently, is also sound economics for the OAC, helping to "stretch scarce resources."[52]   In defending its own management practices and decisions, the OAC is attempting to prevent further cuts to its budget. But its claims are couched in the discourse of the marketplace which has become a goal in and of itself, an absolute that has swallowed up culture.

The populist direction of OAC policies can be noted everywhere, the successful democratization of programmes providing justification for the disbursement of public funds on cultural activities. Everyone is involved. Proof is no longer the child on the cover but a letter from a parent grateful for an arts education programme.[53] Faced with a difficult choice, the OAC has chosen to spread more than to raise, to involve more and more people in the arts, rather than to develop the skills of a few to a higher level. This democratization is evident in the emphasis on the number of communities involved in programmes. Regionalism is not the only discourse of inclusion in this report. Language and ethnicity figure prominently – under the sign of difference. Gender, however, is minimized. Culture becomes a mode of disjunctive synthesis yoking contraries. What is at stake is not culture, but culture*s*. The 1992-93 report is bilingual (written in French and English) and focuses on the autonomy of the Franco-Ontarian Office. A page of visual images, the only one in the report, features the poster from *True Colours*, a festival organized by Full Screen in Toronto to present new works by film and videomakers of colour. The heading "From Oshweken to Muskrat Dam" announces an onomastic remapping of provincial topography by First Nations communities involved in the First Nations Artists in the Classroom Program.[54] The question has changed from "Which Culture?" (high or low) to "Whose Culture?" Fictions of identity are no longer thought within the frame of nation, or province, or even region, but of language or race. Culture versus nationality: this changes the frames of affiliation. There is no singular fixed meaning for culture or nation, but a localized field of contesting struggles mutually constituting meaning.

The understanding of the cultural and the political in Canada as framed by idealism is frequently expressed in terms of Frygean archetypalism with its myths of concern and identity that carry out operations of symmetrization. Through government reports or legislation, these figurations of unity work to produce unification by rendering uniaccentual and hierarchized, the dynamic heteroglossia of cultures.[55] Against such figurations of culture as singular as evident in the OAC report of 1963-4, the report of 1992-3 operates under the sign of difference. The heading "Mirror, mirror, on the wall," for example, figures identity as resemblance only to reconceptualize it as mobility and diversity: "Ontario reflects a world of difference that touches every aspect of the arts...Ontario isn't what it used to be. Not that there was anything 'wrong' with the old Ontario – the one we all grew up in..." "Nostalgia" for this Ontario leads to "stagnation" or "death."..Now, there are not only "more of us" but there are "more kinds of us too." Immigration has brought a richer diversity of people from the world to Ontario. "The gay and lesbian community has become a potent and recognized cultural force." The First Nations peoples here from the beginning "are creating a cultural renaissance of their own."[56]

There is an ambiguity of address in this document in the shifting "we" that continually realigns the boundaries between inside and outside, between speaking subject and addressee. Who is this "we"? Women or "lesbians"? Old Anglo-Ontario? Or newcomer? Or conquered other? Ontario has the renaissance promised thirty years ago, though not at a site which its culture as absolute could have conceptualized, and in the image of a "Bronze" rather than "Golden Age". The mobile boundaries redistribute around the category of artist as well as of citizen so that by turns "we" are all artists wherever "we" come from. It is art that unites "us" in a common activity. The emphasis on "participaction" rather than on glorification displaces the question of the artist's political responsibility, although in fact it creeps in through the back door in fleeting references to artistic excellence and the importance of work on "the cutting edge."

"Opening our minds to new possibilities" means making "contact with people who have felt distanced from OAC."[57] Innovation is introduced in relation to racial and ethnic diversity, but the report stresses formal and technological innovation as a way of bridging differences within continuous change. This is a revolving door policy – of constant rotation of juries, of grants to new individual artists – that involves everyone in the web of the OAC, keeping everything mixing, everyone blurring. This figure of unifying mixture contrasts with the balance in the 1963-4 report among discrete fields that was medically or juridically regulated. Artists now are seers and guides to new technologies, producing hitherto unimaginable fields of art practices that "blur out the neat little compartments we all learned about in school."[58] This blurring prepares for alignments with industry that constitute a new figuration of unity in a high-tech society. Youth may help "identify new trends." However, Murray Schafer, "accomplished and celebrated composer," is the metonymic artist that sanctions the equalizing effects of the technological imperative. As keynote speaker at a conference on art education, he connects the technological world of young people to the challenges of cross-cultural education which both require radically new forms of intervention. Through quotation, the OAC casts itself in Schafer's transformative view of art as "destructively creative."[59] Recognizable here is the Modernist version of the Orphic myth of dying into creation, of fragmentation merging into a new formal unity on a higher level of resolution. Technology rather than education has become the means to a collective project of society. Diversity is managed by social morphing. This contrasts with the care and tending to produce balance among discrete elements in the 1960s project of civil society. Incidentally, the current figuration of the artist as dissident, as rebel outsider, is a fleeting glance backward to the Peace Corps vision where the elitist scorn and disruption of the romantic are brought into the service of society to contain dissent. Technology not art now defines the model of incorporation of citizens. This function is officially accorded to the arts in the OACs present institutional positioning where it reports to the Ministry of Citizenship, Culture and Recreation.

Constants in the reports of the OAC for 1963 and 1993 is the triumvirate of state, education and business through whose partnership culture is articulated and managed. This power/knowledge nexus orders specific practices affecting what and who gets funded to constitute symbolic capital, so mobilizing desire for cultural recognition in the work of subject constitution and class differentiation. If knowledge gleamed brightest in the 1963-64 report, where the arts create new forms of understanding, money talks loudest in that of 1992-93. That business has been the hesitant partner reluctant to recognize the ties of community is indicated in the oppositional language of the first report. That business has become the dominant force to be courted is indicated in the discourse of the 1992-93 report which is framed in the truth claims of the balance sheet. In the interval, "balance" has been reconfigured so that instead of being a figure of mediation among competing claims, it has become the restrictive figuration of a single framing of the social: the bottom line. Since the eighteenth century, the idea of an autonomous, unregulated marketplace that could adjudicate among social purposes has fostered a faith in the market as a progressive institution in which self-serving individual choices will ultimately benefit all. Now, the invisible hand of the market is poised to grab complete sway over public mind and public policy. In doing so, it labels all value except that of exchange as of "special" rather than of general "interest."

There are many documents from the arts councils I could subject to such a symptomatic rereading of tropes, reading for the contradictions, moments when the text turns back on itself. I have attempted to approach these by way of genealogy which, for Foucault, is an examination of descent that does not attempt to go back in time to a fixed point of origin in order to restore an unbroken continuity, but focuses instead on dispersion, "the minute deviations – or conversely, the complete reversals." Such shifts in a "relationship of forces, the usurpation of power, the appropriation of a vocabulary," constitute historical events. Events occur in tangled profusion, for origin or "emergence" is never singular and visible, but occurs in interstices at different points, producing unstable assemblages, disjunctive syntheses. Seeking to re-establish "various systems of subjection, not the anticipatory power of meaning but the hazardous play of dominations" in the subtle traces that might connect to form a network, a genealogy would "sort out" lapses, differences, piecemeal fabrications, contradictory versions...[60]

***

Anticipating the contradictions of the OAC was the Canada Council whose complex orientation may be read in terms of shifting lines of institutional accountability from Secretary of State to Minister of Communications, then Canadian Heritage. How far back in the past does one unravel its genealogy? To the 1941 Kingston Conference of the Arts where 150 artists from across the country gathered to denounce the federal government for its apathy with regard to the arts? To the 1944 March on Ottawa by sixteen artists' organizations to make a presentation to the Special Committee on Reconstruction and Re-establishment (1939-1951), demanding $10 million for the arts from the federal purse? The groups formed the Canadian Arts Council in 1945, which became the Canadian Conference of the Arts in 1958. So many men had sacrificed their lives during the war. For what? The national independence they had fought for would be meaningless if Canadians did not have an established and distinctive culture. Can we trace this genealogy to the Massey Commission on National Development in the Arts, Letters and Sciences (1949-1951) whose report inventoried the underdeveloped state of Canadian culture, the absence or neglect of cultural institutions making them vulnerable to the threat of American invasion on the airwaves, in magazines, films, and advertizing? To the British Arts Council, founded in 1947 to make permanent the support to the arts which had been an important boost to morale during the war effort, and a model of government arms-length intervention adopted by the Canadian government in response to the Massey Report? To the British tradition of government support for the arts which, since the founding of the British Museum in the eighteenth-century, had tentatively entered a kind of international competition for national glory?[61]   In contrast, republican France, which had launched this competition for prestige through the state as patron of the arts to enoble its new form of government in the international sphere, supported the arts directly through a ministry of culture. The network of traces surrounding the beginning of the Canada Council is dense.

It was none of these examples, petitions or reports, with their appeals to romantic nationalism, however, that prompted the enabling legislation from the federal government in 1957, but rather the death of two business tycoons, James Hamet Dunn and Isaak Walton Killam, whose succession duties were used to set up a $100 million endowment fund for the Canadian arts and university capital grants. Though the Massey Report framed the need for support in the strongest terms of national interest in face of an American cultural invasion, and theorized culture as the perfecting of the mind through the arts, letters and sciences – a theorization of culture as absolute, so as to avoid the problem of the division of powers and the provincial jurisdiction over education – this was not effective in securing government action until the estates were available. While the arms-length principle of peer adjudication was adopted from the British Arts Council for the regulation of aesthetic value, it was the model of the American private foundations established by "robber barons" to perfume their money that was adopted to finance the project. Representatives from the Carnegie, Ford and Rockefeller Foundations attended the Canada Council's official opening ceremonies. The Council's current ambiguous position owes much to the legacy of dual models: its partial autonomy from the state results from the remnants of this endowment which gave it complete freedom from state intervention in the early years, though not from parliamentary criticism: "$100 million for eggheads; six bucks for old-age pensions."[62] The tension between the vast and expanding scope of the Council's mandate, however – which included support of educational institutions and research funding for universities as well as responsibility for culture in the international arena in support of UNESCO initiatives – and its fixed budget in what was to become a period of rapid inflation, quickly exposed the contradictions of this partnership of the state and business. In 1965, with the institution of government appropriations, the Canada Council entered a period of rapid expansion which coincided with the massive spending on culture for the centenary of Confederation. This first ad hoc government funding became an annual appropriation by the end of the decade.

The combination of national and international mandates distinguishes the Canada Council's delineation of culture from that of the Ontario Arts Council. Culture is enlisted in the support of national unity and identity in an era of increasingly forceful demands for "provincial" rights and subsequently of "globalization." Fostering a national culture became a primary function of the Canada Council's policies in the seventies of intervention in the debate over Quebec separatism, an explicit objective of such initiatives as the funding of translation between English and French established in 1971 on the heels of the October events involving the FLQ. More recently, in a shift of focus to the exportation of Canadian culture internationally, direct intervention of the ministries of External Affairs and of Trade and Commerce have effectively limited the Canada Council's role to the fostering and preservation of culture internationally in UNESCO and nationally by nurturing individual artists or arts groups. On the other hand, provincial responsibility for education complicates the relation of culture and personal development in the discourses of the Canada Council, which was assigned the role of expanding intellectual resources and stimulating research. The provincial mandate to educate citizens has lead to the emphasis of the Ontario Arts Council on artists as teachers in primary and secondary schools. Conversely, the Canada Council pursuing a distinction made by the Massey Commission between education and culture has focused on the professional development of artists in support of their continuing pursuit of excellence through travel grants for further training often outside Canada. Stimulating the imagination necessitates a move beyond the local, the parochial. The decentralization of the federal system tends to diffuse contradictions by separating them into national elitism (excellence) and regional populism (participation).

At the opening ceremonies of the Canada Council (1957) held, significantly, in the Rooms of the Senate Committee on Banking and Commerce, a number of such contradictions emerged in the address of its Chair, Brooke Claxton. In his first paragraph, Claxton focuses on the past, calling upon Thomas D'Arcy McGee's vision of the role of art in nation-building as civilizing to unify – the "great new Northern nation" that will emerge if "every gleam of authorship" is fostered so as to "keep down dissension" and "cultivate that true catholicity of spirit which embraces all creeds, all classes, all races." Yet in his second paragraph, he centres on the future. He forecasts that by 1980 a GNP of $74 billion will bring problems both of "more leisure" and of "more complexity," which may be solved with "higher skills" and "more education" – that is, by technology.[63] Claxton perspicaciously foresees a number of problems the council will face, such as constant public criticism and bureaucratization. However, he minimizes the potential conflicts between the claims of artistic and scientific contributions to nation-building, with their opposed agendas of imaginative stimulation and social engineering. Indeed, the order in which he frames their relation is significant, beginning each time with the engineer and scientist before referring to the humanist and artist: "We have long felt that material things cannot alone make a great nation ... we must hope to advance, too, on the spiritual front, advance in our artistic expression as a nation, advance so that we can 'lift ourselves to the level of our destinies'." And our destinies are figured in material terms, in metaphors of profit, as the "dividend" realized from "investment."[64]

A potential clash arises in the contrasting vision of the co-chair, Père Georges-Henri Lévesque, who speaks of "cooperation," of the "Truth" and "Beauty" that will result from the "expansion of humanism in Canada" through the work of the Council. Deploring cultural, intellectual and spiritual poverty in spite of great wealth, he prophesizes an important role for artists "the cherished children of God," "la fine fleur de culture d'une société" through whose works will appear the "veritable image of the people." Materialism is introduced only within an ethic of concern in response to the poverty from which artists "suffer," a state of privation that prevents them from bringing forth beauty for the "delight of their fellow men."[65] Is the Council a response to their great need? Or guarantor of their equitable share of the public purse? Does the state intervene to meet needs or to assure rights? What is clear in Lévesque's formulation is the responsibility of the state to create a climate for creativity.

Between beauty and profit, between art as the glory of the nation and the marketplace- this is the complex relation in which the Council is designed to mediate as a "powerhouse,"[66] its arms-length status providing the requisite checks and balances. The Council has generally been squeezed, but now is in a stranglehold between the competing claims of its diverse partners. And the number of underemployed cultural workers has grown rather than decreased. For the increase in arts activity over the last forty years has not been translated into higher incomes for individual artists.

***

The crisis in the arts councils has been perennial, I would suggest, because there have been three models in competition from the first: market, welfare, and nationalist. The divergence among the contending objectives of profit, where value is determined by supply and demand through the exchange of works with *consumers*; of access, where the aim is to reduce cultural inequity of regional, ethnic or linguistic varieties among *citizens*; of collective identity, where the aim is to develop national awareness of *patriots* where it has been distorted by colonialism, is constitutive of the contradictory tropes in the documents I have been examining. Thelma McCormack has outlined a number of distinct models of the relationship between culture and the state with regard to broadcasting in her analysis of the Applebaum-Hébert Report on Federal Cultural Policy as a response to a crisis of underemployment.[67] She introduces as corrective a post-nationalist model that would consider artists an *occupational group* and apply principles of affirmative action to equalize disparities. This model of artists as workers with equal rights introduces the important issue of symbolic capital constituted by grants, the recognition, in other words, of the social production of creativity by the regime of power. However, this valorization is complicated by the involvement of audiences in McCormack's communication model of art as interactional process, which thus returns to a model of consumption, to the marketplace. A sense of the demands of the polity as more than an aggregate of individual preferences, is what is at stake in the present renegotiation of the social contract. Reframing interaction in a field of power relations as struggle, rather than communication as transparent interchange, would recognize difference in relation to the symbolic as a matter of politics and posit culture as constitutive of the polity, and so contestatory. The state in this model is not impartial but an arena of discursive struggle. In the absence of such a theory of difference, McCormack's fragmentation of "public" into "audience" or consumer works to undermine a concept of "public interest" or "common good," the understanding of artistic activity as an integral part of public life demanding an equitable share in the distribution of public funds. Feminist theorizations of difference as desiring relation of connection with, rather than as incorporation of, an other[68] offer alternatives to current figurations of culture as morphing. Such recognition of radical alterity within symbolic forms of power frames claims to public access as rights, as political, not as "special interests" in a discourse of needs.

In the 1940s, it was the artists' articulation of the significance of the arts in the understanding of the polity that placed the arts on the public agenda. In an ongoing discursive struggle over "culture" and "interest," artists' resistance with regards to the specific claims of the arts is critical political action if the body politic is to be reordered. The entire post-World War II contract of the Canadian people with the state regarding social and cultural practices is under the threat of tectonic pressures. New coalitions must be forged by artists with other groups so that the state's function of maintaining balance can be reasserted. The transformative potential of art would be reconnected to the social responsibility of the artist. This is all the more crucial in that the Canada Council, in opting to preserve grants to individual artists and cut funding for arts organizations – sites for the articulation of artists' political discourse – is preparing the terrain for an arts community dominated by a few heroic individuals rather than providing continued support for a depth and breadth of talent and the institutional forms which have translated artists' discourse from the symbolic to the political with the power to affect the world around it.

Reconfiguration of the artist as hero undermines the struggle of women artists for recognition of their creative productions at the very moment when through communities such as the Women's Art Resource Centre they are increasingly exercising self-determination. Through its journal, *Matriart*, this centre is attempting to make public its work of documenting women's art making. In an attempt to redress a gendered hierarchy of value, these women are demanding accountability from art institutions through the collection of statistics demonstrating the low status of women's art. Through the regular column on the status of women artists, "Who Counts and Who's Counting," the inequitable representation of women's art in public art galleries and commercial galleries (only 22 per cent women in 1990) is being recorded. Women's work constitutes just 12.5 per cent of the Canadian collection of the National Gallery, for example. This profiles a gendered difference in exhibition histories that would account for the great disparity in women artist's incomes. As demonstrated in the Ontario Women's Declaration, these women are also obliging the State to accord women artist's full rights as citizens by assuming responsibility for working to correct the distortion of distribution of (symbolic) capital.[69]

The claims of the marketplace along with those of equalizing regional disparity among citizens and of decolonizing the collective identity have shaped cultural policy at least since the 1950s. The end of a period in which "culture and state relationships were shaped by nationalism" did not come about in 1980 with the cultural policy recommendations of the Applebaum-Hébert Report as McCormack suggests, though this was a moment of acceleration in the process along with the 1982 promulgation of the Charter of Rights. The ideal of balance in the distribution of resources has not been fully met with the abdication of business from "investment" in the arts, and its weakening sense of the obligations of the polity. At the same time, it imposes its concept of value as exchange as absolute. In the privileging of a single fiction or frame (monetary exchange) as constituting the "real," the kind of exploration that makes demands beyond the instrumental, beyond the individual, and of any transformation other than exchange, is constricted which in turn has a repressive effect on diversity and dissent. The sense of collective belonging withers in the current proliferation of metaphors of "cocooning" and "dispersed systems." A force of private interest threatening to overflow its limits and to dissolve the bonds of the state is what Hegel considers the most significant menace to a civil society.[70] Bringing what is now habitual to a crisis through critique in an articulation of the limitations of practice, as I have attempted to do, reframes this as a political struggle over discourses organizing the social in which the arts play a key role. The discourse of exchange value is only one potential fiction framing the real.

Notes

1. Barbara Sternberg, Graffiti, Posted in mid-town Toronto in November 1995 after she read this essay.
2. Virginia Woolf, *Three Guineas* (Harmondsworth: Penguin, 1977), p. 115.
3. *Culture Slash Nation*, curated by Lorraine Johnson and Cheryl Sourkes, on view at Gallery TPW, Toronto, October 21 to November 25 1995, began as a response to the Canada Council's failure to consult artists in December 1994 but became a more general investigation into cultural policy. The exhibition raises the question: Slash, s/lash, sl/ash. Does cutting cultural policy produce a desert? An abridged version of this essay was prepared in August 1995 for the exhibition and published as "Writing on the Wall" *Border/Lines* 38/39 (1995): 98-103.
4. Kate Taylor, "CBC Under the Knife," *Globe and Mail* April 8 1995, p. C1; Judy Stofman, "Budget Cuts to Grants will Force Shutdowns Book Publishers Say," *Toronto Star* (April 11 1995), p. C4; "Telefilm Shuts Foreign Offices, *Toronto Star*, (August 5 1995); Robert Crew, "Arts Voice. Petition PM to Rescue Harbourfront," *Toronto Star* (April 25 1995), p. B5; Robert Crew, "Arts Council Faces the Dark Realities," *Toronto Star* (August 17 1995), p. C8; Sid Adilman, "Tory Cuts 'Disas-

trous',"*Toronto Star*(August 18 1995), p. D1; Henry Mietkiewicz, "Arts Groups Fear the Sky is Falling," *Toronto Star* (July 20 1995), p. C8. Since the 28 per cent autumn cuts to OAC funding, headlines have focused on the effects of cutbacks, such as the struggle of Ontario publishers to keep printing books in light of both federal cuts and provincial cancelation of the loan guarantee programme. Publishers will be forced to do "bottom-line publishing," putting out more hockey books than poetry and pursuing foreign rather than Canadian markets. Anita Flash, "Grant-Slashing Reshapes List," *Quill & Quire* 62, no. 1 (January 1996): 10-12.

6.   Judith Baldwin, "Gender Representation in Canadian Commercial Galleries," *Matriart* 4, no, 1 (1993): 14 and17. While the number of women graduates of the Ontario College of Art and York Univerity has been between 54

per cent and 65 per cent in recent years and the MFA programme at York graduated six women and four men in 1996, only 22 per cent of artists exhibited across the country in commercial galleries in 1990 were women. In the National Gallery of Canada, women's works account for 12.5 per cent of the Canadian collection and 6.1 per cent of the International collection. This gendered difference in exhibition histories would account for the income differential among artists at mid-career when in 1985, for example, women earned about half as much as men. Penelope Stewart, "Who Counts and Who's Counting?" *Matriart* 4, no. 1 (1993): 13. This column on the status of women artists has become a regular feature of *Matriart* since 5, no. 2 (1995).

7. *Occupation: Artist. A Profile of the Demographic, Economic and Employment Characteristics of Artists in Ontario* (Toronto: Ontario Arts Council, 1992), p. 56 and 21. The situation has changed little since 1978 when the Canada Council called artists an exploited "sub-proletariate" in which 60 per cent of the worst paid were women. Laurent Mailhot and Benoit Melançon, *Le Conseil des arts du Canada 1957-1982* (Montreal: Lemeac, 1982), p. 48 and 92.

8. Karl Marx, *Grundrisse: Foundations of the Critique of Political Economy*, trans. Martin Nicolaus (New York: Vintage Books, 1973), p. 163.

9. The many changes in monetary and fiscal policy which occurred under Mulroney's Conservative government (1984 -1993) include shifting the burden of public financing from the Bank of Canada to private banks with high interest rates, and shifting the indebtedness from Canadians to foreigners through a decreased reliance on Canada Savings Bonds and an increased use of Government Treasury Bills to finance government business. This gave increased power to New York bond traders in the arbitration of Canadian government policy. As well, the tax burden has been shifted since the 1960s from an equal weight on individuals and corporations to the present when individuals contribute nearly 90% of the public revenue while a number of corporations earning huge profits benefit from a tax holiday. For more details about such changes consult Linda McQuaig, *Shooting the Hippo: Death by Deficit and Other Canadian Myths* (Toronto: Viking, 1995).

10. Michael Walker, "Disarming Special Interests is Key to Re-engineering Ontario Economy," *Financial Post* (22 July 1995), p. 15. Public sector unions, tenants, farmers, and welfare recipients are those "seekers after privilege" ("special interests")

Walker considers most likely to protest their "loss". During the Ontario election campaign, the special-interest label was attached to non-white racial groups and to women, preparing the terrain for the quick abolition of employment equity legislation.

11. Andrew Cardozo, "Opposing Voices Aren't the Villains," *Toronto Star* (8 August 1995), p. A13.

12. Jocelyn Harvey, "Closed Council," *Canadian Forum* 836 (January 1995): 19-20.

13. "Government Expenditures on Culture," *The Daily* (Ottawa: Culture Statistics Program) August 1, 1995. Judy Stofman, "162 Magazines Lost Since 1989, StatsCan Reports," *Toronto Star* (9 August 1995), p. D1.

14. Susan Walker, "Professional Arts Nags Had Work Cut Out For Them," *Toronto Star* (30 December 1994), p. C14.

15. Guy Laforest, *Trudeau and the End of a Canadian Dream* (Montreal: McGill-Queen's University Press, 1995), p. 189-90.

16. Advisory Arts Panel, *The Future of the Canada Council* (Ottawa: Canada Council, 1978), p. 17.

17. The speeches of Roch Carrier and Donna Scott of the Canada Council on the occasion of the 1995 Governor General's Awards presentations in Toronto indicate the trend of the Council to become a broker of arts-business alliances: its "new mission," according to Scott, is to "develop a whole range of programs for businesses so they can express their love of the arts." Paul Dutton, "Amputating Arm's-Length," *Quill & Quire* 62, 1 (1996), p. 10. This contrasts greatly with the Canada Council's 1981 rejection of the term "cultural industries" as a contradiction in terms. *Le Conseil des arts du Canada*, p. 114. The new Ontario Minister of Citizenship, Culture and Recreation used the word "business" seventeen times in a September speech to cultural agencies and the word "culture" only six times, as reported in "Index: Art Facts," Programme Notes, Theatre Passe Muraille, November 1995.

18. While women received 6.4 per cent of Ph.D.s in 1969, the increased support of Canada Council, then of SSHRCC grants, meant that they received 32.8 per cent of doctoral degrees granted in 1988. Council of Ontario Universities, 1988.

19. John Buttrick, *Public Funding of the Arts: An Economic Examination*, Working Paper 90-1 (Toronto: York University Department of Economics, 1990), p. 17.

20. *Le Conseil des arts du Canada*, p. 25.

21. Toronto Children's Players 1931-1960; Hart House Theatre, University of Toronto, founded in 1919; Crest Theatre 1953-1966; New Play Society 1946-1971; Spring Thaw satiric revue 1948-1971. The latter's theme song, "Let's All Hate Toronto," speaks volumes about the frustration of artists with Toronto's provincialism at the time. The Arts and Letters Club, of which my musician father was a member, was at the centre of arts activity in Toronto. It was a club for men only. Margaret Atwood, b. 1939, and Gwendolyn MacEwen, 1941-1987, subsequently became major Canadian poets.

22. *Ontario Arts Council Annual Report 1963-64* (Toronto: Queen's Printer, 1965), p. 55-7.

23. *Ontario Arts Council Annual Report 1992-93* (Toronto: OAC, 1994), p. 2.

24. *OAC Annual Report 1963-64*, p. 45.

25. *Ibid.*, p. 18.

26. *Ibid.*, p. 13.

27. *Public Funding of the Arts*, p. 27-8. This change occurred between 1971 and 1985. According to the 1985 census, artists in Ontario have more years of schooling, and are more likely to be bilingual than the general population. What should be a recipe for success, however, results in incomes well below provincial averages, and the poverty line. Within this general profile there is a gender gap. Women are more likely to have had postsecondary education than men (81 per cent as opposed to 75 per cent) but they earn only 63 per cent of what men do. The gap is especially pronounced in the 35-54 age group, artists' peak years, when among visual artists, men earned an average of $16,165 to women's $9,871. Women visual artists were the group most likely to be self-employed and hence least paid. *Occupation:Artist,* p. 16, 21, 38.

28. *Public Funding of the Arts*, p. 20.

29. Heather Robertson, "Starving Slowly: Notes from the Reservation," in David Helwig (ed.) *Love and Money: The Politics of Culture* (Ottawa: Oberon, 1980), p. 91.

30. Parliamentarians took the Canada Council to task for a 1978 grant awarded to Blewointment Press for publishing "revolutionary" bill bissett, whose work was judged by an MP to be "Disgusting, trashy and vulgar," and over the awarding of the 1970 Governor General's Award to b p nichol's "obscene" *The True Eventual Story of Billy the Kid. Le Conseil des arts du Canada,* p. 250, 254, 264.

31. Julia Kristeva, *Black Sun: Depression and Melancholia* trans. Leon S. Roudiez (New York: Columbia, 1989), p. 6. Melancholy is characterized by the failure of a subject to constitute itself by separation from a primal object of desire, from the mother's body, resulting in a borderline instability for a subject, in this case between the knowing subject and the object of knowledge so that the personal bleeds into the analytical.

32. *Three Guineas*, p. 115.

33. Virginia Woolf, *Moments of Being: Unpublished Autobiographical Writings* (London: Chatto & Windus, 1976).

34. Barbara Hepworth's sculptures were on exhibit at the Art Gallery of Ontario, summer 1995. Seeing them brought back memories of woodworking I had done as a teenager which had made me want to sculpt. When I did take a course, it was in an age of conceptual and constructivist art and there was no carving.

35. Jill Conway, *True North* (Toronto: Vintage, 1995), p. 136.

36. *OAC Report 1963-64*, p. 6.

37. Raymond Williams, *Culture and Society 1780-1950* (Harmondsworth: Penguin, 1961), p. 16-7.

38. *OAC Report 1963-64*, p. 49.

39. *Ibid.*, p. 44.

40. Matthew Arnold, *Culture and Anarchy* (London, 1869). For the legacy of Arnoldian theories denouncing the "external, mechanical tendency" of culture in Canada see David Staines, *Beyond the Provinces* (Toronto: University of Toronto Press, 1995). For the Arnoldian influence on the Massey Commission, see Paul Litt,

Muses, Masses and the Massey Commission (Toronto: University of Toronto Press, 1992), p. 99-103.

41. *OAC Report 1963-64*, p. 44.

42. *Ibid.*, p. 47.

43. *Ibid.*, p. 44.

44. Henry Hubert, *Harmonious Perfection: The Development of English Studies in Nineteenth Century Anglo-Canadian Colleges* (East Lansing: Michigan State University Press, 1994), p. 137-8.

45. Roy MacSkimming, *For Arts' Sake: A History of the Ontario Arts Council 1963-1983* (Toronto: Ontario Arts Council, 1983). Was the Council indeed founded for "Art's Sake"? That is, for Gelber's (business') sake?

46. *OAC Report 1992-93*, p. 2.

47. *Ibid.*, p. 3.

48. *Ibid.*, p. 2.

49. *Ibid.*, p. 3.

50. *Ibid.*, p. 2.

51. *Ibid.*, p. 18.

52. *Ibid.*, p. 17.

53. *Ibid.*, p. 18.

54. *Ibid.*, p. 8 and 9.

55. Northrop Frye, *The Bush Garden: Essays on the Canadian Imagination* (Toronto: Anansi, 1971), p. iii, vi. A neo-Arnoldian, Frye postulates a divergence between myths of identity and of concern in the shaping of culture. Identity is local, regional, pastoral, and imaginative, whereas concern is romantic, idealistic, exploratory, and unifying. In the tension between concern (unity) and identity, an arrangement privileging the former would produce "cultural nationalism" whereas privileging the latter would produce "separatism." The impact of Frye's archetypalist universalism on the exclusion of a consideration of Canadian and women's difference in literature has been explored by Priscilla Galloway, "Sexism and the Senior English Curriculum in Ontario Secondary Schools," Ph.D. Dissertation, University of Toronto, 1977. Loretta Czernis has explored how his conceptualization of unity shapes the discourse of the task force on Canadian unity. "The Report of the Task Force on Canadian Unity: Reading a (Re)Writing of Canada," Ph.D. Dissertation, York University, 1988.

56. *OAC Report 1992-93*, p. 23.

57. *Ibid.*, p. 11.

58. *Ibid.*, p. 23.

59. *Ibid.*, p. 23.

60. Michel Foucault, "Nietzsche, Genealogy, History," in *Language, Counter-Memory Practice,* trans. Donald F. Bouchard and Sherry Simon (Ithaca: Cornell U P, 1977), p. 145-6, 148.

61. Janet Minihan, *The Nationalization of Culture* (London: Hamish Hamilton, 1977), p. 11.

62. John Diefenbaker, quoted in *Le Conseil des arts du Canada*, p. 34.

63. Brooke Claxton, *Opening Proceedings* (Ottawa: Canada Council, 1957), p.8-9.

64. *Ibid.*, p.9.

65. Georges-Henri Lévesque, *Ibid.*, p.17, 19.

66. Brooke Claxton, *Ibid.*, p. 14.

67. Thelma McCormack, "Culture and the State," *Canadian Public Policy* 10, no. 3 (1984): 267-77.

68. Luce Irigaray, among others, has critiqued the theorization of the subject constituted within a symbolic order (a masculine imaginary ordered around discrete entities) and relating to fetishized objects in sovereign isolation. She has attempted to think relationality otherwise, within a different order of mutual constitution or fluid boundaries. Within the Hegelian dialectic, the discrete self-other relation of master-slave has been characterized as one of incorporation or cannibalism within a sublation to a higher order that in turn instantiates an order of sameness that cannot recognize difference. Irigaray articulates difference as a series of potential creative relations, not as domination of one over another. *Speculum of the Other Woman* trans. Gillian Gill (Ithaca: Cornell University Press, 1985). For development of this position in respect to feminist discourse see my "Translating (With) the *Speculum*," *TTR* 4, no. 1 (1991): 85-121.

69. The Women's Art Resource Centre has sponsored the fact-findingcolumns "Who Counts and What's Counting?" in *Matriart* since 1993. A politicized discourse of self-assertion through opposition characterizes the Ontario Women's Declaration (1995).

70. Charles Taylor, *Hegel* (Cambridge: Cambridge University Press, 1975), p. 453.

Bibliography

Allor, Martin and Michelle Gagnon. L'Etat de Culture: Généalogie discursive des politiques culturelles québécoises. *Montreal: Concordia University, GRECC, 1994.*

Grant, George. Lament for a Nation: The Defeat of Canadian Nationalism. *Toronto: McClelland and Stewart, 1965.*

Helwig, David ed. Love and Money: The Politics of Culture. *Ottawa: Oberon, 1980.*

Innis, Harold. The Strategy of Culture. *Toronto: University of Toronto Press 1952.*

Schafer, D. Paul. Review of Federal Policies for the Arts in Canada, 1944-1988. *Ottawa: Department of Communications, 1989.*

Sullivan, Mary C. Arts Councils in Conflict. *Ottawa: Canada Council, Research and Evaluation, 1988.*

The Third Strategy. *Ottawa: Canadian Conference of the Arts, 1984.*

Not a Woman within Coo'ee: An Encounter with Cultural Policy on the Superhighway

Patricia Gillard

I don't recommend writing articles as a means of debriefing after an intense experience. Yet now, over a year since the Broadband Services Expert Group (BSEG) first met and a month after the prime minister launched our final report, I still can't write dispassionately. A few events keep bursting through the ordered, analytical account.

This is an article about one year's work on BSEG (it came to be pronounced bee-seg), a group of twelve experts who had been appointed in December, 1993, by the Commonwealth Minister for Transport and Communications to "examine the technical, economic and commercial preconditions for the widespread delivery of broadband."[1] It had a term of one year to accomplish this brief. Members came from relevant industry sectors, with mainly engineering or commerce backgrounds, as well as a scientist, a chairman, Brian Johns, with wide knowledge of media industries and regulation a unionist, and a technology writer/academic who had become a senior administrator. The two major telecommunications companies and a television network were represented. I was the only woman, and the only social scientist.

BSEG's work involved monthly meetings of the twelve members, presentations by companies and overseas experts and brainstorming sessions with invited audiences. We were supported by a full time secretariat of six men, mostly economists, who were joined by a woman graduate trainee halfway through the year. BSEG called for submissions and produced an interim and a final report both titled Networking Australia's Future.

They were widely circulated beyond the groups directly involved.

In other circumstances, a technically oriented group such as BSEG would not have been involved with cultural policy. However, in early 1994, two previously distinct government departments with responsibility for culture and communications were united in the new Commonwealth Department of Communications and the Arts. With this marriage our work on new broadband technologies was brought into the arena of cultural policy. One suggestion from our interim report, to foster a creative infrastructure and to develop Australian multimedia product, became a central notion in *Creative Nation*, a major cultural policy statement released in October 1994. Suddenly Australian cultural policy was high-tech. Broadband would enliven the possibilities of making money from our creative talent.

This article will discuss the progress of BSEG's work during its life of twelve months. Tensions arose when discourses of technology and economics were applied to areas of social and domestic life a necessary engagement, since broadband technologies will be closely involved with everyday activities. Industry, economic, and technological concerns dominated, but they were also reshaped by new understandings of human networking for social and recreational purposes. Women's involvement in these debates is crucial because the task involves a redefinition of how communications industries are to serve their populations. The linear, reductionist thinking still dominating telecommunications is one of its biggest limitations.

In this time of convergence, it seems that the very names we invent to describe new fields are themselves combinations of previously unrelated notions. The three main areas of BSEG's work to be outlined here reflect such awkward marriages: creative infrastructure, the communications platform, and future demand.

Creative Infrastructure

The prime minister launched *Creative Nation* on October 18, 1994, claiming: "No government has ever delivered a national cultural policy for Australia on anything like these dimensions."[2] A central concern of *Creative Nation* was the development of a creative infrastructure whereby Australian cultural products would be created in multimedia form to provide for citizens who might otherwise be swamped by incoming product and, especially, to create exports for the new information age.

Two months earlier BSEG had highlighted the creation of content as a major opportunity for Australia: "The Group believes that the most exciting aspect of convergence is the opportunity to create content the information carried by broadband networks."[3] A sophisticated delivery system and service providers would be essential to this development and together they defined a "source of commercial opportunities for Australia."[4] The prime minister referred to BSEG and to these ideas in a speech soon afterwards: "Australia can be at the forefront of change in the global economy and the information superhighway, because of the fact that we have natural skills in content...we are a content--strong country."[5]

This emphasis on content, as well as on the development of the skills, collaboration, and industry structures required to produce it, emerged over time. A presentation in February by Philip Corman (an adviser to Clinton's National Information Infrastructure Advisory Council in the U.S.) had highlighted content as a major aspect of convergence and one which the U.S. government was emphasizing. The importance of maintaining an Australian cultural presence in futureprograming had arisen in the first BSEG brainstorming session on social impact.[6]

However, it was the brainstorming session entitled "New Creators", conducted on May 13, which decisively set this agenda. The concept of two types of laboratories was suggested in this session, one type providing experimental and production facilities for small companies and individual artists, the other a site for generating ideas from people with different backgrounds, which would hopefully work to "break down the cultural barriers between artists and scientists and engineers."[7] The creative talent in Australia and the fact that it is a multicultural society were seen as resources which provided a competitive advantage.

In *Creative Nation*, these ideas had been developed so that multimedia initiatives were synonymous with cultural production in an information age. Government funding was to be provided for six cooperative multimedia centres, and the Australian Multimedia Enterprise would provide financing for interactive products and services. The linguistic mix was curious: "multimedia products will be the drivers of these vast new services,"[8] "[there will be] new ways of accessing the storehouse of our intellectual and creative inheritance,"[9] and perhaps most succinctly, "good ideas can be turned into commercial product."[10]

The power of an idea, when it has captured the imagination of senior ministers and garnered support across government departments, was evident in this cultural policy statement. A great deal of background research had already been conducted the economic benefits of such a move had been looked at, and export earnings estimated.[11] However, there was little that was creative in such an approach. The disciplines of economics and politics, relying on measurement rather than an opening up of meaning and experience, seem unlikely to make an equal match with cultural activity unless they define themselves as supporting the main drama. There seems to be no evidence that this will happen. Indeed, one critique of Creative Nation recounts rumours that "industry lobbied hard and long to ensure that artists wouldn't get their hands on the money."[12]

As a representative of BSEG I spoke in December 1994 to a meeting of the National Association of Visual Artists (NAVA) in Sydney about the opportunities and problems of multimedia. Artists saw a major opportunity to make a living from multimedia art, if copyright was properly structured. However, the cultural mix of artists, scientists, and engineers was not a joyful prospect to artists if they were expected to fill the pipelines in pre-ordained ways and as part of teams in which they had little control and scant remuneration.

The position of artists and writers (many of whom are indeed women) in relation to engineers and technologists seems to parallel the position of women in the debate about new communications technologies. Both are either not mentioned at all, or described as part of a team put together by someone else who is running the show. Artists, writers, and women, however, are the people who will transform multimedia and make possible new forms and uses. Without their inspiration and forceful participation, we may have pipelines carrying information we don't care to access.

At this stage, the marriage of hi-tech communications and culture seems an unequal one for the artists and cultural workers who find themselves incorporated into an industrialized notion of cultural production, with themselves at the bottom of a technical hierarchy. The infrastructure does not seem to have creativity as its central purpose.

The Communications Platform

The report of the Broadband Services Expert Group was only part of an explosion of advice to the Commonwealth Government. During 1994, there were at least fourteen major publications; from BSEG, from the Communications Futures Group which was set up in the Bureau of Transport and Communications Economics and from other associated groups concerned with telecommunications policy.[13]

Early in our work, members of BSEG came to the understanding that it was industry, social, and cultural issues that would be our focus. Technical matters were already being decided by the main companies involved, Telstra and Optus. Their rollout of cables had begun.

In the final report, the statement is made that the communications network is a "platform underpinning our society, supporting a diverse and interwoven range of social, business and community activity."[14] The statement reflects a crucial development in our thinking during the twelve months we worked. No doubt other notions will supersede these in time, but the assertion that the purpose of the physical communications network is to support and reflect human relationships and enterprises is a significant basis for the recommendations that follow in the report.

Comparisons with other countries show Australia's emphasis on the social, communicative importance of telecommunications infrastructure to be unusual. Singapore talks of its vision of an intelligent island, Japan of the information society and of itself as a "life-style superpower," and Canada of a "network of networks" which will transform the economy to one based on information. The United States has coined the word "information superhighway" and thinks in terms of "information infrastructure." A broader understanding of what is involved in the shift to advanced communication systems may prove to be important in Australia's industrial, cultural, and social development.

From the first discussions in December 1993, the chairperson expressed the wish that the report be bold and imaginative. Members emphasized services rather than technologies, and spoke of cultural and industrial creativity and the sense of excitement that this field created, particularly in young people who associated it with leisure. At the second meeting in January, I circulated a short paper which used the term "human ecology" to describe the social and cultural context of telecommunications use.

Members shared values of fairness and equity, and agreed that the government had a major role to play in the maintenance of a just society in a new communication age. There was initial disagreement about the particulars of funding and regulation, reflecting the organizations from which people came. Because of the shared basic values, a number of events and submissions had a major effect on the final report. The brainstorming session on the social impact of broadband services was the first to be held, in March. The meeting was begun by making a list of desired social outcomes, which included strengthening a sense of community, increasing participation in the democratic process, and maintaining Australian cultural identity.[15] A later brainstorming session in May considered universal service.[16] The emphasis on social values in relation to broadband developments was assumed to be an important feature of the group's work.

BSEG'S interim report began with a description of convergence but looked at its wider implications: "the transmission of digitised information on broadband networks provides the opportunity to communicate in a number of ways (video, audio, text and data) simultaneously and interactively. But the convergence of technologies...is only a forerunner of many types of social, cultural and commercial convergences."[17] This approach was welcomed by many, and ten thousand copies were circulated, necessitating a second printing. Industry and community groups seemed to welcome the approach and there was a hint of surprise and relief in some quarters that we had not simply talked technology.

In the same month, a group of communications academics and consultants were invited to report to BSEG on the work they had been developing, "Communication Scenarios for the Twenty-first Century." The academic papers presented two scenarios, one a market-driven model with many players in a highly competitive market with low consumer appeal, and another which integrated commercial interests with community and government intervention to meet both social and economic goals. The social consequences of each approach had been elaborated. This work has since been further developed by Hearn and others.[18] It is referred to in BSEG'S final report.

The positive response to BSEG'S interim report, which emphasises a social approach and carefully eschews technological jargon for its own sake, referring to the information superhighway sparingly, encouraged the group to continue with this perspective. This was reinforced by a presentation, Communication Scenarios, which gave the members their first extended contact with the thinking of a group of academics about the social implications of our work. The problem of my wearing a number of "hats" on this committee, that of social researcher and academic as well as that of the only woman, meant that my views could be seen as singular and unsupported. The presentation gave a broader authority to such views. Moreover, the presentation to BSEG was by Susan Oliver, previously managing director of the Commission for the Future. While she was in the room and presenting the two scenarios she was the object of attention and scrutiny. The fact that she was both female and an expert made this combination seem everyday. For a while I could comfortably assume the role of just an ordinary member of BSEG and enjoy having another woman contributing to the meeting.

Emphasis on the "communications platform" is an achievement for BSEG. We understood that the nature of the network would evolve over time, but that there needed to be a continuing concern with the kind of society we wanted to build through it. The recommendation that a Commonwealth research body "be funded to coordinate a program of social research to identify the needs of particular groups of telecommunications consumers that are not currently being met"[19] was a crucial part of this understanding. It was a way of informing policymakers that they must know what is happening during our society's shift to more mediated forms of communication in particular, that they must realize the need to track the disparities in purchase and usage by different income groups, and by those positioned by their gender, cultural background, or physical location in ways that work against access.

The term, "communications platform," with its solid, material second word, encapsulates the difficulties of a group of experts looking for new ways of thinking about social change but limited by their technical background. Social engineering always was a derogatory term, used against social scientists who wanted to plan a future society. Planning for future communications is equally impossible for technologists to do unless it is in partnership with those who understand social and cultural approaches.

Critics are correct in finding the BSEG report vague about the details of ensuring access to different groups of users. While BSEG may have adopted new metaphors, we were unable to relate this thinking confidently and systematically to the realities of social and cultural life. As a group we could not take the step of conceptualizing our society itself as a resource with which to build a communications infrastructure. Conferences and seminars have since pushed for the next steps in creating a communications platform accessible to all Australians.[20] Unfortunately the language of policy statements increasingly implies that this is wishful thinking. A news release titled "A New Era in Telecommunications" from the Federal Minister for Communications and the Arts outlined the new policy framework in telecommunications after July 1997 in Australia. With regard to universal service it said: "Full access to the widest possible range of telecommunications services for all Australians remain[s] the goal, but this can only be pursued with due regard to cost and overall national priorities."[21] The opposing of cost and national priorities to new telecommunications services in the structure of this sentence shows that broad access is itself not yet a national priority. Economic considerations areoften mentioned alongside universal goals, modifying their meaning and preventing serious consideration of how such policies could be implemented.

It is possible to think of Australian people as a nation of leading edge users and to provide the opportunities for them to become producers of their own content in the form of organizations and social relationships. A country of advanced communicators would provide a unique test bed for the development of new kinds of products. Different groups of consumers would begin to define their own interests and needs. In many cases they would produce solutions to problems in the course of their daily work or become more intelligent seekers of new services. Members found it hard to imagine how this could be done. They were unused to reasoning about domestic spheres, and thought only in terms of supplying expensive equipment to individual homes, an option that was dismissed as impractical. The membership, which had been constructed according to industry sectors represented by men, proceeded to formulate policy in the terms of industrial development with which they were most familiar.

The limits of understanding and the narrowness of what could be accommodated and developed by the group became clear when I suggested we consider some of the debates concerning women, media and technology. The suggestion was welcomed by the chair and I gave a brief presentation at the July meeting. I used research on the family viewing context to discuss the differential power of family members and to raise the notion of the cultural power of males within families, as researched by Morley.[22] I referred to work by the Australian Broadcasting Corporation[23] on women as audiences and my own research within families to relate this to an Australian context.[24] All viewers are not equal. Men's choices dominate when they are at home, particularly with genres such as news and sport. Serial dramas are often considered inferior and viewing of them needs to be justified to the male in the family. Men "guard" the remote control. When men are not at home, childen's preferences dominate. Women watch their own chosen programming when they are by themselves.

A second brief paper by a student, Milly Fels looked more generally at the absence of women within the development of technological artefacts and patriarchal definitions of what technology is and is for, which are patriarchal, are built into the machines and the ways we use them.

As a social scientist, my language and concepts differed from others' in the meeting so that sometimes I had the experience not of being misunderstood but of not being heard at all. On this occasion there was some good discussion and interest from individual members, and one member made the request that I keep them informed throughout the process about the issues I had raised.

Weeks later when I received the minutes of the meeting, I found that this whole item and the discussion that ensued had been omitted. Originally not listed on the meeting outline, it was not picked up (or remembered) in the record of the meeting. Despite the papers and the discussion, it had disappeared. At the time it seemed an eloquent and devastating response to my major argument that women's perspectives in this area were different and should be made visible.

Reflecting on my own position, the lone woman in a room of eighteen or more men (until a woman was added to the secretariat), what now stands out is that the one thing I could not do effectively was to speak explicitly about women. In such an environment I was so conscious of being different because I was female that to speak of women created too much of a focus on myself as an individual. It even made me physically uncomfortable, aware, as some cultural theorists would put it, of my "female sexed body." The men knew this at an intuitive level too. It operated to circumscribe a number of our discussions. During the whole twelve months, for example, we didn't discuss pornography or sex, one of the main content areas of new network services, about which there is much public and media debate.

I was grateful for this courtesy on a personal level. However, I regretted it was necessary. It seemed that when sex was tacitly ruled out as an area of debate and policymaking, so was the discussion of women and their particular needs and perspectives.

Future Demand

There was one particular area, future demand for broadband services, where my expertise in consumer and user research should have been used and was not. There were a number of reasons for this. The most immediate was particular ideas of future demand espoused by economists and their reluctance to think differently about what might be required to study the ways people use and adapt to communications technologies. There was also an implied necessity to keep some control over future possibilities, rather than admitting their complexity and indeterminacy. Future demand was to be corralled in the economic and technological discourse of the present.

The question of what people will want from broadband networks when they are in place was part of BSEG'S original terms of reference. It was one of the most difficult questions. In the first meeting, three members of BSEG directly challenged the use of economic projections and suggested different ways of gaining information. In spite of this, a press advertisement was placed in March, 1994 which emphasized the possibilities for revenue and cost reductions and called for consultants to predict and measure future broadband services. The work was to be done in industry sectors which had been defined in advance. Domestic uses were originally not going to be studied in relation to the home environment and were labelled as entertainment. Telecommuting was listed separately.

It seems mundane to discuss definitions and procedures. However, in these areas of new technology, the way that research is defined is crucial. Assumptions built into measures are directly expressed in the findings. In this case, a disregard for the domestic context led to some bizarre findings, which treated the home as neutral ground receptive to new contents of all kinds. Arthur D. Little [25] estimated future demand for broadband services based on the current revenues in relevant sectors and predicted that home shopping and home gambling would be by far the most profitable residential broadband services. People now spend large amounts on shopping and betting, though mostly not from home. However, the consultants ignored their own logic when it came to the potential of an electronically networked sex industry, which they didn't consider. Although estimates of revenue were probably available, they did not seem to think it a fitting subject for their report.

There was no consistent methodology used to study present and future demand across the various sectors. Since they did not have a strong basis for comparison or a consistent rationale for predicting the future, these studies cannot be used to answer the overall question of which industries showed the greatest potential demand for broadband services. Research which interviewed key players in the manufacturing industry[26] and the health sector[27] was the most productive in linking current uses with future demand. Information from these demand studies does not feature in the final report because the group was not confident to draw firm conclusions. There was disagreement within the group about their usefulness and accuracy. The various studies have been published separately.

If based on the business and residential studies, the final report would have put domestic adoption of broadband ahead of most other industries, and downplayed the interest of business in the short term. Overall, the pattern of results supports the argument about the primacy of social uses in the building of future telecommunications networks, since the strongest interest was from residential and public sector areas. However, the methodological shortcomings cast doubt on the conclusions.

The acceptance of a predominantly economic approach to future demand demonstrates a readiness by government to define the whole field of technological and cultural change as one that is about the supply of commodities, rather than the transformation of living and business practices. Restricting information in these matters to aggregated consumption figures hides and controls the real complexity of the situation. Yet we know that cultural change is both embedded in particular contexts and interpreted from particular subject positions. The simplistic use of economic statistics to furnish information about complex social phenomena needs to be fundamentally challenged.

For women, the consequences are serious. Those managing the information and scheduling the content of networks predominantly men decide what the numbers measure and how they are interpreted. With such data, new categories cannot be discovered. Assumptions already existing in the field are locked both into the parameters of the research and into its explanation. These discourses and what they silence are rarely made explicit or accountable.

In the field of telecommunications there has been little research-based discussion of users and consumers at the levels of industry and policymaking. Telephone companies keep their market research to themselves, and government research has almost exclusively been concerned with economic and technological issues. Social research is not yet readily accepted as a basis for policymaking in telecommunications, despite the fact that there is a growing body of writing in the public sphere about the needs and concerns of consumers, including women, and the social implications of widespread changes.[28] Those places to which social research gains admission are limited to preventing the appearance of a class of information poor.

For women, this means that there is as yet no recognition of difference in terms of use, of particular social and cultural values, or of the need to adapt communications technologies to the environments and relationships that sustain them. This is despite a very significant body of research by Moyal,[29] Rakow,[30] and others which shows that women in particular are using the phone to create community life parenting, providing support for working families,[31] "visiting" the sick and disabled,[32] and keeping active links with friends and families in ways that make a functioning society possible.[33]

Future demand is itself a problematic term. It implies something that is waiting to be activated by the circumstances, requiring merely a matching of equipment to need. It ignores the question of how particular consumer groups are targeted in the process of designing and marketing new technologies and the importance of training and familiarity in their adoption. These aspects are possibly more important when women's uses of new communications are considered.

Conclusion

A reluctance to consider the characteristics of women's uses of new technologies may be predictable in a committee named an "expert" group and given the task of reporting to the prime minister. According to Benston, in technology areas, "men are experts, women are not."[34] Certainly, the lack of female representation on BSEG was not noteworthy for most of the committee. At the first BSEG meeting, the chair even commented on how balanced BSEG was. He was referring to the industry sectors involved. Narrow definitions of technological concerns and relevant expertise produced a small list of industries and disciplines from which the "experts" were drawn. Women were casually filtered out because they were not at the top of these industry sectors: engineering, economics, banking, science, and the media.

On BSEG I was sometimes shocked at what was taken for granted. Many assumptions did not accord with my research or industry and everyday experience. At an intellectual level, perhaps I should not have been so affected. According to Smith, "the break between a world known, acted, and lived" and "objectified knowledges built into the relations of ruling" is to be expected. It is, indeed, "socially organized."[35]

There was one meeting where the conflicts between my personal history and my role as a member of BSEG were dramatized. As the day progressed I could find no way to accomodate both. My keen sense of alienation, which I took pains to hide, was reinforced by the behaviour of those men who were hosts and presenters to the BSEG group.

I arrived a few minutes late from the airport to a morning briefing prior to the afternoon BSEG meeting. A U.S. company was giving a detailed presentation of its broadband trials. I walked into a rather fancy boardroom packed with men, towards a single empty chair with my name, literally, in front of it. I looked for another woman, and there among the strangers was one other, wedged into a corner.

Outside the door, I had just passed four women, smiling, with silver tea and coffee pots held at the ready. Their teapots and smiles reminded me of myself when I was much younger, demonstrating for women's ordination to the priesthood in front of St. Andrew's Cathedral in Sydney while the male priests lined up for the procession. I was part of a tableau of five women, one of them a bound and gagged female priest, and I smilingly held an enamel teapot and porcelain cup and saucer. This teapot image was reproduced in the local newspaper and has become one of the many symbols of resistance by women within the churches.

Women are now Anglican priests in Australia. However, the sense of exclusion I experienced in my teens and twenties in the church returned on this occasion in the boardroom with BSEG. I was not surprised when none of the American consultants or salesmen spoke to me over the lunch they hosted. They focused their energies on the other members of BSEG and some of the secretariat. Women are not going to be admitted easily as leaders, experts, or advocates in the new communications age. The conventional relations of ruling will be scripted all over again in new fields if we do not intervene.

The experience I describe is very different to the metaphors of family life and even echoes of the marriage service in the prime minister's speech launching BSEG'S final report:

> "So, despite our reasonable doubts about the capacity of technology to change the things that really matter like love, laughter, life and death we say 'Yes'. We're not sure that technology gives us much more than a stress-related illness and a sense of inadequacy but we say 'Yes'...We really do have to embrace them now, so that we, our children and future generations of Australians will not be left behind." [36]

Curiously, in this affirmation, in the embraces and the talk of children, there is no mention of those women who will be working hardest to maintain communications and produce cultural work. The 'yes' is said on behalf of us, and our compliance is assumed but women are not spoken about.. So now that the vows have been exchanged, we need to start speaking for ourselves. Women must gather their resources and shape this communications future themselves. It is within the world of the everyday, in the details of interaction, that the new technologies will be placed, tested, and adapted. Women are experts here, and in all of the other industry sectors. We must say so.

Notes

1. Broadband Services Expert Group (BSEG), *Networking Australia's Future: The Interim Report of the Broadband Services Expert Group* (Canberra, 1994), p.85. Broadband is used as a general term describing the capacity to communicate information at a high rate. Broadband services are a range of services using image, sound, text, data or video singly or in combination. It was assumed that these services would need the greater bandwidth of broadband to be provided, but developments in the Internet, which is a narrowband service, have shown that some services can be developed without broadband capacity.

2. Paul Keating, speech by the prime minister at the launch of *Creative Nation: Commonwealth Cultural Policy*, Parliament House (Canberra, 18 October) 1994, p.12.

3. BSEG, *Networking Australia's Future: The Interim Report*, p.32.

4. Ibid.

5. Paul Keating, launch of *Creative Nation*.

6. BSEG,"Social Impact of Broadband Services," brainstorming session report (Canberra, 1994).

7. BSEG, "New Creators," brainstorming session report, (Canberra, 1994), p. 5.

8. Department of Communication and the Arts, *Creative Nation: Commonwealth Cultural Policy* (Canberra, 1994), p. 57

9. Ibid., p. 55.

10. Ibid., p. 57.

11. Cutler and Company, Commerce in Content, Building *Australia's International Future in Interactive Multimedia Markets*, a report for the Department of Industry Science and Technology, Commonwealth Scientific and Industrial Research Organization, and the Broadband Services Expert Group (Canberra: DIST, 1994).

12. Paul Brown, "Cargo cults and Technofetishism," *Media Information Australia* 75 (1995):88.

13. See, for example, Bureau of Transport and Communications Economics, *New Forms and New Media: Commercial and Cultural Policy Implications*, Communications Futures Project, work in progress paper no. 3 (Canberra: Department of Transport, 1994); Department of Communication and the Arts, *Beyond the Duopoly*, issues paper (Canberra: Australian Government Publishing Service, 1994); and Telstra Corporation, *Population Group and Policy Issue Papers: Planning for an Information Society Project*, (Melbourne, 1994).

14. BSEG, *Networking Australia's Future, The Final Report of the Broadband Services Expert Group* (Canberra, 1994), p. 3.

15. BSEG, "Social Impact of Broadband Services," p.1.

16. Universal service is the notion, built into Australian telecommunications legislation, that all Australians should have access to a standard telephone service at a reasonable price. BSEG wanted to consider the implications of developments in broadband technologies for the definition of a standard telephone service and access to new technologies.

17. BSEG, *Networking Australia's Future, The Interim Report*, p.5.

18. Greg Hearn, David Anthony, Leanne Holmen, June Dunleavy, and Tom Mandeville, *The Information Superhighway and Consumers*, the Communication Centre Research Report Series, no. 1 (Brisbane: Queensland University of Technology, 1994).

19. BSEG, *Networking Australia's Future, The Final Report*, p. 53.

20. For example, the Australian Council of Library and Information Services/ Australian Library and Information Association Forum, "Networking Whose Future?" Melbourne, May 23, 1995; the Consumer Telecommunications Network Conference, "Crossed Lines," Sydney, August 8, 1995; and a workshop convened by the Commonwealth Office of the Status of Women to examine policy implications for women of new technologies, Canberra, August 23 and 24, 1995.

21. Michael Lee, "A New Era in Telecommunications," Press Release by the Minister for Communications and the Arts and for Tourism (Canberra: August 1, 1995).

22. D. Morley, *Family Television: Cultural Power and Domestic Leisure* (London: Comedia, 1986).

23. *Australian Broadcasting Corporation, A Female Audience Development Study*, (Sydney: Australian Broadcasting Corporation, 1987).

24. Patricia Gillard, "Insight from the Inside: A New Perspective on Family Influences over Children's Television Viewing," in J. O. Milner and C. A. Pope (eds.), *Global Voices: Culture and Identity in the Teaching of English* (Illinois: National Council of Teachers of English, 1994).

25. Arthur D. Little, "Demand for Broadband Services in Australia: Entertainment and Information Services and Domestic Transactions." final report to BSEG (Canberra, 1994).

26. Marina Cavill, "Broadband Demand Study: Manufacturing Sector," report prepared for BSEG, (Glen Waverly, Victoria: Consulplan, 1994).

27. David Anthony, Tom Mandeville, Greg Hearn and Leanne Holman, "Demand for Broadband Services in the Health Sector," report prepared for BSEG, (Brisbane: The Communication Centre, Queensland University of Technology, 1994).

28. See, for example, Greg Hearn and Thomas Mandeville, "The Electronic Superhighway: Increased Commodification or the Democratisation of Leisure?" *Media Information Australia* 75 (1995): 92-101; and Karen Wale, and Patricia Gillard "The Impact of New Telecommunications Services on Family and Social Relations,", in *Population Group and Policy Issue Papers, Planning for an Information Society Project* (Melbourne: Telstra, 1994).

29. A. Moyal, "The Gendered Use of the Telephone: An Australian Case Study," *Media, Culture and Society* 14 (1992) 51-72.

30. L. F. Rakow, and V. Navarro, "Remote Mothering and the Parallel Shift: Women Meet the Cellular Phone," *Critical Studies in Mass Communication* 10, (1993) 144-157.

31. Eva Cox and Helen Leonard, *Weaving Community Links* (Sydney: Distaff Associates, 1993).

32. K. Williamson, *Drinks on the phone at five o'clock: Telecommunications and the Information and Communication Needs of Older Adults*, (Melbourne: Telecommunications Needs Research Group, Royal Melbourne Institute of Technology, 1993).

33. Patricia Gillard, Amanda Bow and Karen Wale, *A Major Line From the Outside World to the House* (Melbourne: Telecommunications Needs Research Group, Royal Melbourne Institute of Technology, 1994).

34. Margaret Lowe Benston, "Women's Voices/ Men's Voices: Technology as Language," in Cheris Kramarae (ed.), *Technology and Women's Voices* (New York: Routledge & Kegan Paul, 1988), p. 24.

35. Dorothy E Smith, *Texts, Facts and Femininity. Exploring the Relations of Ruling* (London: Routledge, 1990), p. 3.

36. Paul Keating, speech by the prime minister at the launch of *Networking Australia's Future, Final Report of the Broadband Services Expert Group*, (Lindfield: Film Australia, March 1, 1995) p.1-2.

Bibliography

Australian Science and Technology Council, *The Networked Nation*, Canberra: AGPS, 1994.

Broadband Services Expert Group(BSEG)."Universal Service and Broadband Services." Brainstorming session report, Canberra, 1994.

Bureau of Transport and Communications Economics (BTCE). *Emerging Communications Services: An Analytical Framework*. Communications Futures Project, work in progress paper no. 1. Canberra: Department of Transport, 1994.

—.*Delivery Technologies in the New Communications World*. Communications Futures Project, work in progress paper no. 2. Canberra: Department of Transport, 1994.

—.*Costing New Residential Communications Networks*. Communications Futures Project, work in progress paper no. 5. Canberra: Department of Transport, 1994.

Gillard, Patricia. "What Do We Really Want? Rethinking Media and Telephone User Research" *Media Information Australia* 74(1994): 27-33.

Gillard, Patricia, Amanda Bow and Karen Wale, *A Major Line From the Outside World to the House*, Melbourne: Telecommunications Needs Research Group, RMIT, 1994a.

—"Issues of Access and Equity in New Media Services for Residential Consumers." Paper presented at the "Consumer Perspectives on New Media" conference, Sydney, 9 March, 1994.

Keating, Paul. "The Global Economy." Speech by the prime minister at the launch of the Open Learning Agency of Australia's internationaltelevision production, Parliament House, Canberra, 16 August, 1994.

Rakow, L. F. *Gender on the Line. Women, the Telephone and Community Life*, Urbana: University of Illinios Press, 1987.

WATERFALL

ELIZABETH GERTSAKIS

PHANTOM FALLS, LORNE.

WATERFALL

SOUTHERN CROSS SERIES 2328.   CUMBERLAND FALLS, MARYSVILLE, VIC.

CATARACT

The Cascades. Katoomba

WISHING YOU A MERRY CHRISTMAS
AND A HAPPY NEW YEAR

CASCADE

B. SERIES NO. 2. LADY HORDERN FALLS N.S.W.

TORRENT

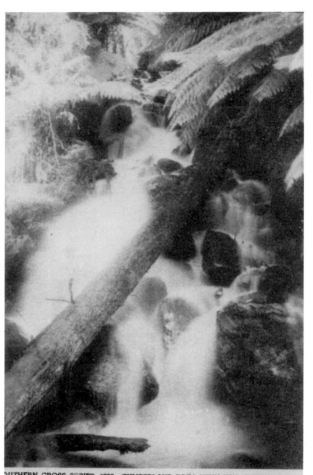

OUTHERN CROSS SERIES 4938. CUMBERLAND-CORA LYNN TRIP, MARYSVILLE, VI
AT THE MEETING OF THE WATERS.

DELUGE

W. Series No. 4. FITZROY FALLS, N.S.W.

OVERFLOW

1843 D   MISSES ZENA AND PHYLLIS DARE.   ROTARY PHOTO. E.C

Minnie Ha Ha Falls Katoomba

FLOOD

FALL

Building Blocks: Recent Anti-Racist Initiatives in the Arts

Monika Kin Gagnon

Instead of relying on the 'kindness of strangers' to open doors for us, the conference was part of a process of strengthening, and opening the doors ourselves.

— Mina Shum on *About Face About Frame*

I'm not sure we want to go through that door. Our task may be something like ripping off the door.

— Dionne Brand at *Writing thru Race*

ANNPAC is a house that simply must be rebuilt.

— Lillian Allen, "Transforming the Cultural Fortress"

Three comparable cultural events which occurred between 1992 and 1995 are illustrative of some strategies of political activism concerning issues of race and cultural difference in Canadian cultural production. *About Face, About Frame*, *It's a Cultural Thing*/Minquon Panchayat, and *Writing thru Race* could be characterized as nationally based in intent, and occurring within alternative cultural networks. Although these events took place within different disciplines—film and video production, visual arts, and writing—they are essentially related in having been initiated and organized by people of colour and First

Nations peoples working to address racism and cultural inequity in the contexts of national cultural organizations.

As it is impossible within this essay to comment fully on all three events, I have generally contented myself with briefly describing and addressing specific initiatives, strategies, and conflicts in each. Primarily, all three were developed in relation to already established cultural organizations, alternative or otherwise. They functioned within a strategy of identity politics, that is these events were organized by and for artists or writers, self-identified as First Nations or of colour, who presented a challenge to white-dominated cultural organizations.[1]

Providing "access" to excluded or underserved communities identified by race, gender, or sexual orientation characterizes the dominant rhetoric of most cultural organizations tackling issues of gender and cultural equity. This essay considers the implications of negotiating as self-defined communities of colour with largely all-white organizations. I was a participant in all three events and my experience with the Minquon Panchayat/ ANNPAC in particular proved instructive in several ways. It demonstrated how an equity rhetoric which ostensibly invites diversity and embraces change can continue to maintain a paternalizing approach and leave existent relations of power intact. It revealed how equity enters the vocabularies of institutional bureaucracies and organizations as a response to pressures from communities self-organizing to challenge their exclusion from the resources and discourses of mainstream culture. But it also revealed that the way in which this new vocabulary is practically interpreted is another matter. Measures such as the introduction of anti-racism workshops focus on an organization's own needs for awareness and education, but effectively operate as delaying tactics. Dionne Brand has argued:

> Notions of access, representation, inclusion, exclusion, equity, etc., are all other ways of saying "race" in this country. country. So it's made it comfortable to talk covertly about race in this country without saying that we live in a deeply racialized and racist culture which represses the life possibilities of people of colour.[2]

I would contend, however, that the terms of negotiation are rapidly shifting as social inequality is revealed to insidiously permeate all levels of the language, structures, and procedures which allow these organizations to operate. As Lillian Allen has said, "Those of us who do this [equity] work are about to keel over from the censorship of tact, constantly negotiating the infested waters of white guilt, liberalism, power addiction, fear, ignorance, arrogance, sabotage, stupidness and sometimes walls of plain hatred—walls and walls and sheets and walls of it."[3] If the three conferences I discuss seek first to empower and affirm their participants, it means that the constraints of politeness and educating allies in the struggle are giving way to an impatience with the very terms of current arrangements. As Ahasiw Maskegon-Iskwew has said of his work as Canada Council First Peoples Equity Coordination Intern, his goal was to allow various communities—and not the Canada Council—to define what constitutes an artist and art worthy of funding.[4] As Allen concludes: "There are two significant litmus tests for [the success of] anti-racism work: meaningful change and critical mass."[5]

The first of the events I will discuss is the closed conference *About Face, About Frame*. It was organized by President Premika Ratnam and an *ad hoc* committee of artists of colour within the Independent Film and Video Alliance/L'Alliance de la vidéo et du cinéma indépendants (IFVA/AVCI) in June 1992. The Alliance is comprised of approximately fifty independent film and video production and resource centres across Canada.[6] The second event is the formation and subsequent formation of the Minquon Panchayat caucus within the Association of National Non-Profit Artists Centres/Le Regroupement d'artistes des centres alternatifs (ANNPAC/RACA) in 1992-93. Founded in 1976, ANNPAC was an association of approximately one hundred artist-run centres across Canada. It was considerably re-structured in 1993, and is now the Artist-Run Network.[7] The third event is a one-time conference that occurred in June 1994, *Writing thru Race*, organized by the Conference Planning Committee of the Racial Minority Writers' Committee of the Writers' Union of Canada. The Planning Committee was made up of about fifteen Vancouver writers of colour and First Nations writers, most of whom were not members of the Writers' Union of Canada.[8]

Moving chronologically from 1992 to 1994, my descriptions summarize some different ways of addressing institutional racism. Language and procedure are pivotal points of conflict. I also explore how issues of race interact with the cultural mainstream. It is not coincidental that the impact of events gradually broadens: from the insulated effects of *About Face, About Frame* within IFVA and the independent film and video community; to the Minquon Panchayat caucus inadvertently prompting a radical restructuring of the seventeen-year-old organization, ANNPAC; and finally to hysteria in the mainstream media and a minor crisis in cultural funding policy within the Canadian House of Commons as a result of *Writing thru Race*. In my view, this broadening demonstrates not only the extent to which issues of cultural equity are now inevitably affecting the cultural mainstream in Canada, but also how repressed histories which have erupted in the Canadian social fabric are now coming to bear in the cultural domain.

About Face, About Frame :
Identifying Arenas of Discussion

About Face, About Frame was conceived as a closed conference of approximately forty participants from across the country involved in the production of independent film and video. Over the course of four days, participants made presentations of their work, and contributed to a series of facilitated workshops and sessions pertaining to the "distribution, funding, the negotiation of difference and the forging of solidarity, programming and exhibitions, employment equity and professional development, as well as a caucus on anti-racism strategies for artist-run centres."[9] The broad aim of the sessions was to define working needs and to develop a strategy for providing support for First Nations artists and artists of colour.

Many of the sessions were particular to the concerns of film and video producers. On day three, facilitator Anne-Marie Stewart created a more general forum of analysis, which is interesting to consider as a point of departure here, for the way that it identified how subjective knowledge can be used to illuminate the operations of systemic racism. Stewart introduced three factors that interplay within institutions: the first is policy and proposed beliefs surrounding issues of racism; the second is individual experiences and behaviour with regard to policy and proposed beliefs about racism within an organization; and the third is the jobs, systems, and decision-making structures that arise around policymaking and the individuals functioning within them. She then proceeded to outline the historical development of anti-racist policy in organizations: from an archaic "no way" position, in which considerations of racial inequality in the workplace were nonexistent; to a "kindness of strangers" phenomenon, in which some acknowledgement of the impact of racial discrimination on work environments was possible, but addressed only because of the goodwill of random individuals; to the more recent affirmative action and employment equity strategies, which fundamentally recognize sexual and racial discrimination in the workplace, and designate programs to increase diversity, ideally countering the historical impact of inequity with proactive structural change.

The fact that job creation programs frequently result in the perception of affirmative action as a hiring policy for individuals defined by their colour (or gender) over and above their skills was addressed. This often creates marginalized ghettos in the lower echelons of hierarchical institutions and a situation in which class and gender issues distort the realities of racism. In other words, the creation of "optics" means that people of colour are involved in institutions, but in menial positions that can do little to fundamentally challenge organizational structures. Thus a hiring policy based on skin colour means that affirmative action can be perceived as an internal threat to quality work and to existing and potential white employees.

Further, it was pointed out how frequently equity policy is formed without access to increased monies. The necessity to adhere to strict rules, guidelines, and categories of funding for such projects often results in the gradual absorption of anti-racist politics into the broader organizational structure. Competition for funding then effectively silences voices of opposition. As with affirmative action, target-group hiring is illusory and frequently creates backlash. In addition, training programs are often implemented without the possibility of actual jobs. Overall, equity policy seems to remain an "appendage" project unrelated to other systems within a given structure.

At an individual level, both types of policy—affirmative action and equity programs—result in experiences of tokenism, which frequently means scapegoating, being used as a pawn in political matters and, more personally, being the object of resentment. Individuals carry the burden of limited public definitions of who they are or what they are capable of without having any access to the power of actual decision-making regarding issues pertaining to race and racism (particularly if these entail structural change). This particular workshop effectively established a broad framework of analysis that evolved into a concrete strategy and resolution session later that afternoon, with the formulation of a document of recommendations for IFVA.

Minquon Panchayat: Cultural Equity Strategies Devised for Alternative Cultural Spaces

At the 1992 conference, "Contemporary Arts in Canada at the End of the Twentieth Century," organized by ANNPAC/RACA in New Brunswick, the keynote speaker, Lillian Allen (a dub poet and cultural activist) challenged the audience to acknowledge the dismally low number of people of colour and First Nations participants present. On a later panel (somewhat unfortunately, if revealingly, entitled "Anthropological Aspects of Contemporary Arts and Culture"), Allen invited First Nations individuals and people of colour to caucus. What would emerge from this seven-person group after several early morning and late night meetings was a caucus named Minquon Panchayat and a concrete document for the implementation of an anti-racism strategy specific to ANNPAC, entitled "Principles and Responsibility of the Advisory Committee for Anti-Racism."[10] The broad goal was to transform ANNPAC as an organization by bringing significant numbers of artists' groups and centres of colour and of First Nations into ANNPAC's membership; educating and transforming already existing member centres and their memberships; and networking those First Nations individuals and people of colour already working within the current ANNPAC centres.

The caucus "Principles" drew (if only implicitly) on a "Restructuring Proposal" drafted internally for the organization in 1991. As a participant in the fine-tuning of this "Restructuring

Proposal" it was instructive to observe how the caucus' "Principles" initially depended on the space provided by the role of a proposed equity coordinator, but accelerated both the coordinator's pace and tasks. The proposal for an equity coordinator acknowledges the progressive intentions of ANNPAC and its membership. But more significantly, it also reveals the gulf between a predominantly white organization (albeit an alternative one) such as ANNPAC, and people of colour, their groups, and organizations who have a wealth of knowledge and experience from their work toward cultural equity. Notably, six of the seven members of the caucus were not officially affiliated with ANNPAC in any way. This suggests that an organization's attempts to deal with cultural inequity within its own frames of reference and without a radical examination of how it constitutes itself as an organization may be (despite ostensibly honourable intentions) completely ineffectual, or at worst, merely symbolic or tokenistic. Cosmetic modifiers, such as an equity coordinator, give the illusion that an organization is prepared to accomodate diversity. The danger is that it in fact simply remains trapped—ideologically, strategically and practically— within the very structure that excluded people of colour from the cultural process to begin with. As I re-read the "Restructuring Proposal," a document I had already read a dozen times, very early one morning in Moncton, I was struck by the fact that the terms racism and anti-racism were not uttered once throughout, despite being its *raison d'être*. I had merely assumed their presence before, without noting their absence. It was as if an organization that was willing to acknowledge the necessity of an equity coordinator was still unable to speak of racism.

Central to a consideration of the wide gap between a mainstream cultural organization and First Nations artists/artists of colour, is the issue of "access," for access should be understood to be flowing both ways. It is only once the balance of cultural values and priorities shifts, and mainstream cultural organizations understand their potential enrichment that meaningful change can occur. And these values and priorities fundamentally depend on definitions of power, knowledge, and language. The caucus was a spontaneous eruption within the structured parameters of a conference. Politically, that eruption had concrete effects in providing what Allen described as a vision and a road map for change over the ensuing year. For example, Shirley Bear, a Minquon Panchayat member, introduced a talking circle, trans-forming the usual modes of address and conduct at a conference in a simple but powerful and productive way.

The Minquon Panchayat was empowered to implement its principles by a modest budget allocated over the following year, and, by the 1993 ANNPAC Annual General Meeting in Calgary, Minquon Panchayat had invited some artists of colour and First Nations artists to attend, as well as organizing a conference to precede the main event. The conference, *It's a Cultural Thing*, highlighted the work of forty artists of colour and First Nations artists in a three-day event attended by over 250 ANNPAC members and non-members.[11] During the ensuing meeting, how-ever, events irreconcilably erupted with regard to the Minquon Panchayat's work over the previous year, through a form of resistance that can only be considered covertly racist. As I have described elsewhere, these conflicts were dominantly focused on procedural violations and alleged violations, which ultimately wore through the highly formalized process of the meeting.[12] When Minquon Panchayat reported on its activities, questions of how monies were spent were both unusual and inappropriate to the forum, particularly since all spending had been previously approved by ANNPAC's management committee. The introduc-tion of new member centres was rapidly met with interrogations as to their qualifications as artists' groups—again unusual as new members are always nominated by existent members and this process had not been violated. Questions of legitimacy were perhaps prompted by the racializing context of the Minquon Panchayat.

Procedural language was thus used to reinforce the status quo of ANNPAC, enabling interrogations and exclusions in barely-veiled language of discrimination; violence masquerading as bureaucratic formality. As a consequence of increasing com-plications, the caucus departed from the meeting table. Many members subsequently resigned from the association. As I com-mented later, "Minquon Panchayat left the AGM table because what was clear to each of us was that it was not our responsibility to defend or justify our [volunteer] work."[13]

Writing thru Race: Creating Closed spaces, Redefining the Terms of Negotiation[14]

Writing thru Race: A Conference for First Nations Writers and Writers of Colour brought together 180 delegates from across the country for three days in Vancouver. Conference events included panel presentations, plenary discussions, round-table and caucus sessions, and workshops. The conference was sponsored by The Writers' Union of Canada, conceived by the Racial Minority Writers' Committee (RMWC) of the Writers' Union (formed in 1990), and organized by a working committee of Vancouver-based writers—including Chair Roy Miki, Larissa Lai, Joy Hall, Charmaine Parkins, Scott McFarlane, Anne Jew, Susan Crean, and Mark Nakada—who were predominantly writers of colour and First Nations writers.

Writing thru Race can be seen as part of an ongoing process precipitated by challenges which have repeatedly brought issues of racism to the Writers' Union forum over the last decade. In 1983 Makeda Silvera's address to the *Women and Words* conference in Toronto foregrounded issues of race and racism in Canadian writing. In 1989, protests against the lack of representation of writers of colour and First Nations writers in the Writers' Union of Canada and in P.E.N. by groups such as Vision 21: Canadian Culture in the 21st Century, and Women Writers of Canada, took on a national profile in the media as a result of June Callwood's involvement; her reputation unfortunately became the focus of discussion and eclipsed any analysis of the systemic dimensions of racism which was the integral content of the challenges.[15] Then in May 1992, the RMWC organized "The Appropriate Voice," a gathering held in Orillia, Ontario, which brought seventy writers of colour and First Nations writers together for three days to identify common concerns and barriers to writing and publishing in Canada. *Writing thru Race* emerged as a recommended strategy from this event.

Writing thru Race's policy of restricting participation in workshops and panels to writers who identified themselves as First

Nations writers and writers of colour was designed (according to the original call for participation), to "ensure a milieu in which writers directly affected by racism [could] engage in candid and personal discussions." *Writing thru Race* effectively created this milieu in which writers, editors, theoreticians and publishers networked and exchanged ideas. Implicit in the conference policy was the fact that participants themselves could establish the parameters of discussion without having to attend to the white guilt, anger, and defensiveness that have characterized and often dominated so many past discussions of race not only within the Writers' Union but in other cultural contexts in which race politics have come to the fore. Rather than a mixed forum in which a negotiation of politics, vocabulary, and strategy frequently dominate, the conference allowed instead for a focus on the production of bodies of work which, broadly defined, challenge traditional categories of writing and language, as well as conventional notions of history and culture.

Panel sessions were often held simultaneously (with up to four running concurrently), actually making it impossible to take in more than 25 per cent of the discussions. This tended to have the adverse effect of fragmenting any collective discussion or even experience of the conference. The shortcoming became evident during the scheduled caucus sessions and the two plenary sessions, and particularly affected attempts during the last day's plenary to focus on recommendations. While over seventy recommendations were brought forward by participants, it became unclear how and why the conference was identifying itself as a unified group in order to produce such recommendations. And also, to whom were these recommendations being directed—to ourselves as representative of our own communities? to the Writers' Union? to cultural institutions, such as funding bodies or publishers?

In other words, the conference did not automatically produce a homogeneous politic with regards to self-identification, self-definition, or strategy. Contentions about "process" during the last hour of the plenary further accentuated the conference's "identity crisis," which had mostly gone unaddressed during the conference itself. Particular motions began coming forward,

suggesting an adherence to voting procedures and formal process that had neither been declared nor agreed upon by conference participants. That the motions were largely being made by
Union members had the dangerous effect of directing and defining the conference in relation to the Writers' Union, and could be
perceived as an ideological hijacking of the conference in the
interests of a handful of Writers' Union members.

In response to suggestions by some Union members that
there should be a massive influx of membership by conference
participants, Program Committee member Larissa Lai pointed
out that many *Writing thru Race* participants were in fact
ineligible for membership without the publication of a "book
with a spine." She further remarked that the Union's definition
of what constituted a writer was restrictive and explicitly challenged by large amounts of work published in magazines and
chapbooks. Writer Sky Lee stated that she had no interest in
joining the Union despite her eligibility. Yet Union members
continued to espouse the virtues of the Union. A small group of
speakers on the floor attempted to challenge and interrupt the
implicit assumptions operating through the making and passing
of motions by Union members. But many more conference
participants had in fact already registered their response to the
direction of the plenary, as many had left the forum out of
disinterest or confusion.

Writing thru Race is also notable for the level of mainstream
backlash that resulted from its participant policy. In the months
preceding the conference, there were repeated claims made by
Toronto *Globe and Mail* columnists Robert Fulford and Michael
Valpy that it was "racist against whites."[16] Then in June, only
weeks before the conference, Minister of Canadian Heritage
Michel Dupuy withdrew $22,500 of crucial funding for the
conference. Dupuy's announcement came in the House of Commons after Reform MP Jan Brown's simplistic accusations that
the conference workshops were "racist and discriminatory."
Brown's comments completely denied the intense effects of
racism experienced by First Nations peoples and people of
colour. It also reaffirmed the current social and political climate,
which is increasingly hostile to cultural organizations defining

themselves or their projects on the basis of race, gender, and/or sexual orientation.

Dupuy's decision has been criticized as contrary to both *multi*culturalism and the principles of affirmative action in the Canadian Charter of Rights, and cryptically underlines the Reform Party's ability to influence cultural policy in spite of its reductive and uninformed critique. While an emergency fundraising campaign within the cultural community and trade unions was overwhelmingly successful in bridging the budgetary shortfall and making the conference possible, the double-edged implication of such private support is that it alleviates the government's ideological responsibility to proactively develop and support affirmative cultural policies.

The Power and Limits of Cultural Identity Politics

The problem with race as special event is that like all specials— lunch special, special of the day, flavour of the month—they are, by definition, not the staple, not the norm. On the other hand, without such events, the issue may never be raised at all.

— Richard Fung

Without transforming core values around power and diversity, the culture of domination will always frame the agenda and shadow the relations between individuals.

— Lillian Allen

For the master's tools will never dismantle the master's house.

— Audre Lorde

About Face, About Frame, the Minquon Panchayat, and *Writing thru Race* forged collective spaces for many artists and writers who are East and South Asian, Aboriginal and Black. By creating a critical mass at an intersection with established cultural organizations, these events, in different ways, made the significant first step of facilitating increased access to the tools of cultural production, exhibition, and distribution. Integrationist strategies might further include redressing the exclusion of artists of colour in written histories, and countering the enduring misrepresentations that proliferate within the cultural mainstream. As the points of intersection proliferate, it has also become increasingly important to analyze how and why such absences and exclusions occur and become contained. In other words, how have racialized identifications impinged on practical strategies of cultural production? And how do alternative representations become, as Trinh Minh-ha puts it, "narrow, predictable representation"?[17]

What is becoming increasingly evident, as forums such as these are provided for debate, is that to empower certain identities does not mean that they must merely be integrated into existing dominant (white) structures. One implication of all three conferences is that it is possible to challenge ideological notions of what constitutes the Canadian public and the ways in which national funding bodies distribute funds. The three events described overtly challenged notions of cultural universality. By applying for public cultural funding the conferences insisted that the government recognize the politics of cultural difference functioning in Canada: that gatherings of First Nations artists/writers and artists/writers of colour are culturally productive spaces that should be valued by institutions which historically have worked according to simplistic notions of multiculturalism, or else through cultural erasures which homogenize and define culture within Eurocentric traditions and criteria.

What the conferences also implicitly recognize to varying degrees is that bureaucracies and existing cultural organizations are not neutral sites, but themselves (even inadvertently) perpetrators of racist practices. *About Face, About Frame* created a temporary collective space which sought to strengthen its participants, to identify the needs of its communities in a multi-layered way, and to bring recommendations back to IFVA. The Minquon Panchayat operated as a caucus within ANNPAC, using its resources to attempt a transformation of ANNPAC's adminstration and member centres. The *Writing Thru Race* Planning Committee targetted resources toward an event that, initially, had no overriding agenda in relation to its funding organization, but rather was focused on creating a space of dialogue for First Nations writers and writers of colour.

The concluding sessions of this latter event, however, profoundly revealed the radically different ideological positions that First Nations writers and writers of colour occupy in relation to dominant culture and cultural organizations: from assimilative to radically transformative. If all three conferences implicitly challenged dominant notions of what constitutes a Canadian citizen and valid cultural production, the procedural wranglings of Minquon Panchayat with its "host" organization, and of *Writing Thru Race* amongst its own delegates of colour, foreground the various stakes and struggles now occurring at the level of meaning and interpretation. Initial optimism for a shared politic must give way to different, if more dramatically effective, crises of representation. For as these events also affirm, it is only once we might speak of the impact of self-representation that the radical possibilities of cultural transformation will have been truly explored.

Notes

1. As a result of the broad strokes of my approach, some complexities have been left out. It would be productive to consider the specificities of the different media and their contexts of production and dissemination (i.e. writing and publishing vs. independant film, etc.). It would also be interesting to examine the historical trajectories of these organizations and their inception within broader social and cultural contexts.
2. Dionne Brand, "Notes to Structuring the Text and the Craft of Writing," *Front* 6, no. 1 (September/October 1994): 13.
3. Lillian Allen, "Transforming the Cultural Fortress: Imagining Cultural Equity," *Parallélogramme* 19, no. 3 (Autumn 1993): 52.
4. Ahasiw Maskegon-Iskwew made these remarks in an unpublished paper delivered at *Parallel Tracks*, one of two preconference panel discussions organized by the Programing Committee and held in Vancouver prior to *Writing thru Race*.
5. Allen, "Transforming the Cultural Fortress," p. 50.
6. In its bi-monthly *Bulletin*, The Alliance described itself as incorporated in 1980, composed of approximately fifty groups engaged in the production, distribution, and exhibition of independant film and video, and representing over seven thousand individuals. The primary objective is to provide a national network linking these groups and individuals.
7. For a brief overview of ANNPAC's history and a focus on its attempts to with issues of gender, sexual orientation and most recently, cultural difference, see Lynne Fernie, "Editorial," *Parallélogramme* 19, no. 3 (Autumn 1993): 10-13. Fernie

resigned as editor of *Parallélogramme*, published by ANNPAC, in solidarity with the Minquon Panchayat in the fall of 1993. She produced a final special issue entitled "Anti-Racism in the Arts" (Autumn 1993), based on the events that had transpired at ANNPAC's Annual General Meeting. *Parallélogramme* is now published as *MIX*.

8. The Writers' Union of Canada is composed of nine hundred members and was founded in 1973. The Union published a detailed final report on *Writing Thru Race*, authored in part by members of the Conference Planning Committee, who also appended relevant media coverage. See *Writing Thru Race Conference: Final Report* (Toronto: The Writers' Union of Canada, 1995) available through the Writers' Union of Canada, Toronto.

9. Kwame Dawes, "Negotiating Difference: *About Face, About Frame* Coalition formed at Historic Banff Meeting," *Parallélogramme* 18, no. 2 (Autumn 1992): 12-14. For another descriptive review, see Mina Shum "About Face, About Frame," *Fuse* 16, no. 1 (Fall 1992): 10-11.

10. "Minquon" is a Maliseet word meaning rainbow, and is also present in other Native languages, while "Panchayat," originally Sanskrit, exists in various South Asian languages to mean council. The Minquon Panchayat was conceived by Lillian Allen, Shirley Bear, Marrie Mumford, and Gloria Eshkibok; Zool Suleman and Sherazad Jamal of the Rungh Cultural Society, and myself. We were joined by David Woods, Paul Wong, and Dana Claxton, and later, by Cheryl L'Hirondelle, who became interim coordinator for the caucus and a main organizer of the 1993 conference *It's a Cultural Thing*.

11. For an animated description of *It's a Cultural Thing*, see Cheryl L'Hirondelle's "It's a Cultural Thing," *Parallélogramme* 19, no. 3 (Autumn 1993): 28-35.

12. See Monika Kin Gagnon, "How to Banish Fear: Letters from Calgary," *Parallélogramme* 19, no. 3 (Autumn 1993): 36-47.

13. Ibid., pp. 44 and 46.

14. Sections of my discussions of *Writing thru Race* draw on previously published material. See my "Landmarks and Landmines," *Front* 6, no. 1 (September/October 1994): 6-8, and "Writing Thru Race," cowritten with Scott McFarlane in *Parallélogramme* 20, no. 2 (Autumn 1994).

15. See Scott McFarlane, "The Haunt of Race: Canada's Multiculturalism Act, the Politics of Incorporation, and Writing thru Race," *Fuse* 18, no. 3 (Spring 1995): 18-31, for an extended theoretical exploration of *Writing thru Race* and its emergence in relation to the Writers' Union. On the history of the Writers' Union and issues of racism, McFarlane refers to M. Nourbese Philip's *Frontiers: Essays and Writings on Racism and Culture* (Stratford, Ont.: Mercury Press, 1992), especially her chapter, "Disturbing the Peace." 16. Robert Fulford, "George Orwell, Call Your Office," *The Globe and Mail* 30 March 1994, and Michael Valpy, "A Nasty Serving of Cultural Apartheid," *The Globe and Mail* 8 April 1994. In response to her colleagues, Bronwen Drainie said "Females perhaps have more sympathy for the rationale behind the conference than do white males. For the past thirty years, considerable public funds have been spent in this country facilitating the coming together of women to help them plan strategies that would allow them to take their rightful place in a world dominated by men." Bronwen Drainie, "Controversial Writers' Meeting is Both Meet and Right," *The Globe and Mail* 16 April 1994. These

articles and more are republished in *Writing Thru Race Conference: Final Report.*
17. Trinh Minh-ha, "The World as Foreign Land," in *When the Moon Waxes Red* (New York: Routledge, 1991), p. 192.

Bibliography

Fung, Richard. "Conference Calls: Race as Special Event,"
  Take One 5 (Summer 1994): 38.
Lorde, Audre. "The Master's Tools Will Not Dismantle the Master's House," in *Sister Outsider*. Freedom, California: The Crossing Press, 1984.

The author gratefully acknowledges the financial support of the Social Sciences and Humanities Research Council.

From Theory to Practice: Some Reflections on Cultural Planning in Australia

Deborah Stevenson

Introduction

In Australia, the adoption of a cultural planning perspective by local governments has frequently been restrained by unwieldy definitions of culture and the territoriality and conflicting agendas of those involved in traditional arts and cultural practice. Arguably, however, a more significant factor limiting its adoption has been the entrenched organizational practices of local government, which have often made sure that cultural planning and the resulting cultural planning documents occupy a marginal status in local government policy making, planning and implementation.[1] This marginalization has not been addressed through a systematic evaluation of the relationship of cultural planning to the operational and enterprise cultures of Australian local governments.

In March 1994, Newcastle City Council launched the City of Newcastle Cultural Review under the stewardship of its director of Community Development, Deborah Mills. As head of the Community Cultural Development Unit of the Australia Council, Deborah Mills had been influential in introducing cultural planning to Australia and was now well placed institutionally to see the principles of cultural planning adopted by a city council. I was appointed the consultant responsible for undertaking the Cultural Review and was thus afforded a rare opportunity to build on previous research into inner-city redevelopment and cultural planning, to test theoretical assumptions, and to explore more closely the workings of local government.

This article, by focusing on the activities of the Newcastle City Council from 1993-94, considers the potential and some of the limitations of current cultural planning processes, particularly with regard to their integration into the strategic and corporate planning practices of local council.The proposition that this integration of cultural planning requires a movement away from the research and formulation of static cultural planning documents to the establishment of ongoing, flexible cultural planning processes is central to my argument. The significant barriers which make these outcomes difficult to achieve should not be underestimated.

The Intellectual Context

The emerging global economy continues to have a considerable impact on urban form and the processes of constructing and reconstructing city space. Cities today, as the (often postmodern) built spaces of a new economic order, do indeed have "a decisively different form, structure and appearance,"[2] from the cities of modernism. Given the magnitude of these changes, one of the most pressing tasks for practitioners of urban design and the authors of urban policy must be the formulation and implementation of imaginative strategies that are capable of meeting the social and cultural challenges presently being posed by globalization and de-industrialization. This task includes addressing such concerns as the increase of homelessness, the decline of the city centre, the relentless sprawl of suburbia, and the abandonment of industrial landscapes.

Cultural planning has been gaining currency in recent years as an innovative approach to the theory and practice of urban policy and city development, capable of addressing such wide ranging issues. It is a perspective influenced by advances in cultural theory and cultural policy studies[3] and, in many respects, is the outcome of an uneasy marriage between the left-wing romanticism of British cultural marxism and the pragmatism of American liberal pluralism. Cultural planning initiatives, both ad hoc and formal, are well established in the United Kingdom and the United States, and have had a profound influence on the way cultural planning is developing in the vastly different Australian context.[4]

As both a practice and a concept,[5] cultural planning is difficult to define precisely. It is clear, however, that cultural planning pivots on the claim that through the coordination of urban and cultural policy formulation and implementation, local government is better placed than any other tier of the state to address the significant urban effects of de-industrialization and to meet the associated challenges of urban decline.[6] Cultural planning aims to facilitate the equitable participation in decision making processes of a wide cross-section of interests, and is presented as a mechanism for placing local cultural activity and the priorities of local communities on the urban agenda. Women, for example, have rarely occupied influential positions from which to define urban development, even when the fabric of their lives is to be most brutally affected by particular development decisions. Frequently, the only opportunities women have to access the mechanisms of planning are through community consultation initiatives which, as has been argued elsewhere, have long had a nebulous and peripheral status in urban planning.[7] Cultural planning, therefore, is being touted by advocates as offering those whose interests are excluded from, or peripheral to established planning practices and discourses the chance to represent the diversity of their urban experiences and to shape the nature of the urban landscape. As an expansive urban discourse, cultural planning endorses the Europeanization of the inner city often through the development of cultural precincts, the promotion of local cultures, and the celebration of a local sense of place. To achieve these ends, urban cultural activities such as the expressive arts are being reconceptualized in conjunction with broader economic and social policies[8] and promoted as effective tools both for animating the urban landscape[9] and facilitating the attainment of wide-ranging social and economic benefits. As has been pointed out by Gay Hawkins,[10] the arts ministries of Australian state governments and the Community Cultural Development Unit of the Australia Council[11] were quick to embrace the idea of cultural planning as a creative approach to community arts policy and a strategy for shifting some of the burden for arts funding away from federal and state governments and onto local governments. The Australia Council and these other government ministries, however, continue to be influential in defining, promoting and shaping the complexion of cultural planning practice in Australia.

A recent consultants report to the Australia Council, *Better Places, Richer Communities*[12] details the optimum role of local government in arts and cultural policy development and funding, and suggests how these initiatives and responsibilities should be strategically positioned within the corporate structure of city councils. Apart from giving insights into the scope and diversity of local cultures and suggesting innovative methods for fostering that diversity, the report argues that a central aim of any successful cultural planning exercise must be its thorough integration into the council's overall strategic and corporate planning. Indeed, it is the introduction of a cultural planning process rather than the writing of a cultural plan per se that is endorsed. Given the wide-ranging social, environmental, and economic objectives of cultural planning, and the underpinning anthropological definition of culture as the entire way of life of a group or population[13] that defines and legitimates the field,[14] the rationale is obvious for claims that strategic integration is crucial to successful cultural planning. It is timely, therefore, to consider some of the factors which currently militate against the integration of cultural planning processes into the decision making procedures of local government.

Integrating Culture

In the following passage Colin Mercer explains why integration is an absolutely fundamental requirement of effective cultural planning:

> Cultural planning cannot come after the fact. It cannot be added on. Cultural planners must persuade other types of planners that what is being planned in cultural planning are ... [n]ot just streets and buildings but conjunctions of habit, desires, accident and necessity. So, cultural planners must be there and make themselves heard from the very beginning: at the first whiff of a town strategic plan, at the first sign of a new residential or commercial development, at the first signal of a new local industry development strategy.[15]

Cultural planning, therefore, must be integrated from the outset if it is to shape development, influence the ordering of priorities, and inform guiding principles. As Mercer has warned elsewhere, cultural planning that is not undertaken thus risks becoming little more than another town arts policy which have long been peripheral, low priorty concerns of Australian local governments.[16] Recognizing the importance of integration prompts a number of questions. It is of particular importance to ask who, institutionally, is, or should be responsible for the incorporation of cultural planning into the overall planning framework of local government? What, for example, is the identity and organisational position of those cultural planners Mercer says "must be there [making] themselves heard" at the outset? And are they, in fact, in a position to make themselves heard from within the field of play, or are they calling inaudibly from the sidelines?

These are pivotal issues especially when one considers that, to date, the majority of cultural planning activity in Australia has been undertaken by consultants (who by definition are outside the strategic decision making mechanisms of local councils), or by cultural planners who, although situated within the council bureaucracy, are lowly-placed institutionally and thus command limited organizational or strategic influence. For example, local council cultural planners are often located in recreation or community development departments which, historically, have occupied marginal positions in the council corporate structure where the perspectives of urban planning and civil engineering have long been privileged. In effect, then, the operational understanding of cultural planning, the nature of the cultural planning processes that this understanding structures, and the cultural plans which result from these processes, have either been determined before the cultural planning consultant is commissioned, or are initiatives of cultural planners or other council bureaucrats who are peripheral to the policy making process.

Recently, however, there have been a number of encouraging developments, in particular the adoption of principles of cultural planning by the Australian Local Government Association and those of state local government associations including, New

South Wales, Tasmania and South Australia. The aforementioned report to the Australia Council (*Better Places, Richer Communities*) moves to place cultural planning practice at the core of recent Australian Local Government Association initiatives to foster the policy and planning principles of Integrated Local Area Planning (ILAP). Theobjectives of the ILAP method relate the responsibilities of the various divisions of local government to the concerns and activities of different federal and state agencies; these activities are then connected in various ways to the concerns of local communities. The idea is to foster vertical and horizontal integration of the three tiers of government and their constituents.[17] The linking of cultural planning to the principles of ILAP is encouraged through the Local Government Cultural Development Strategy, which is based on a formal agreement between the Australia Council and the Australian Local Government Association to provide resources for the better integration of cultural considerations into local area planning."[18]

This agreement includes a commitment by the Australia Council to provide funds to local government through its Community Cultural Development Board and the Community, Environment, Art and Design Committee (CEAD) for undertakings which will assist in changing the perception and use of the arts and cultural activity within local government areas. Also endorsed by the Australia Council are initiatives which will further the integration of cultural development objectives with other local planning practices, including urban planning. It was in this context and with a commitment to these principles, that moves were made to establish integrated cultural planning practices in the de-industrialising New South Wales city of Newcastle.

Cultural Planning Comes To Town

Suggestions that Newcastle City Council should develop a cultural plan began to gain currency after Labor councillor Greg Heys attended the Cultural Planning Conference in Sydney in December, 1991. Despite a general acceptance that a cultural plan would be a good idea, however, few people, including Councillor Heys, had any practical concept of what formulating a cultural plan might entail nor how this formulation might best be undertaken. Indeed, it would be reasonable to suggest that a cultural plan was seen as a one-off policy that would have a strong expressive arts and community cultural development focus. In early 1992, responsibility for developing the cultural plan was given to the then director of Community Development Keith Swan, whose department was in charge of administrating the local councils arts and cultural resources, facilities, and programs. These include the Newcastle libraries, the regional art gallery, the community arts centre, and the regional museum. The assignment of the cultural planning problem to the Community Development Division signalled that cultural planning was seen by the council to be an extension of its traditional arts and cultural activities that is, part of the council's soft community development portfolio of duties.

The cultural planning initiative stalled at this point. Mr Swan seemed to have little understanding of, or interest in,exploring the possibilities of cultural planning and nothing more was done until the budget session for 1993-94 when, again at the instigation of Councillor Heys, an arbitrary amount of money ($A40,000) was allocated for the development of the cultural plan. Very soon after this the position of Community Development director became vacant and Deborah Mills was chosen to fill it in August, 1993.

Deborah Mills came to Newcastle City Council saying that the Community Development Division would not be, as she was apt to say, "the ministry for silly walks" a department traditionally regarded as not being involved in the real concerns of council (roads, rates, or rubbish), but in unimportant or messy issues, such as the operation of museums, libraries, parks, and beaches. Not surprisingly, given her previous association with the Australia Council, Deborah Mills expressed a commitment to the principles of ILAP and that the local council should adopt a cultural planning approach to urban and community development, and strategic planning. It was of concern, however, that if responsibility for formulating the cultural plan remained solely that of the Community Development Division, as had originally been proposed, Newcastle's cultural plan would effectively be marginalized and, like so many other instances of cultural planning in Australia, achieve little of its innovative potential. As director of Community Development, therefore, Deborah Mills claimed to be particularly concerned that organizational responsibility for the cultural plan should be shared by all divisions of the council.

I have had an ongoing research interest in cultural planning, particularly as it relates to urban policy, and I was at the time a member of the influential Newcastle City Council Social Impact Consultative Panel. Deborah Mills, therefore, regarded me as a potential collaborator in the initiation of Newcastle's cultural planning process and, within weeks of her becoming director of Community Development, we began to work towards this end.

As funds had been set aside for the formulation of the cultural plan, we were in a position to begin the process without referring the matter back to the council for discussion or approval. However, our objective was to initiate an integrated cultural planning process that would influence the perspectives of urban, corporate, environmental, and strategic planning and development. If the Community Development Division was to set about formulating the plan in the context of its organizational position, the result would be effectively irrelevant to these other areas of planning practice. No matter what exciting suggestions and recommendations might be made regarding the use of cultural diversity and activity to arrest the decline of the inner city, to facilitate suburbandevelopment that would incorporate the cultural priorities of residents from the outset, or to create a vital and socially responsible replacement for the industrially redundant Honeysuckle site (a forty-five hectare waterfront area currently being redeveloped by the state government as part of the federal Labor government's Building Better Cities program), these ideas would be trapped in documents that before long would be gathering dust in the council archives.[19]

To lessen the likelihood of such a fate it was necessary to consider how best to situate the planning process within the council's organizational and decision making structure, and how to foster understanding and support for the outcomes and recommendations that would emerge. The first priority was to make the cultural planning process the product of the council's Social Impact Consultative Panel. This panel, chaired by the Lord Mayor, administered by the Urban Development Division and including as members three councillors, the general manager, the directors of Corporate and Urban Development, and community members from a cross section of interests, is the most powerful committee of council. The director of Community Development is not a member of SICP but attends meetings as an invitee. Making the cultural plan an initiative of this panel automatically made it the concern of the divisions of Urban Development and Corporate Development and of the general manager's office. It also put the initiative at arms length from the Community Development Division, a move deemed strategically useful.

The proposal to formulate a cultural plan was put to the Social Impact Panel for endorsement. The details of this submission were based on a longer and more general discussion article on cultural planning that had been considered by the panel and the council, and which had generally been well received.[20] The Social Impact Panel endorsed the proposal and a subcommittee was formed which included Councillor Greg Heys, Debroah Mills, me, and three other members of the panel one of whom who at the time was chairing a series of ILAP (Integrated Local Area Planning) meetings for the Hunter Region Association of Councils. This subcommittee met on a number of occasions in late 1993 and was an environment for exploring the ideal focus of the plan and for developing a proposal which would go to the Community Development Strategic Committee in March 1994.

Strategic committees are meetings of all councillors and directors and provide a forum in which the initiatives of each division can be workshopped, often with an expert facilitator, in an atmosphere that is less formal and confrontational than regular council meetings. From our point of view, going to the Community Development Strategic Committee was an opportunity to make the councillors feel involved in the process, and thus, hopefully, to foster some sense of intellectual ownership and commitment to the outcomes and recommendations of the final report. It was also an opportunity to hear councillors' objections to cultural planning in an arena where council was not being called upon to endorse or reject the proposal. As explained above, since the money had already been allocated for the plan, taking the proposal for how the money would be spent to the Strategic Committee was not a procedural necessity but was important politically. We calculated that if objections could be expressed at the outset we would have a clear sense of who was supportive and who remained sceptical. We would also have a fair idea of what the objections were, for example, one quite hostile right wing councillor believed that if the council had forty thousand dollars to spend on culture the money should be used to acquire library books. Another felt that support for the arts was to be commended but that it should be expressed in kind rather than financially.

There was never any need to deal directly with these objections in the initial phase of the Review because the funds had already been allocated. However, for the ongoing objectives of the Review to be achieved, subsequent funding was esential which meant working continually to maintain the support of the majority of councillors. In effect, enormous amounts of my time (as the Cultural Review consultant) was expended keeping councillors informed and involved. Inevitably, undertaking this essentially political work was often at the expense of the more important information gathering tasks associated with the Cultural Review and was, thus, an unfortunate use of resources.

The proposal that went to the Strategic Committee was to undertake the City of Newcastle Cultural Review in association with the Social Impact Consultative Panel (of which I was no longer a member). It should be noted that it was decided to abandon the terms cultural planning and cultural plan in order to counter the perception that a one-off document would be produced at the end of the process. Rather, a review of the range of cultural resources currently available in the city, suggestions for ways in which these resources could be applied to the changing needs of residents, and information about residents' participation in cultural activities outside the home (which would, in turn, highlight any barriers to that participation) were being proposed.[21] The Cultural Review was also intended to initiate the establishment of an inventory of cultural resources and to begin a process of ongoing consultation with local communities. These objectives were difficult for councillors and officers of officers of the council to grasp, as most were used to thinking in terms of tangible outcomes and clearly delineated, time-bound procedures. Even those sympathetic to cultural planning, like Councillor Heys, continued to think in terms of a plan rather than a process.

After the proposal for the Cultural Review had received the endorsement of the council, I was appointed the consultant responsible for imnplementing it. A steering committee was formed to provide advice, oversee the process, ensure a level of community participation, and generate widespread commitment to the Review and its outcomes.[22] The Cultural Review involved a series of community forums, in-depth interviews, an extensive literature and policy review, a four hundred household phone survey, and the collection of census data. It considered the heritage, identities, and landscapes of Newcastle, the performing arts, the visual arts and crafts, festivals and events, creative writing, musical expression, dance, indigenous cultures and the work of indigenous artists, the activities and work of people from non-English-speaking backgrounds, youth, and local residents. It also considered the current financial and administrative involvement of the city council in fostering local cultural activity and diversity. Some of these areas were researched in detail, others, such as the complex artistic practices and cultures of indigenous people and youth, were undertaken as pilot studies which raised a host of issues requiring far more comprehensive investigation. Suggestions regarding the potential of cultural tourism and the cultural industries were also discussed.

In October 1994, I submitted a draft report to the Cultural Review Reference Group. The recommendations contained in the report were then workshopped by the Reference Group and a summary of key issues and recommendations was written. This summary document along with my full report, was placed on public display for a month. After this period the summary document and its recommendations were edited and amended for presentation to the council for approval and further action.

It would be misleading to give the impression that this process was unproblematic. Much has been written about the relationship between the consultant and the commissioning body and these arguments will not be rehearsed here.[23] It is important to note, however, that the process of workshopping the final report and its recommendations, and of compiling a summary document that set out to be both innovative in its recommendations and scope (like the final report) and sufficiently unthreatening to be sold successfully to the council, was a highly political process of compromise and negotiation. Aspects of the final report were modified because it was feared councillors would be alienated by perceived and actual insinuations of incompetence or lack of foresight on their part, or by suggestions that Newcastle had still not overcome its negative industrial image. For example, suggestions that the council should demonstrate a commitment to integrated cultural planning and establish a range of initiatives designed to nurture local cultural activity had to be built on statements that the council was already supporting cultural diversity and artistic endeavour successfully and the valuable insights of the Review would help the council continue this good work. The evidence, however, pointed to a council which was seriously alienated from local cultural communities and which administered its cultural and artistic portfolios on the basis of favour and historical precedent.

Discussion

As the initiative for undertaking the Cultural Review came first from someone in a relatively powerful position within the council corporate structure who had an incisive understanding of and commitment to integrated cultural planning, and then from an influential bipartisan committee of the council, Newcastle has probably been more successful in achieving the objective of integration than most Australian local councils. For example, a recent review of the impact of the Honeysuckle Development on Newcastle includes, alongside land-use and economic considerations, a requirement that the impact of the development on local cultures, and the relationship of the Honeysuckle Development to the recommendations of the Cultural Review, be assessed. Having studied both the Honeysuckle Development and urban policy, I can vouch that this incorporation is a significant break-through. But it is a break-through that has come from having the cultural planning cause promoted from senior positions within the council and its committee structure, and by explicitly involving councillors, council directors, and senior bureaucrats in the Review process in as many ways as possible, for example, allowing them to as as group facilitators at the community workshops conducted for the Review. In effect, whenever possible, key council personnel were exposed to the ideas of cultural planning in direct but unthreatening ways, and most became sympathetic to the process as a result. There were also other positive outcomes from this involvement, such as the adoption of the model used in community workshops which involved the participation of hundreds of local people and organizations by other divisions within the council.

To many within local government, cultural planning is a radical, even revolutionary approach to city planning and the management of urban space. It seems to threaten established practices and is underpinned by theoretical propositions and assumptions that are either difficult to grasp or at odds with those which have so far prevailed in local government. One-off exposure to the principles and potential of cultural planning, therefore, is insufficient. The Newcastle Cultural Review showed that people must repeatedly be confronted by the ideas of cultural planning in a range of contexts and in familiar situations. Approached thus, cultural planning can gain wide acceptance and support. At the same time, it is necessary for more fundamental changes to the culture of planning and local government to be initiated. These processes are lengthy and the obstacles, both bureaucratic and historical, considerable.

Despite some exciting achievements, Newcastle City Council like other Australian local governments still has a long way to go before the necessary comprehensive changes are made and the cultural planning process is truly integrated into the strategic and corporate decision making structures of the city. The mechanisms of integration must transcend the initiatives of particular individuals and it is difficult to determine the significance or extensiveness of the progress that has been made to date. Indications are, however, that the necessary autonomous procedures and frameworks have not yet been sufficiently established and the place of cultural planning remains tenuous.

For those who believe in the principles of cultural planning, the lessons from the City of Newcastle Cultural Review are many. In particular, it is clear that there must be an assault on the very core of local government its practices and values if fundamental change is to occur. This assault must be conducted on a number of fronts, both inside and outside the bureaucracy. For example, we still have little idea of the long-term effectiveness of cultural planning in Australia or elsewhere, and a critical survey ofthe achievements and failures of cultural planning practice from which lessons can be learnt and strategies for the future devised is way overdue. In particular, much more research into the mechanisms of local government (the most under-researched tier of the Australian state) is urgently needed.

The promise of cultural planning to shape the form, function, and livability of futures cities creatively and positively is considerable. Until its current peripheral status in local policymaking and planning practice is addressed, however, this promise is destined to remain unfulfilled and established discourses and conventions of planning and development will continue unchallenged. Also unchallenged will be the hegemonic, limited patterns of inclusion, exclusion, and separation of responsibilities on which established local government discourses and conventions are built.

Notes

1 . Deborah Stevenson, "Cultural Planning and Urban Redevelopment," in EIT Pty Limited (ed) The Cultural Planning Conference. (Mornington: Engineering Publications, 1991) pp 4.1-4,11.

2. Paul Knox, "Capital, Material Culture and Socio-Spatial Differentiation," in Paul Knox (ed.), *The Restless Urban Landscape* (Englewood Cliffs: Prentice-Hall, 1993), p.1.

3 . Franco Bianchini, "Models of Cultural Policies and Planning in West European Cities," in EIT Pty Ltd (ed) *The Cultural Planning Conference*, p.10, 26.

4 . For example, see Culture and Policy, special issue on "City Cultures,I.4 (1992).

5. Colin Mercer, "Brisbane's Cultural Development Strategy: the Process, the Politics and the Product," in EIT Pty Ltd (ed.), *The Cultural Planning Conference*. pp 2.1-2.16

6. For example, see Franco Bianchini, Mark Fisher, John Montgomery and Ken Worpole (eds.), *City Centres, City Cultures: The Role of the Arts in the Revitalisation of Towns and Cities* (Manchester: Centre for Local Economic Strategies, 1988); Geoff Mulgan and Ken Worpole, Saturday Night or Sunday Morning: From Arts to Industry New Forms of Cultural Policy (London: Comedia, 1986).

7. Deborah Stevenson, *Agendas in Place: Cultural Planning for Cities and Regions* (Rockhampton: Rural Social and Economic Research Centre, 1997).

8. Gay Hawkins and Kathie Gibson, "Cultural Planning in Australia: Policy Dreams, Economic Realities," in Kathie Gibson and Sophie Watson (eds.), *Metropolis Now: Planning and the Urban in Contemporary Australia* (Leichhardt: Pluto Press, 1994), p.217.

9. Robert McNulty, "Cultural Planning: A Movement for Civic Progress" in EIT Pty Ltd (eds.), *The Cultural Planning Conference*. pp 1-19.

10. Gay Hawkins, *From Nimbin to Mardi Gras: Constructing Community Arts* (St. Leonards: Allen & Unwin, 1993).

11. The Australia Council, a statutory authority of the federal Government, is the principal government arts funding body in Australia. Prior to the restructure of the Australia Council in 1996, the Community Cultural Development Unit was an executive unit of the Council answerable to the committees of Community, Environment, Art and Design, and Development. Both these committees were chaired by a member of the Board of the Australia Council..

12. Graham Sansom Pty. Limited and Praxis Research, *Better Places, Richer Communities: Local Government, Integrated Planning and Cultural Development* (Redfern: Australia Council, 1994).

13. Bianchini, "Models of Cultural Policies and Planning in West European Cities".

14. Deborah Stevenson, "Urban Re-enchantment and the Magic of Cultural Planning" *Culture and Policy* 4, (1992), p8.

15. Colin Mercer, "What is Cultural Planning?" *Network News*,15 (Winter, 1992).

16. Colin Mercer, "Little Supplements of Life": Cultural Planning and the Management of Urban Populations" (paper presented to the Institute for Cultural Policy Studies Seminar, Brisbane, 1991), p.8.

17. Graham Sanson Ltd. and Praxis Research, *Better Places, Richer Communities* p.9.

18. Ibid, p.19.

19. Stevenson, "Cultural Planning and Urban Redevelopment," Deborah Stevenson, *A Review for the Future: The City ofNewcastle Cultural Review*. (Report to Newcastle City Council, 1994).

20. Deborah Stevenson, "Towards a Cultural Plan for Newcastle" (Discussion paper prepared for Newcastle City Council, 1993).

21. Stevenson, A Review for the Future, p.8.

22. The Cultural Review Reference Group included all members of the Social Impact Consultative Panel along with people chosen because their specific experiences and proficiencies informed the Aboriginal Community Arts Officer, a representative of the Tourist Office, and the theatre critic for the local morning newspaper.

23. Eva Cox, Fran Hausfield and Sue Wills, "Taking the Queen's Shilling: Accepting Social Research Consultancies in the 1970s," in Colin Bell and Sol Encel (eds.) *Inside the Whale: Ten Personal Accounts of Social Research* (Rushcutters Bay: Pergamon Press, 1978).

Community, Public, Audience: Complex and Critical Transactions

Jennifer Barrett

In the 1990s, rhetoric similar to that of community arts has been used, mostly unconsciously, by art museum professionals and exponents of public art to promote notions of a democratic culture. In some instances this has been employed to convince both the Australian public and the government that a particular type of organization, or a particular cultural form, is more accessible and relevant than others. Yet these claims of relevance and accessibility are often based on nineteenth century didactic notions about generating a cultured, educated, and intelligent population, signifying a developed nation.[1] They also involve the promotion of public art to physically and culturally "improve" the public environment. There is an absence of writing and analysis which articulates these changes in the rhetoric used within major cultural practices and institutions and their signifi- cance. In this sense, the changes of emphasis would appear to be unquestionably accepted. It seems to be assumed that the shifts are inevitable and that concerns for more democratic cultural practices within our institutions and by practitioners have some- how occurred naturally, as distinct from being constructed.

There also appears to be a significant relationship between these developments in public cultural policies, cultural practices and cultural institutions. The desire to be more publicly relevant is expressed by art museum curators and directors, and the increasing numbers of local governments developing cultural plans and public art policies. These developments focus on community consultation, accessibility, and participation, and community and public accountability for cultural programs. It is not always clear whether this desire for public relevance is instigated by shifts in federal government policy and the rhetoric of economic rationalism, or by the desire to develop a more cultured public.

Perhaps it is feasible to assert that community arts can and does affect mainstream cultural institutions and forms as they seek ways of representing diversity and ways of enticing diverse audiences to engage. Either way, the practice of community arts within the discursive formations of the art museums and public art contradicts the perceived marginal position of the genres. It also reveals significant problems in defining and articulating cultural difference, what it means and how it means. Consideration of these problems can assist in illuminating issues of representation and cultural difference in practice and in the construction of cultural policy, which concerns itself with these issues.[2]

Analysis of the notion of community has hardly occurred within the arts. Notions of community are fluid and the relationship of community to state varies within different historical contexts.It is increasingly difficult for cultural institutions simply to claim that they represent a public culture without first indicating which community they represent and therefore, their policies of inclusion and exclusion. This article will consider the problems of using terms such as community, public, and audience as ways of approaching difference in the arts, particularly in relation to the praxis of community arts and cultural policy in Australia. It will consider community arts concepts and the ways in which the notion of community has underpinned a strategy to locate, define, advocate, and understand cultural difference. What is known as the community arts movement in Australia[3] has resisted simple definition even within its own terms of reference, for political reasons relying instead upon an ascribed identity of cultural resistance, usually to high culture.[4]

The relationship between community, art, and government in Australia is often interpreted as being peculiar to community arts. It has been argued by critics such as Gay Hawkins, that community arts was/is constructed by the state, and that communities were constructed in terms set by this relationship, which in turn significantly affected cultural policy in Australia. Yet it is also possible to argue that the state has significantly and similarly influenced other areas of the arts and their communities, such as the visual arts and correlating cultural institutions.

During the 1990s a number of significant directions have emerged in the areas of museums and public art practices that converge with political philosophies of community arts from the 1980s. This article seeks to identify and analyze these directions by considering the points at which selected articulations of community arts practice intersect with perceived notions of community and public, and cultural difference in the visual arts. Many of the central issues addressed by community arts are common to visual arts criticism for example (particularly around identity politics), and an analysis of commonalities and differences has productive possibilities, particularly in relation to the general tendency to essentialize community and the public sphere.

This line of argument seems to lead inevitably towards a crucial question: If contemporary artists are now increasingly concerning themselves with issues of representation, the politics of privileging identity, and the politics of marginalized cultures, how can community arts continue to identify itself as a resistant and alternative cultural practice and philosophy? In other words, if the parameters against which community arts has attempted to define itself have shifted significantly or even disappeared, what can community arts resist? Can it be differentiated from the so called mainstream art world by its collaborative practices? by its creation of employment opportunities for artists? or by its blurring of the distinction between audience and subject matter?

The notion of community used in discussions about culture is generally an idealised, nostalgic, and romantic one. Closer analyses of community, particularly as elucidated in Jean-Luc Nancy's "Of Being in Common"[5] and in recent reviews of Jürgen Habermas'[6] notion of the public sphere can challenge such simple interpretations. Community, as constructed by the state, detracts from or dissolves certain political possibilities of community as formed through choice, and, as Nancy argues, is the site where notions of democracy are acted out, or tolerated in various *de*formations.

Policy development and implementation has been used by federal government arts and culture organizations to build certain preferred cultural forms within Australia. Community arts has, to some extent, been funded to compensate for a perceived lack of interest amongst so called dominant cultural organizations in addressing the issues of community, access, and equity.

Art, Community, Public

Community arts and public art are each embedded in Australian art communities and cultural institutions in different ways.[7] In the 1990s, community arts and public art in Australia are both key elements in the strategies of government and visual arts organizations to democratize culture, as opposed to promoting a culture of democratic diversity and difference.

Public art and community arts intersect significantly within the visual arts. Both, it could be argued, are informed by similar periods of art history in Australia, such as the postwar period (1945-1948), and the most influential period for public art practice, the 1960s and 1970s.[8] The term community arts has now become synonymous with community cultural development. Public art seems to enjoy a greater status within the visual arts than does community arts; the avenues for validation of public art are more widely recognized and, generally, there is little reference to community art in writing on public art in Australia. Theorizing on public art has also become easier with the availability of texts on notions of the public within a specific arts context as well as within urban and social theory.[9]

The Public Sphere

The public sphere tends to be constructed as made up of private citizens, who form communities, that, as an aggregate, in turn constitute the public sphere. A bourgeois notion of the public sphere has traditionally deemed some cultural forms, practices, and issues as private, therefore not qualifying for inclusion in the public sphere. The process of exclusion also enabled the bourgeoisie to construct a distinctive public culture which distinguishes it from other private cultural forms and practices, the familial, domestic, or community spheres. It seems that currently in Australia, community art, public art and the art museums are all critiquing the exclusive notion of the public sphere to varying degrees, with differing publics and practices in mind, and with an inadequate understanding of the actual complexities of the public sphere.

Alexander Kluge, in his writing on the concept of public, makes the point that, while a bourgeois notion of the public sphere has many shortcomings, it is still a fundamental element, or condition of, and for, social and political change. "[C]hanging and expanding, increasing the possibilities for a public articulation of experience..."[10] the public sphere exists in binary opposition to the private sphere which is characterized by private ownership and individual experience. The more obscure, and less defined sphere among these discussions is the community sphere, although it is clear that an oppositional, or contested, public sphere seems dependent upon the production of a community sphere, or realm.[11]

All of these discussions on the public sphere are different yet similar. While Habermas' interprets the public sphere as being inclusive to all, there are others such as Nancy Fraser and Alexander Kluge who argue that there are many opposing and inequitable characteristics internal to the public sphere, particularly as it is articulated by Habermas. Significantly such discussions on the public sphere are attempting to develop a model of democracy which deals with actual cultural differences and more hybrid forms of social formation and the subsequent impact on democracy as it functions. Fraser and Kluge are attempting to develop a more productive public sphere. A community sphere is not used explicitly in any of these conceptsof thinking about the public sphere. Discourses on community cultural politics in Australia and its relation to democracy tend to do the very same thing with the term community that is done with the term public that is they either use it in vague generalist ways, or they specify or essentialise community groups into legible units for governments to manage.

An oppositional public sphere consists of what Nancy Fraser

calls competing public spheres in the bourgeois public sphere.[12] Fraser critiques the limitations of Jürgen Habermas' authoritative notion of the bourgeois, liberal public sphere because he stresses, particularly in his earlier writing on the public sphere, that it is open to all.[13] Habermas, according to Fraser, conceptualizes the public sphere as:

> the space in which citizens deliberate about their common affairs, hence, an institutionalized arena of discursive interaction. This arena is distinctively different from the state; it [is] a site for the production and circulation of discourses that can in principle be critical of the state. [14]

The "liberal model of the bourgeois public sphere" is historically understood in terms of exclusions, constructed on the basis of universalizing ideas of the bourgeois European male in the nineteenth century. Gender is the central basis of exclusion here. Fraser, (drawing on Joan B. Landes authoritative text on women and the public sphere during the French Revolution), argues that "despite the rhetoric of publicity and accessibility, that official public sphere rested on, indeed was importantly constituted by, a number of significant exclusions" and that it involved the "formal exclusion of women."[15] Fraser also cites the misuse of the term "public sphere" by many feminists, particularly as it is misinterpreted to mean anything outside of the "domestic, or familial sphere." It is interesting to note these critical interpretations of and debates about the term, and the problem with conflating notions of the public sphere, as there are "at least three analytically distinct things: the state, the official economy of paid employment, and arenas of public discourse."[16] Despite identifying the shortcomings of Habermas' notion of the liberal public sphere Fraser considers it a significant "conceptual resource that can help overcome such problems" which eventuate through generalization of the term.

Public and Audience

Issues of public and audience are increasingly central to arts institutions, particularly in the current cultural policy rhetoric of access and participation. It is, however, important to recognize that this is not a new concern for cultural institutions, although the way in which it is articulated differs from the early 1980s. The Bienniale of Sydney in 1979, for instance, was the focus of a great deal of agitation within the visual arts community.[17] Artists argued for a broader, more inclusive, and diverse interpretation of what contemporary art was and is.[18] More recently, many museumshave been seeking to develop their audience or public, in terms of numbers and in terms of type of audience and type of work exhibited.[19] In this context, "to develop" has multiple meanings, including the expansion of the intellect and cultural capital of the audience, increased museum attendance, and the attraction of a range of cultural groups who have formerly been disenfranchized by the nature of the art museum.[20]

Part of the trend of seeking wider audiences partially in opposition to museum practice, but at the same time complementary to it is the resurgence in public art projects. Aspects of public art, at least historically, are critical of the art museum. Public art carries the implication that it is somehow more accessible, and more interactive with the public than art in a gallery or institution.

The idea of a *critical* public art practice is advanced by such theorists as Rosalyn Deutsche, who claims that public beautification projects are undemocratic and mask the underlying power structures and social contradictions of the urban environment. Deutsche interprets artists, such as Krzysztof Wodiczko for instance, as being more critical of public space and the competing institutional and public interests found within the public sphere than that of the majority of public artists. The institutional role of public art could also be interpreted as more functional in urban societies. An example Deutsche identifies as typical in this instance is an artist "whose work, primarily pieces of furniture designed for public places, epitomizes the position repeatedly stated that 'utility' is the principal yardstick for measuring the value of public art."[21] This tendency is distinct from a more critical public art practice which intervenes in public space by questioning the social relations constituted and concealed by such spaces.

Deutsche also cites examples of writing on community sponsored public art programs (which she considers are now the dominant discourse on public art), where the "consistent invocation of 'the community' ... [to be] terminological abuses pervading discussion of public art [by] endowing the new type [of public art] with an aura of social accountability."[22] Deutsche argues that:

> "Community" conjures up images of neighbourhoods bound together by relations of mutual interest, respect, and kinship; "community sponsored" connotes local control and citizen participation in decision making.[23]

A shortcoming of Deutsche's argument is that she does not consider in sufficient detail the possibilities of community as the site of resistance, nor as a site of cultural production.

> Redevelopment converts the city into a terrain organized to fulfill capital's need to exploit space for profit; if anything, clashes rather than confluence, between communities and state imposed initiatives are more likely to characterise urban life today [in the United States]. [24]

She outlines how the notion of community is co opted to signify, or represent, local control and decision making, at least in rhetoric, by the state and by those desiring to invoke a united sense of identity rather than to recognize inherent differences. Within an Australian context such a distinction is, as I have been arguing, productive in relation, not only to community arts, but also to areas of the visual arts where the issues of representation and cultural politics are central concerns.

The history of public art reveals many parallels to the history of community arts in Australia, while at the same time highlighting fundamental differences. Greater clarity about the purpose and implications of both public art and community arts is derived from more extensive analysis and comparison of the two practices in terms of their institutional forms and affiliations, and the nature of their audience engagement. Common to both critical public art and community arts, even as defined in terms of cultural development, is the assumption that artists are an important element in public discourse and planning and that they too are concerned about who may speak in these spheres. As noted above, the profile of public art is also becoming sharper in the public sphere. Public art has become a popular form of civic enhancement, as evident in most state government cultural policies.[25]

Art Museums, Public, and Community

The public museum has played a significant role in the aestheticization of community culture in Australia. In the 1990s museum exponents are articulating a desire for more relevance to an undefined audience/community/public. This change seems to be due to pressures from government policy, and from arts organizations, artists, critics, and other internal forces within museums.[26] However, the term community is often used to describe an undifferentiated audience and/or public for museums to which culture is presented.

Those who attend a museum as viewers/observers, the audience of the exhibit/s are known simply as visitors. Implicit in the word visitor is transience; the notion of visitor is not at home, is away from his/her usual or common environment. The transient visitor, or, in aggregate, the Australian public, provides the main support for museums in the 1990s. The vague term *the Australian public* is increasingly being used interchangeably, with the term *the Australian community*. This conflation shifts and obscures the power relations that underlie the terms community, public, audience, and visitor.[27] The most obvious contradiction in such a context is that *the community*, as suggested above, is predicated on very different ideas about being at home than those invoked in a great deal of museum policy and promotional material.

It is also true that community arts is a conduit for more equitable distribution of cultural funding. But at what cost? Exponents of the community arts movement propose that the whole area of art museums needs to significantly alter its relationship with the public, and not simply in terms of increasing audience numbers. On the one hand community arts seems to suggest ready-made publicity and marketing strategies for art museums. Yet on the other, are the art museums also willing to take on the inherent difficulties of the terms *community* and *public* such as the potential opposition between access and equity, and artistic excellence as community arts and public art practices have attempted to do?[28]

Community

The tendency within community arts in recent years has been to affirm and support cultural diversity and cultural difference within communities, focusing on factors of gender, class, ethnicity, or geography. Historically, community arts has been identified by its strong emphasis on the process of community participation in and access to the project; on redressing so called cultural disadvantage before addressing aesthetics and formal issues. Community arts projects have generally been the product of a specific community, primarily for consumption by that community, although it may have other, secondary audiences.

What most clearly distinguishes community arts from any other arts activity is the emphasis on the community. Yet this concept has hardly been theorized at all within discussions on community arts. This has meant that institutional constructions of community such as those that appear within local, state, and federal government, have filled the conceptual vacuum.

Gay Hawkins, in her important work on the history of community arts, asserts that the contradictions within community arts are a consequence of the combination of the terms *community* and *arts*. She correctly claims that the "category community arts produces confusion" and that it has no "apparent meaning as the two terms can seem so disparate and un related." What does art have to do with the community? More traditionally associated with rarefied notions of excellence, art seems to work in contrast to popular interpretations of "community as amateurish and with an implicit idea of being an alternative form of social politics," as argued by Williams.[29] This stance makes an easy definition of the term community impossible.

> With so many assumptions attendant upon 'community' and 'art' how is it possible to fix some boundaries around possible meanings?[30]

Community arts invokes many meanings: democratization of art; democratic art; art in community; art for the community; art about the community; art by the community. The word community within an arts context can also imply the community as audience/s for art. Community arts seems to defy any singular form of characterisation and classification, as either art, welfare, culture, or indeed cultural development.

> When the "community" entered the discourses of arts policy previous assumptions were inevitably disrupted; what the ambiguity and apparent innocence of "community" allowed was an onlsaught of new forms, new constituencies, new methods of patronage and new purposes for art.[31]

The contemporary use of the term community arts refers to an artist working in a community context on an issue of particular relevance to that community. It can take the form of a commissioned work, where the artist uses the community as subject material or inspiration; or the artist can work with a specified community to produce cultural material which expresses the views of that community on an issue or issues of general concern to that group. In the latter model the community is not meant to be constructed as the noble subject for consumption by an outside community; it entails involving the community in all (or most) aspects of the production of the work, whereas in the model of the commissioned artist, the aesthetics of the project tend to be more important and the artist has more control over the work.[32] As I noted earlier, in both these models of practice the cultural product is intended for consumption by the specific community concerned, although the work may have an audience beyond that specific community. The emphasis is often on process, although this varies from project to project, artist to artist, community to community, and so on. The differences between different strands of community arts are immense this however, can often be a profound aspect of the genre.

Much writing on community arts has focused on attempts to define it, or the difficulties in defining it. Definitions and theories of community arts range from descriptive material on community arts practice and projects which is available from various organizations, institutions, and individuals to more obtuse attempts which argue for a dynamic, less bureaucratic, interpretation of the term. Arts bureaucrats have played a major role in articulating and interpreting community arts. Definitions have also focused on the supposed commonality of interest in community arts: location, gender, ethnicity, occupation, age, sexuality, for instance. Identity of some form is thus a defining feature.[33] Community arts then becomes a creative contribution to the identified common interest, although at times particularly recently, the notions of community arts have focused community as a site for audience development.[34]

Previous directors of the Community Arts Board of the Australia Council, such as Jon Hawkes and Ros Bower, did not seem to discern community as being an enforced entity (or commonality). Although this involves a somewhat rudimentary notion of community, both Hawkes and Bower argue that the distinct and fundamental feature of community arts is community identity and control of projects. (Hawkins would disagree, arguing strongly that the State *constructed* communities for its community arts program.) What Hawkes and Bower seem to have overlooked here is that the state is central to their notion of community. Despite this limitation, which threatens to contradict the basic premise of the funding program, the Board was much more focused on ways of developing cultural policy for diverse forms of cultural practice than other programs of the Australia Council. The interpretation of community here also falls loosely within the parameters of the term as defined by Raymond Williams:

> Community can be the warmly persuasive word to [used to] describe an existing set of relationships or the warmly persuasive word [used] to describe an alternative set of relationships. What is most important perhaps, is that unlike all other terms of social organisation (*state, nation, society, etc.*) it seems never to be used unfavourably, and never to be given any positive opposing or distinguishing term.[35]

In contrast, Jean Luc Nancy sees the notion of community constructed by the state as being an interpretation of community which detracts from or dissolves certain political possibilities. He argues for a community which is formed by choice, producing a meaning of community where "the political is the place where community as such is brought into play."[36] Community is thus not always distinct from other forms of social organization, such as ideas of nation. While community arts has claimed to critique the homogenizing effect of a national culture, arguing for a culturally diverse Australia, its relationship to the state and the rhetoric it employs undermines this claim.

Some writers, such as Giorgio Agamben and Jean Francois Lyotard, imply that community is not necessarily recognizable or knowable. Such a concept of community is not considered in writing on community arts, where the primary interpretation of community is community as constructed by the state. Significant here is Nancy's attempt to re interpret, or expropriate, the term community by articulating the distinct differences in definitions of the term community and the need for the differentiations to be identified and re thought in a more specific way.[37]

In contrast to this view Hawkins identifies the tendencies of the Whitlam government (1972-1975) as a "classic social democratic response and an important indicator of the broader political context in which Labor's arts policy was implemented."[38] So how does Hawkins place community arts within this context? It seems that community invoked for the Whitlam government the fundamental site for its policies as it was the site of "ordinary Australians."

The notion of community within this context was constructed in terms of the identification of a constituency for the community arts program. The most desirable constituency was, according to Hawkins, "culturally disadvantaged... both silent and invisible."[39] "[T]he ambiguity of community was strategic."[40] Communities were constructed around shifting sites that were unified made an essence by their common so-called *lack* of culture. This identification of lack presumes a more competent cultural community, a more dominant constituency, which utilized and mobilized its values and notions of culture to measure both the so called culturally disadvantaged and, at the same time, the cultural competence of mainstream culture.[41] Perhaps Nancy would agree with this definition, but would add that to assign community a common being (commonly lacking in culture) confines (and limits) the political and cultural possibilities of that community.

In Australia, therefore state, federal, and local governments are constantly redeveloping strategies to ensure that their cultural policies and public monies can better serve their constituencies, both quantitatively and qualitatively, through an increasing number of public and community programs. With such an emphasis on community and public at all levels of government, it is important for these terms to be more closely scrutinized so that their specificities and commonalities, their potentials and their limitations, can be better understood.

Notes

1. Carol Duncan, "Art Museums and the Ritual of Citizenship," in Steven D. Lavine and Ivan Karp (eds.), *Exhibiting Cultures: The Poetics and Politics of Museum Display* (Washington: Smithsonian Institute, 1991), pp. 88-104.
2. Sneja Gunew and Fazel Rizvi (eds.), *Culture Difference and the Arts* (Sydney: Allen and Unwin, 1994), and Elizabeth Grosz, "Feminist Theory and the Politics of Art," in Catriona Moore (ed.), *Dissonance. Feminism and the Arts 1970-1990* (Sydney: Allen and Unwin and Artspace, 1994), pp. 139-54.
3. Gay Hawkins, *From Nimbin to Mardi Gras: Constructing Community Arts* (Sydney: Allen and Unwin, 1993), and Vivienne Binns (ed.), *Community and the Arts: History, Theory and Practice* (Sydney: Pluto Press, 1991).
4. Rachel Fensham, "Why Do Angels Fly Anti-Clockwise?" *Artlink* 10(Spring 1990): 10-13.
5. Jean-Luc Nancy, "Of-Being-in-Common," Miami Theory Collective (eds.), *Community at Loose Ends* (Minneapolis: University of Minnesota Press, 1991).
6. Craig Calhoun (ed.), *Habermas and the Public Sphere* (Cambridge: MIT Press, 1992).
7. "Special Supplement: Aspects of Socially Engaged Art", Michael Dolk (ed.), *Art Network* 5(Summer/Autumn, 1982): 17-53. Australian art journals, such as *Art & Text* and *Artlink* have produced thematic issues focusing on public art during the last four years. Jeff Gibson (ed.), "Public Address: Art & Urbanism," *Art & Text*, 42 (May, 1992); "Art in Public," *Artlink*, 9, no. 2(Winter 1989); "*Special Issue: Community Art*," *Artlink*, 10, no. 3 (Spring 1990); and "Arts in a Multicultural Australia," *Artlink*, 11, no.s. 1 and 2 (Autumn/Winter 1991). The latter two *Artlink* issues received specific funding from the Community Cultural Development Unit of the Australia Council.
8. Jenny Barrett and Michael Crayford (eds.), *Hypothetically Public* (Lewers Bequest and Penrith City Council Regional Art Gallery, 1993).
9. Rosalyn Deutsche, "Uneven Development: Public Art in New York City," in Dianne Ghirardo (ed.), *Out of Site: A Social Critique of Architecture* (Seattle: Bay Press, 1991), pp. 157-219.
10. Alexander Kluge, "The Public Sphere," in Brian Wallis (ed.), *If You Lived Here: The City in Art, Theory, and Social Activism: A Project by Martha Rosler*, vol. 6 of *Discussions in Contemporary Culture*, (Seattle: Bay Press, 1991), p. 67.
11. Kluge "The Public Sphere," pp. 67-68.
12. Nancy Fraser, "Rethinking the Public Sphere: A Contribution to the Critique of

Actually Existing Democracy," in *Social Text* 25/26(1990): 56-80.

13. Nancy Fraser refers here to Jürgen Habermas' earlier work on the public sphere, *Jürgen Habermas, The Structural Transformations of the Public Sphere: An Inquiry into a Category of Bourgeois Society*, trans. T. Burger and F. Lawrence (Cambridge: MIT Press, 1991).

14. Fraser "Rethinking the Public Sphere," p. 57

15. Ibid., p. 59. Early definitions of the word 'public,' according to the *Oxford English Dictionary*, include "pertaining to a people of a country or locality, or of or pertaining to the people as a whole that belong to, affects or concerns the community or nation; common, national or popular." The Australian *Macquarie Dictionary* and the American *Webster Dictionary* seem to concur with this definition. See Joan. B. Landes, *Women and the Public Sphere in the Age of the French Revolution*, (Ithaca: Cornell University, 1988).

16. Ibid., p.57.

17. See the discussions on the inclusion of community arts on the Sydney Biennale in *Sydney Biennale: White Elephant or Red Herring Comments from the Art Community*, (Sydney: Alexander Mackie College of Advanced Education, 1979).

18. Ann Stephen and Charles Merewether (eds.), *The Great Divide,* (Melbourne: The Great Divide, 1977).

19. Catherine Lumby and Craig McGregor, "The Art Starts Here," *Sydney Morning Herald,* (February 2 1991), pp. 8-21.

20 For a detailed analysis of the "theory of culture as a form of capital," see Pierre Bourdieu and Alain Darbel, *The Love of Art: European Art Museums and Their Public,* trans C. Beattie and N. Merriman (Stanford: Stanford University Press, 1990). For a critique of the limitations and implications of Bourdieu's theories of cultural capital, see John Frow, "Accounting for Tastes: Some Problems in Bourdieu's Sociology of Culture," *Cultural Studies,* 1, no. 1(January, 1987), pp. 59-73. Frow critiques Bourdieu's continual privileging of bourgeois aesthetics as the yardstick for measuring the cultural capital of his subjects.

21. Deutsche, "Uneven Development," p. 173.

22. "Inaccuracies of language, demonstrating indifference to the issues of urban politics, resemble other distortions pervading discourse about public art collaborations, distortions that confuse the issues of aesthetic politics as well. Like the appropriation of urban discourse, these misrepresentations try to invest the recent marriage of art and urban planning with social justification, using the vocabulary of radical art practice." Ibid., p.175-76.

23. Ibid. p. 176.

24. Ibid.

25. See the South Australian and Western Australian Departments for the Arts, Public Art, and Art in Public Places funding program guidelines and brochures from 1989 onwards.

26. There has been a great deal of research in this area carried out by the Australia Council for the Arts and the Institute for Cultural Policy, Griffith University, Queensland, Australia. Most of the research investigates the numbers of people attending the art museums and other types of museums generally. Accessibility and the cultural diversity of visitors have also been researched. Much of this research has been based on the work of Pierre Bourdieu and Alain Darbel in *The Love of Art:*

27. Benedict Anderson, "Census, Map, Museum,' in *Imagined Communities* (London and New York: Verso, 1991), pp. 163-185; and Eilean Hooper-Greenhill, *Museums and the Shaping of Knowledge* (London: Routledge, 1992).

28. It should also be noted that, like other instrumentalities of the state, the museum acts upon, and is acted upon, particularly in relation to government. See Ian Hunter, *Culture and Government: The Emergence of Literary Education* (London: Macmillan, 1988).

The National Gallery of Australia has a collection of political posters produced in a community arts context (as do other art museums, such as the Queensland Art Gallery). Alice Hinton-Bateup's poster, *Lost Heritage* (Garage Graphix, 1986), is a good example here. Although *Lost Heritage* was produced for a specific audience in a local community, it can also be seen in the Australian National Gallery, at the State Library of New South Wales, and in some international collections. The work was sold to the gallery by Garage Graphix, which is a community-based visual arts organization located in a suburb west of Sydney, where Bateup was working as community artist. The funds from such a sale help the Garage to survive and allow it to continue to operate as a community organization. While it could easily be argued that on one level Garage Graphix is complicit with the dominance of major cultural institutions such as the National Gallery, Bateup (and Garage Graphix) are also critiquing the institution of colonialism from within the cultural (and social) edifices of the state because in the national context they are representing cultural difference within a culturally diverse community, and undermining notions of a homogeneous national identity.

29. Raymond Williams, *Keywords: A Vocabulary of Culture and Society* (Glasgow: Fontana, 1976), p. 65-66.

30. Hawkins *From Nimbin to Mardi Gras*, p. 3.

31. *Ibid. p. 4.*

32. This view implies that the involvement of community in the production of art work compromises the aesthetic credibility of the commissioned work.

33. Jon Hawkes, "Definitions," *Artlink*, 4, no. 4 (1984):8.(

34. Ros Bower, "The Community Arts Officer: What Is It All About?" Paper presented at the National Community Arts Conference, 1980, reproduced in *From Vision to Reality*, *CAPER 10*, (Sydney: Australia Council, 1981).

35. Williams, *Keywords*, pp. 65-66.

36. Jean-Luc Nancy, *The Inoperative Community*, vol. 76 of *Theory and History of Literature* (Minneapolis: University of Minnesota Press 1991), p. xxxvii.

37. Jean-Luc Nancy interprets the notion of community as having multiple meanings. In the first instance, he refers to the idea of community coming from the left (which is also a term he argues needs significant reviewing). To the left, "the political as such, is receptive to what is at stake in the community," as opposed to the right where "the political is merely in charge of order and administration." Jean-Luc Nancy, *The Inoperative Community*, p. xxxvi.

38. Hawkins, *From Nimbin to Mardi Gras*, 1993, p. 32.

39. Ibid., p. 35.

40. Ibid., p. 36.

41. Ibid., p. 37.

Gendering the Nation: Symbolic Stations in Quebec and Canadian Film History

Brenda Longfellow

> As a woman I have no country, as a woman I want no country,
> as a woman my country is the whole world.
> —Virginia Woolf, *The Three Guineas*.

Woolf's remark in *The Three Guineas* appears with amazing consistency in recent feminist interventions into theories of nationhood. I believe its currency develops precisely because of the way in which Woolf's statement highlights both the disparity between women's desire and the nationalist enterprise and the consonance between patriarchal social and symbolic relations and the relations of the nation state. Within the logic of the sentence, wanting no country, having an internationalist perspective (Woolf wrote the line on the eve of a World War) follows from the fact that women do not have a place as equal political subjects and citizens and are not provided with the symbolic or the economic means of experiencing ownership of the national.

While it is now a commonplace to insist that the nation state, as a political, juridical formation only comes into being (and continues to receive support) through symbolic processes, what is only beginning to be addressed is the way in which these imaginary formations are highly coded with respect to gender. Feminists working in areas as diverse as postcolonial theory and Eastern European feminism have pointed out how the female body is assigned an absolutely central position within the symbolic regimes of nationalist discourses, most classically as maternal womb, mother of the nation, matrix of creation.[1] This particular coding of the feminine within the public register of nationalism both recalls and leans on the fantasmatic construction of Woman[2] within the patriarchal imagination where the female body, stripped of its materiality, its subjecthood, and its desire is rendered as transcendent, holy, a vessel for divine insemination, the ground of representation. The superimposition of this fantasmatic body onto the body of the nation invests political territory and landscape with the same holy, transcendent and mythological qualities.[3]

The centrality of the maternal body within the symbolic regimes of nationalism has a particular resonance in the context of new ethnic and religious fundamentalist versions where national identity is increasingly constituted through the fantasmatic body of Woman. This is a point insistently remarked upon by Muslim feminists and by feminists writing from all sectors of the former Yugoslavia who have observed first hand how the intensifying mythological elaboration of the nation in maternal terms is always and everywhere accompanied by the real and drastic erosion of women's reproductive and political rights in the sphere of everyday life.[4]

I believe that it is no coincidence that the most powerful appropriation of the maternal body as site and ground of the nation occurs in contexts where the nation is symbolically constructed on principles of ethnic, religious or racial homogeneity. I'd suggest, in fact, that forms of nationality predicated on a rigid binary delineation of gender roles (women-Mother; men-soldiers, leaders) are structurally and ideologically dependent on a modernist conception of the nation or what I'll call strong nationalism where national identity is defined in terms of a fixed set of unifying characteristics. According to Homi K. Bhabha, it is precisely the stress on singularity and purity that facilitates the merging of modernity's justifications with those of the nation: "progress, homogeneity, cultural organicism, the deep nation, the long past ... [rationalizing] the authoritarian, "normalizing" tendencies within cultures in the name of the national interest or the ethnic prerogative.[5]

What follows are some exploratory journeys into the gendered formations of the nation within Canadian and Quebec cinematic histories. The stops on this journey are, for the most part, arbitrary. My intention here is not to construct an exhaustive study but to trace certain iconic representations of the nation (in particular, the transcontinental train) as this image circulates through discrete and historically specific cinematic conjunctures. This always somewhat erratic itinerary is guided by the desire to explore how nationalist discourses are crossed by gendered considerations and determined by distinct historical and political economies of cinema.

Let me hazard the first generalization which is that the powerful symbolic gendering of the nation (which, I've argued is the quintessential characteristic of modernist versions of nation) makes an appearance only in Quebec, during the cinematic revolutions of the nineteen seventies, the decade of the most intense effloresence of cultural nationalism. The representation of Woman as the embodiment of the Nation is, perhaps, most evocatively captured at the end of Gilles Groulx's *Le Chat dans Le Sac* (1964), the film long considered the inaugural moment of Quebec feature filmmaking, there in the figure of the lone and silent woman skating on an outdoor pond. In this final sequence, the woman's body is registered in an organic relationship to the landscape, her grace and ease contrasting powerfully with the ineffectual nationalist sentiments of the male protagonist, who can only observe her body, the figuration of the nation-yet-to-be. A similar figuration of Woman occurs in Jean Pierre Lefebvre's *Les Maudite Sauvages* in the Tekacouita character, the "native" woman who, in the diegetic sequences of the film is completely silent, the ultimate colonized victim, given to the fur trader by her father, cast into the baffling world of civilization (which humorously includes a melange of contemporary and historic signifiers including a television interview with Jean Talon, the 18th century Intendant of New France) and finally degraded as a go go dancer in a sleazy bar on rue St. Catherine. While her story functions in the film as an obvious allegory of the colonization and commodification of Quebec culture, she is also differently figured in the lyrical and non-diegetic sequences which interupt the narrative with a black and white still image of Tekacouita riding a horse through a snow covered forest. In these passages the voice of Tekacouita is finally heard, but only as a disembodied voice off. Here the promise of the nation is mediated not so much through the body of the Woman as through her gendered voice. Framed as a representation of native spirituality, her voice embodies a utopic vision of an an unmediated relationship to nature. It is a voice radically exterior to any social real.

In both these instances, woman's relationship to the nation is perfectly consonant with the classical modernist articulation: she does not create or shape the nation as political subject, she can only incarnate it as a body (or as a voice). I'd like to suggest that in Quebec what enables this particular symbolic circulation of Woman within nationalist discourse is the long and deep Catholic religious tradition with its cult of the maternal.[6] Catholicism is not so simply superseded by the more secular versions of nationalism which emerged during the Quiet Revolution. As the principal arbiter of the communal and organicist values of the Quebec nation for over two hundred years, Catholicism lives on as a form of public imagining and as a repository of rich symbology. This residue is evident in secular nationalism's appropriation of the female body as holy vessel and medium of the nation's spirit. It is also what enables the allegorical impulse in Quebec cultural nationalism which, like Catholicism, points to a meaning which is transcendent and beyond any literal object, text, or image.[7]

By contrast, (English) Canadian films of the same period are completely devoid of that powerful allegorical impulse which structures the imaginary constitution of the nation in Quebec cinema. Influenced by the social realist traditions of documentary, the inaugural moments of Canadian feature film, *Going Down the Road* and *Nobody Waved Goodbye* are far more engaged with issues of individual alienation and social "problems" than with the than with the symbolic constitution of the communal body of the nation. In these films, the quintessential national subject, as Robert Fothergill[8] et al, have pointed out, is the badly oedipalized, ineffectual and emasculated male. Women have only a marginal presence within these films, and certainly lack any of the mythologizing resonance or transcendental status which infuses the figures of Teakacouita and the woman skater in *Le Chat dans le Sac*.

The absence of an allegorical impulse and mythological representation of Woman in Canadian cinema has a great deal to do, I'd suggest, with the Canada's sense of nation. As Linda Hutcheon has pointed out, the modernist drive toward constructing the nation along the lines of a centring discourse of homogeneity and universal interest has always failed in Canada given the fact that there is no singularity of religion, language or ethnicity which could ground a "long" history or "deep" national myth of origins.

Historically dominated by colonial powers and internally colonized by centre/periphery inequalities of wealth and resources, the centre in Canada is, as Hutcheon observes, de-centred, "always elsewhere."[9] National identity is always articulated *against* the centre and mediated through regional, ethnic, and linguistic identificatory priorities.

What this has meant is that the interpellating power of any centring discourse of nation is extremely weak in Canada. One has only to refer to the Heritage Canada "minutes" which have been broadcast on television and projected before the (American) "real" movie in cinemas across the country. What these glossy and overproduced moments reveal is the very nearly transparent operation of what Marcuse defined as repressive sublimation: that appropriation of marginal or subversive discourses into the centre. Each of these moments, in fact, is articulated around a recognition of the existence of alternative national narratives: the women's suffrage movement; the Underground railroad which smuggled American slaves into Canada; Louis Riel, the leader of a Metis revolt in 1890; the mass of Chinese labourers imported to build the "national" railway. Any of the force which might attend a recognition of difference, however, is completely undermined by complete aestheticization of history. Reading like nothing so much as crackerbarrel cheese commercials, the Heritage minutes are all bathed in the golden light of consumerworld where historical struggle, exploitation, class difference and systematic racism evaporate in the glow of nostalgia. While there may be a few aesthetic smudges of dirt on the face of the escaping slave or the pioneer woman, their obstacles are temporary and they are all welcomed into the open tolerant arms of our national family.[10]

Interestingly enough, while most spectators assume these minutes are propaganda produced by the Canadian federal ministry of Heritage and Culture, they are actually sponsored by a leading member of the Canadian establishment: the Charles R. Bronfman foundation.[11]

It is surely no accident that these Heritage moments are produced at a time in Canada's history when the fiction of national unity is most in jeopardy. The upcoming Quebec referendum, Western ultra conservative populism and the general ongoing economic crisis, native land claims movement, all contribute to a deep anxiety regarding issues of cultural identity. These moments have no interpellating power because they are based on an vacuous referents, on a concept of national history and identity that can only return as tv sentiment. Nostalgia, as Falke remarks, is a sign of our postmodern condition, an empty rhetoric which only emerges when "the objects which continually remind one of the past are [irrevocably] gone."[12]

In Canada, the attempt to resurrect or create a singular national narration or highly invested series of emblems, flags etc. is always doomed to failure. Indeed, outside the realm of state propaganda, attempts to do so such as artist Charlie Pachter's Queen on a Moose series, or John Cadiz's depictions of the US/Canada border where Canada is figured stereotypically as a land of snow, dogsleds, Mounted Police and beavers are always ironic. These images are funny to Canadians precisely because, while appropriating the form of a modernist representation of the nation (ie. an emotional patriotic symbol), they utterly lack the mythological resonance of a "long past" or "deep history." At the same time, these ironic national images contain a mild rebuke and retort to the more aggressive and chauvinist displays of nationalism on the part of our neighbours to the south.

What I would like to do in the remainder of this article is to look at two women's films (Joyce Wieland's *Reason Over Passion* (1966) and Lea Pool's *Mouvement de Desir* (1994)) which appropriate one of the more enduring tropes of Canadian nationhood: the transcontinental train, although the effects of this appropriation are markedly different. From its very inauguration in 1867, the Canadian state articulated the symbolic demand of nationhood in terms of economic expansionism. National identity was linked to the implementation of a series of economic initiatives labelled The National Policy, the foremost of which was the state subsidized construction of a trancontinental railway. It was a paradigm that would be repeated throughout Canadian history.

As Craig Brown points out, the use of a discourse of economic instrumentality as the stuff and substance of national identity, had the advantage of ignoring the potentially divisive issues that would disrupt a cultural concept of nationality. "Appeals to a common language, a common cultural tradition or a common religion were simply impossible for Canadians and when they were attempted they were rightly regarded by French Canadians [sic] as a violation of their understanding of Confederation."[13] The railroad provided a technologically mediated form of identity: a national communications system harnassed as the only possible unifying force. Stretching from sea to sea, across vast and diverse regions, the railroad provided the material embodiment, the concrete (and unitary) signifier of the idea of political federation. Like the political federation, its function was to direct immigration, economic exchange and (perhaps, most importantly) semiotic traffic[14] on an east west bias in order to offset the relentless seductions of the money and markets to the south. A more phallic symbolic emodiment could scarcely be imagined.

Joyce Wieland's experimental road movie, *Reason Over Passion* (1969) provides a direct retort to those versions of state nationalism which foreground technology and instrumental reason as the modus operandi of political and cultural nationality, a version much beloved by then Prime Minister, Pierre Elliot Trudeau. While Trudeau, as political icon, is specifically targetted in *Reason Over Passion*, the film, at the same time, offers a subversive send up of various Canadian cliches of nationhood.

The parodic representation of Canadian nationality is a recurring territory for Wieland, a visual artist and experimental filmmaker whose work has frequently involved a playful dephallicization of nationalist discourses. In her visual art practices, this has been most evident in the series of quilts she produced during the late sixties, with titles such as Confedspread (1967), Patriotism (1966-67), O Canada Animation (1970). Employing the idiom of feminine craft work, each quilt is decorated with embroidered or stitched images of Canadiana (a flag or series of feminine mouths singing the national anthem). The juxtaposition between feminine craft and nationalist discourse has the effect of unsettling each, marking the feminine as a space for political assertion and pointing to the gendered implications of most nationalist displays. The most infamous of this series is Wieland's "Reason Over Passion" quilt which hangs in prominent display in Ottawa's National Art Gallery. Here, the slogan's force as a dictate of instrumental rationality is completely undermined by the medium of the "soft" feminine quilt with its pastel colours. Wieland's objects of parody are not only the state authored versions of nationality. In *Rat Life and Diet in North America* (1968), she gently pokes fun at some of the more outstanding left political axioms of that period. Taking on some of the discourse of the anti-(Vietnam) war and new left agenda, Wieland develops a political parable in which a group of rats (really gerbils) decide to escape the "Military/Industrial Complex" and flee to Canada to take up organic gardening, "no pesticides," as the film puts it. In its use of minatures and in its refusal to subsume its politics within the didactic demands of "seriousness," Wieland again forces the issue of a gendered appropriation of nationalist discourse. *Reason Over Passion* represents one of her most extended meditations on this theme.

Reason Over Passion (1967-69) opens with a long shot of waves crashing against the Atlantic coastline and ends with an image of a postcard depicting Canada's west coast. Between those two axes, the one a more realist depiction of a "natural" landscape and the other a mediated and cliched signifier of a touristic vision of nation, the film takes us on a extended cross country journey in which the issue of representation itself is omnipresent.

What we see throughout this road trip are the immediately identifiable images of the Canadian landscape: Atlantic marshes,

Canadian Shield, prairie flatlands, Rockie Mountains. These "scenes," however, are always complexly mediated. Filmed through the window of a moving car or train, the images are doubly framed by the edge of the window and by the varying thickness and transparency of the glass. In addition, Wieland's use of different stocks, filters and optical printing all confound any simple immediacy of the image.The concern with represen- tation distinguishes Wieland's work from the discourses of cultural nationalism, prevalent in the 1970's which leaned heav- ily on the metaphor of the mirror as the founding instance in the formation of cultural identity. For Wieland, seeing, particularly as it is depicted in *Reason Over Passion* is no guarantee of the stability of any identity. Like all of Wieland's work, the film's intention is to parody and subvert existing discourses of Cana- dian nationality without necessarily offering any substantive or alternative content.

In *Reason Over Passion*, the most obvious object of Wieland's parody is the cross country road trip, an enduring cultural (and experiential) trope in Canadian lives. Travelling from the east coast, up the St. Lawrence, to the west, the film follows the established direction of Canada's official national narrative of immigration, settlement and industrialization. While the trans- continental railroad had been a central symbolic device within this narrative, as I've suggested above, here it is not so much the literal image of the train which is significant as the mode of spectatorship involved in travel for the train, itself, is rarely visible and is rather only inferred by the continuous panning movement past each scene.

What we see from behind the window of this moving car and train are the images of an all too familiar Canadian travelogue, where landscape is reduced to its most ritualistic depiction, flattened, commodified and heavily circulated. Images of snow, rocky wastelands, prairie grain elevators and uninhabited north- ern vistas represent a tourist's vision of Canada, where image cliches serve as easy metonyms of Canadian nationality. This exteriorized and stereotyped vision of Canada, as Peter Morris has pointed out, has a long history which begins with the early CPR propaganda films used to lure immigrants to Canada and continues through many of the "scenics" produced by British and American film companies who "moved into Canada to exploit images of 'natural' landscape."[15] Whether produced by Canadians for international export or by foreign producers themselves, the net semiotic effect was the same, as Morris puts it: "As it was, Hollywood's image of Canada quickly became the world's image. And, it might be argued, Canada's image of itself."

Wieland's use of these cliched images recalls the most hallowed and mythologically resonant of Canada's landscape artists, The Group of Seven.[16] While the sanctioned version positions the group as radical innovators who broke with the pastoral traditions of European landscape painting to confront the real rugged terror of the Canadian Shield, recent revisions tell a very different story. In "Race, Wilderness, Territory and the origins of modern canadian landscape painting," Scott Watson argues that the consistent representation of the landscape in Group of Seven productions as "empty, uninhabited, unmapped [and] unnamed territory" not only erases the existence of the first nations people who did, in fact, inhabit the land, but it also supplied a powerful ideological rationalization for northern industrial development and exploitation.[17] As Watson remarks, "it was as if no one could be said to own this emptiness: instead the territory sort of waited for exploitation and ownership that would fill it or bring it into a reality it could not yet be said to participate in."[18] Here, snow and whiteness have a resonance beyond realist descriptions of winter. They become allegorical representations of the racial identity of the implied Canadian subject spectator. As it tropes on this tradition, Wieland's landscape in *Reason Over Passion* is almost always void of human presence and, in a related fashion, void of any indication of urban reality. The camera concentrates on the empty spaces, the spaces between small towns on the transcontinental route, the spaces of archetypal "wilderness."

Within *Reason Over Passion* there are two notable exceptions to the film's non anthromorphic text which, interestingly enough, foreground the manner in which gender is implicated in any discourse of nationality. The first image of a human face, at the conceptual and structural centre of the film, is the rephotographed image of Pierre Elliot Trudeau. Heavily mediated (matted, optically reprinted, seriously underexposed), the image, in its very construction, foregrounds the process by which public figures are transformed into symbolic icons. His silent and reprinted image, the images of Trudeau surrounded by a group of male politicians stand as the official arbiters of national identity as it produced through phallic definition: the belief in the values of efficiency, progress and material expansion; the denial of the body; the faith in the technological version of nationhood.

Wieland's cinematic antics, however, completely disarm the authority of this definition as she visibly links it to the particular interests of the white, male, patrician class. Male political power is playfully diminished as their images are subject to the weathering effects of the optical printing, flicker and reframing. Within Wieland's world reason can no longer maintain its defences against passion.

Trudeau's slogan "La Raison Avant La Passion/ Reason Over Passion," ("la theme de tous mes ecrits") is fed through a computer and reproduced as a regulated permutation of 537 anagrams (aerson over asnsiop; raeson revo spasion..etc.) and then printed at the bottom of each new landscape sequence. While the regulated precision of the variation of the anagrams derives from a certain order and (computer) logic, the semantic sense of the anagrams are pure nonsense. On the other side of the gender divide is the passion of the filmmaker herself, a passion connected to a body. The only other indication of an identifiable body in the film is the image of Wieland, herself, aiming a Bolex camera at her image in the mirror and later mouthing the words to O Canada (the national anthem). Her image counters Trudeau's, a reverse shot in which the body and the flesh are posed against the transcendental and disembodied fantasies of instrumental reason, across the binary of gender difference. Yet, Wieland is not into strict reversals. She does not offer herself or her body as the sites of an alternative concept of national identity. This is never more apparent than in the sequence where Wieland mouths the words to the national anthem. Refusing to take up a (synchronized) position within the official discourse of nationalism, Wieland takes up an eccentric, subversive position, quoting the ritualized words but with the fine and ironic difference of her silence.

While Wieland's embodied authorial presence acts reflexively, as a signifier of the constructedness of the representation, it does so without in any way claiming mastery as the film's originating vision. *Reason Over Passion* refuses a simple assignment of the vision of the film to the subjective, personalized vision of the filmmaker. Individual perspective is always mediated (and displaced in some sense) by the technology of the moving train whose velocity and direction over-determine the frame and landscape vistas of the film.

If the ideological effect of Canada's tradition of landscape painting had to do with the ability of the national subject/ spectator to imagine "him" self as a transcendental subject whose "seeing" implies ownership and control, this subject is radically subverted by Wieland's strategies in *Reason Over Passion*. In the film, the particular representation of the landscape simply does not allow for any contemplative or meditative stance. Flattened out by the continuous movement of the train, the landscape loses depth and "aura," and the subject loses the ability to project the self into deep space.

This is the nature of Wieland's irony as Hutcheon defines it "pretending to speak a dominant 'language' while subverting it at the same time."[19] Like the cardboard Canadian flags she intercuts with their crude renditions of the maple leaf, Wieland quotes the official discourses of nationalism only to empty them of any substantial meaning. Her images of Canadiana are farcical in the weakness of their interpellating power, in their inability to pin a definitive "Canadian" signification onto the landscape. As I have argued above, in the context of Canada's weak form of nationhood, these ritualized emblems and symbols, can only be read as a joke.

Some twenty five years later, Lea Pool's *Mouvement de Desir* takes on the same trope of transcontinental train travel but from a very different perspective. Far removed from the gritty no budget world of experimental film, Pool's film is a product of the international co-production economy, an elegantly produced

35mm narrative feature delivered by French, Swiss and Canadian financial participation. Pool, in fact, has been one of the pre-eminent beneficiaries of the international co-production, with four of her six features produced through international deals and intended for the commerical and art house markets of Europe, a situation that obviously, troubles any easy ascription of national identity to her films. And, indeed, the authorial signature of Pool, a Swiss immigre to Quebec, is marked strongly by the influence of European art cinema and bears a level of textual and symbolic abstraction which, in many ways, runs completely against the grain of the history of Quebec cinema. [20]

As Robert Daudelin and Pierre Veronneau have argued, the singularity of Quebec's feature film tradition is located in the original influence of cinema direct, the documentary movement of the late 1960's which produced such Quebec canonical classics as *Les Racquetteurs* (1958).[21] Translated into fictional filmmaking, the enduring influence of the direct may be read in the abiding concern with social issues and most importantly, in the particular depiction of location and place. Reacting against the staid artificiality of the studio film, cinema direct launched the movement of Quebec cinema into the "real" streets, villages, countryside and city of the Quebec nation. National cinema in Quebec was thus defined, inextricably, in relation to its concrete referencing of place: Ile aux Coudres, the St. Lawrence, the bars and salons of St. Catherine street, the idiosyncratic (and instantly identifiable) quarters of Montreal, the landscape of northern Quebec, etc.

In Pool's films, by contrast, location is rarely given any such concrete specification. For the films set in Montreal, the city represents a kind of anonymous postmodern urban space, viewed primarily through its generic sites of passage: a hotel, warehouse, hospital, asylum, etc. On one level, at least, the absence of geographically specific space in her films is related to the immigrant consciousness of her films with their recurring thematics of wandering, exile and diaspora. While the tone of alienation which marks her films is related to the loss of a home which could root characters within a fixed sense of identity, it is also intimately related to the fluctuating sexual orientation of characters. For the the lesbian characters in her earlier films and the male homosexual in *A Corps Perdu*, condemned and liberated, "home" is often the refuge of another's body. Alienated from the national landscape of both city and country, Pool's characters remain separated from actual geographic backgrounds by their experience of otherness.

Her films, however, absolutely defy any social realist approach to representation by their level of textual abstraction. Signifiers, far from being referential are always and only functions of the hermetic universe of the text itself. Densely symbollic, in a frequently overwrought fashion, characters, places and locations take on a kind of ethereal status. This level of abstraction is what has enraged many Quebec critics including Chantal Nadeau who argues that Pool's "existential mode of treating identity" where women characters appear "out of time, out of place, ahistorical, almost immaterial," [22] repeats a mythological representation of Woman as universal, fantasized subject. While, clearly, articulating the social subject of either Quebec national identity or feminism is not one of Pool's overt concerns, such a critique also needs to acknowledge the specific production and reception contexts of Pool's work - the international co-production which produces its own inherent demands and aethetic criteria.

Mouvement de Desir, Pool's latest film repeats many of her familiar textual moves. Set aboard the transcontinental passenger train, movement and passage articulate every frame of the film as the train snakes its way across Canada to the west coast. Like all characters aboard, the two protagonists are in transition: Catherine (Valerie Kaprisky) a single mother is fleeing the dissolution of a relationship with an "Ishmael" who left her to be with men; Vincent (Jean-Francois Piçhette) a computer salesman who is travelling to Vancouver to meet his Anglo lover.

Mouvement de Desir is a love story between these two protagonists and one which, quite deliberately, reproduces the entirely predictable course of such stories. As Barthes noted in *A Lover's Discourse*, a love story is inherently banal because of its ritualistic nature; it is only alive and new to the lovers themselves, who experience love "as if for the first time." And, indeed, the narrative of *Mouvement de Desir* embodies banality to its very core as it follows the relentless trajectory of desire through its stages of repulsion, attraction, withdrawal, betrayal and passionate consummation. Certainly a good measure of this banality, stems from the heterosexual articulation of desire where penetration, and the artful exposure of the woman's body is coded (almost excessively) by an imagined heterosexual gaze and narrative trajectory.[23]

What rescues the film from its inordinate banality, however, is the use of the train as a trope whose own relentless passage both contains and parallels the narrative movements of desire. As Mary Anne Doane points out, the technology of train travel and the technology of film are perfectly compatabile as "the train embod[ies] film's proairetic codification, its sequencing as a movement from here to there, its assumption of a causal connection, the "coupling" of discrete actions and events, the ultimate termination, terminus, terminal as closure."[24]

As I've argued above, the use of the train also has a particular resonance within the Canadian national imaginary and *Mouvement* very explicitly references this tradition. Like Wieland's *Reason Over Passion*, the privileged signifiers of landscape are the empty spaces of the Canadian Shield, the near deserted Prairie towns, the primeval majesty of the Rocky Mountains. In Pool's film however, these images are are presented without the ironic framing of Wieland's representational strategies which quote the landscape tradition only to displace and disrupt the naturalism of these signifiers as emblems of Canadian nationality. The changing iconography of landscape in *Mouvement* functions less as a concrete reference to place or as a (negative) sign of national belonging than as a kind of two dimensional theatrical backdrop to the passion evolving aboard the train. For the most part, the "scenics" are not framed from the point of view of any particular character. The characters never comment on the scenes that pass on the other side of the train window and any of the subjective traces of embodied vision which animated Wieland's film are absent here. In *Mouvement*, images of landscape are not bound to a body but to the externalized gaze of the camera apparatus itself as aerial shots and shots taken from a prothesis extended out of the train window abound. Mediated by this externalized gaze, the landscape takes on a quality of auratic spectacle, of otherness which operates as an exteriorized frame outside the love story proper.

These two planes of the film, however, (the interior love story and exteriorized landscape view), mirror each other as markers of passage, transition and movement. As the exterior view is continually refigured by the movement of the train itself, the desire between the two characters takes on new shapes, new dimensions and the alternation between these two plans marks the rhythm of the movement of desire, the force moving on the body, the body of the train and the body of the characters.

But what function do these images of landscape have as repititions of the canonical trope of Canadian nationhood ? The separation between the two planes is only overcome at the very end of the film where after a bout of passionate lovemaking, the couple stand stand on the open platform between two cars, gazing at the landscape slowly passing before their eyes: a fog covered glacial lake nestled at the foot of the Rocky Mountains. Within the signifying logic of the film, the landscape becomes the displaced signifier of desire, the banality of love elevated by the transcendental beauty of the scene itself. This scene, however, does not offer any reassurance of national belonging or a concrete specifity of place. The characters can only position themselves before this scene as (*international*) spectators, *as if they were watching a film*. There is a kind of metatextual irony here in the placement of Catherine and Vincent as surrogate spectators to a scene not at all dissimilar to those used by the first foreign film companies in Canada. Here, as in the early scenics, the nation is reduced to a cliched signifier of landscape whose function is defined as the specular seduction of an international spectator.

Notes

1. See, for example: Inderpal Grewal and Caren Kaplan, eds. *Scattered Hegemonies* (Minneapolis: University of Minnesota Press, 1994); Nanette Funk and Magda Mueller, eds., *Gender Politics and Post-Communism* (New York: Routledge,

1994).

2. See Teresa de Lauretis, *Technology and Gender* (Bloomington: Indiana University Press, 1987), pp.1-30 for a crucial elaboration of the ideological construction of Woman.

3. The representation of the nation through the figure of the maternal body, thus, repeats one of the foundational oppositions of western metaphysics between *physis* and *techne*, where the female principle is associated with inert matter, landscape the malleable material that will be shaped by the intervention of *techne* into meaning.

4. Ibid, Funk and Mueller.

5. Homi K. Bhabha, "Introduction" to *Nation and Narration*, ed. Homi K. Bhabha (London: Routledge, 1990), p.4.

6. This particular symbolic intersection is also evident in the epistolary novel *Maria Chapedelaine* which, for generations, was held as the canonical symbolic articulation of the organicist, rural and Catholic values of the Quebec nation.

7. It should be pointed out, however, that that particular valorization of the maternal body which I've argued is characteristic of the 1970's cultural nationalism in Quebec, has been superseded by a vision of the maternal as abject, suffocating, vaguely malevolent in the 1990's oedipal narratives of directors like Jean-Claude Lauzon.

8. Robert Fothergill, "Coward, Bully, or Clown: The Dream-Life of a Younger Brother," in S. Feldman and J. Nelson, eds., *Canadian Film Reader* (Toronto: Peter Martin Associates, 1977), pp.234-250.

9. Linda Hutcheon, *The Canadian Postmodern: a study of contemporary English-Canadian fiction* (Toronto: Oxford University Press, 1988) p.4.

10. Elspeth Cameron and Janice Dickin McGinnis, "Ambushed by Patriotism," *Canadian Forum* (vol.LXXII, no.837, March, 1995), pp. 12-16.

11. Ibid, p.18.

12. Lorne Falke, "The Border Prism," *Semiotext(e) canadas* (ed.) Jordan Zinovich (New York: Marginal Editions, 1994), p.18.

13. Craig Brown, "The Nationalism of the National Policy," *Nationalism in Canada*, ed. Peter Russell (Toronto: McGraw-Hill, 1966), p.161.

14. The railroad, Brown adds, could never be justified in purely economic terms, as a profit generating enterprise: "An expensive and partially unproductive railway through Canadian territory was the price Canada had to pay to "protect" it from American penetration and absorption." A more phallic signifier of nationality could scarcely be imagined.

15. Peter Morris, *Embattled Shadows, A History of Canadian Cinema, 1895-1939* (Montreal, McGill-Queen's University Press, 1978), p.40.

16. Wieland went on to produce a feature, *The Far Shore* which mythically re-enacted the tragic death of Tom Thomson, one of the Group of Seven's most prominent members.

17. Scott Watson, "Race, Wilderness, Territory and the Origins of Modern Canadian Landscape Painting," *Semiotext(e)* (New York: Marginal Editions, 1994), p.93.

18. Ibid, p.97.

19. Linda Hutcheon, *Splitting Images/ Contemporary Canadian Ironies* (To-

ronto: Oxford University Press, 1991) p. vii.

20. It is this singularity which perhaps explains some of the hostile reaction to her work on the part of Quebecois (male) critics.

21. Robert Daudelin, "The Encounter Between Fiction and the Direct Cinema," *Self Portrait* (Ottawa: Canadian Film Institute, 1980).

22. Chantal Nadeau, "Women in French-Quebec Cinema," *CineAction* (no.28, 1992) p.13.

23. Generously pointed out to me by Thomas Waugh.

24. Mary Anne Doane, "When the direction of the force acting on the body is changed" : The Moving Image," *Femmes Fatales, Feminism, Film Theory, Psychoanalysis* (Routledge: New York, 1991) p.189.

"Outside in the Machine"[1]: Institutional Experiences and Strategies of Canadian Women Electroacoustic Composers

Andra McCartney

> La société admet la présence de femmes créatrices, mais n'ajuste aucunement les structures pour les admettre et leur permettre de vivre pleinement au meme titre que les artistes du sexe opposé. *[Society admits the presence of creative women, but does not adjust its structures at all to admit them and to allow them to live fully to the same extent as artists of the other sex.]* Micheline Coulombe Saint-Marcoux.[2]

This article will focus on electroacoustic institutions and gender relations within them. I will discuss first the educational environment, since it is here that an electroacoustic composer's career begins, and is most likely to be social: it is also the time when the composer is most open to influence. After graduation, the electroacoustic composer, theoretically, can work alone in a studio.

The solitude of the studio after graduation, however, can never be complete. Electroacoustic composers need access to expensive equipment. And whether or not they work with performers, composers look for venues in which their works can be played. A commentary on other institutional structures, including the music store, the public studio, the concert hall, and the professional community, will conclude this article, which is derived from a larger research project, in which I interviewed fourteen Canadian women composers of electroacoustic music.

Educational Institutions

Composition classes were closed to women until late in the nineteenth century, and Marcia Citron has documented how this lack of access was both a result of, and a means of maintaining, the gendering of composition.[3] Even a hundred years later, there are still very few women teachers of composition in university departments.[4] Access to courses is no longer the primary concern in the 1990s: electroacoustic composition classes are equally available to men and to women. Despite this, the percentage of women students in these classes is remarkably low, with an overall average of 24 per cent at Ontario universities (see Appendix A). In many cases, there was only one woman in a class.

Low initial enrolment may be a result of the fact that many women are not taught to think of themselves as tool-users. Early socialization through the home, playground, school, and mass media encourages gender conformity: girls are taught to relate, and boys to tinker.[5] A Saturday morning spent watching children's television reveals advertisements and programs that encourage girls to see themselves as passive, warm, soft, and caring, relating to soft toys and dolls; boys, as active, cool, hard, and warlike, manipulating tools and machines. Composer Pascale Trudel remarks that at her secondary school, different technical standards were expected of girls and of boys: "At secondary school, we had to pass orientation tests, and the girls were not given the part about electronics, engineering, and so on. It was, even by that time, discriminating."[6, 7]

The Studio Course

The institutional site discussed most by my consultants is the electroacoustic studio course at university. All of them had been in a minority as students, and many perceive the environment as a difficult one for women. Wende Bartley describes the electroacoustic studio course as "a very macho environment. It's a much more macho environment than composition."[8]

At two of the Ontario universities that I contacted, Guelph and York, there was an introductory course followed by an advanced course. Although in the introductory courses 25 per cent of the students were women, this number dropped to 4 per cent at the advanced level (see Appendix A).[9] Pascale Trudel also mentions this phenomenon of female students dropping out after an introductory course: "All of the women who started at the same time as me dropped out after one or two years"[10]. Turkle's analysis of discrimination in computer culture, which functions "not by rules that keep people out but by ways of thinking that make them reluctant to join in"[11] could help to explain why some women would try an electroacoustic course, but not continue in the field. Susan Frykberg believes that this may be so:

> Really there is a sense of "Go away from here, I don't want you messing around with my technology." It's almost like it's personal, it's an extension of their bodies, their power structures. And it may not be overt, they don't tell you to go away but the kind of teaching and the man talk about technology in a sexual way, a kind of sexual banter. There's a sense that the technology is part of one's own prestige and if you can't do it right then you're incompetent or marginalized. I think it's a really powerful force, in which the male psyche and the technology is intertwined. And one of the things that is very interesting is this whole idea of men and their fear of the woman's fertility, because it comes out of this fear and loathing, in a sense. It's a mystery of creation, it's very psychically intertwined. So a woman will feel that, and even though she might not be able to articulate that that is what's going on, it might be enough to stop her from going into the technology.[12]

Entering the electroacoustic studio course, therefore, a woman student is in a minority, surrounded by language that may seem alienating.[13] In addition, she has been socialized away from machines, and her approach to them may reflect this. Several of my consultants mention differences in the way men and women students approach the equipment. Some of them speak of this from the perspective of their experience as students, while others describe their teaching experience as well (Carol Ann Weaver, Wende Bartley, Helen Hall, Susan Frykberg, and Hildegard Westerkamp have all taught studio courses).

Susan Frykberg, Hildegard Westerkamp, and Helen Hall discuss classroom dynamics. They notice male-female differences in confidence levels, approaches to questioning, and attitudes towards the machines. Their comments are remarkably consistent. Susan Frykberg:

> I can quite often go into a room, and I can tell that both groups of people know exactly the same about the machinery, but the men will sort of swagger up to it and whip up the slider and "wing wing wing, punch in the thing," which is a macho sort of confidence, whereas a woman might come up, and twiddle this and twiddle that. They both know as much or as little as each other, but it's just the apparent approach. [14]

Hildegard Westerkamp:

> The main difference that I noticed was that guys would come in and not ask any questions. They would just go at the equipment and not ever admit that they did not know anything about it, and would start fiddling around with it—would pretend, in many cases, that they knew what they were doing, looking confident, and if they weren't confident they wouldn't have the guts to ask questions. They would just somehow make their way through it with an enterprising approach. Women would either have the courage to ask questions and completely expose themselves and say "I don't know anything about this, can you help me?" or they would be so timid that they would neither touch the equipment nor ask questions. [15]

Helen Hall:

> In the class usually it's the male students who jump in with the sound and lighting technology, and then the women students back off. But when they're alone—when I work with [the women] individually, that's when they really get to know the equipment. They work on projects in the studio, and they use everything possible. [16]

Carol Ann Weaver says that her male students will often come up with a more avant-garde approach, and believes this may be because they have been socialized to be more adventurous: "I mean it's that outside and inside life that men and women have gotten used to [men are used to] going *outside* in terms of ideas" [17]. Monique Jean, however, suggests that male students are able to go further because of the informal support that they receive from each other, and from the (male) professor:

> There is a friendship among the guys. Because they help each other, they go to each other's places. They say "Come over tonight, to organize my tapes," but they don't say that they've never made a tape. I say "I've never done that, come and teach me." It's not the same words, but it's the same reality, nevertheless the result is not the same.[18]

Monique Jean also notes that she was never invited over to her professor's house informally, as the male students were. The male students rarely came to concerts where her works were being performed, never commented on her work or critiqued it. She wanted them to: "Say something to me, a criticism, a comment. But it's always silence. I play my pieces—silence" [19].

Compositional Approaches

Another problem is that the educational system values certain ways of working over others. Claire Piché says: "Men and women have different ways of living, of thinking, that's a fact. But we are often obliged to bend ourselves to their [male] mentality"[20]. Although not all of my consultants believe that men and women have essentially different ways of thinking, several note a lack of tolerance in the electroacoustic studio for a variety of ways of working.

Monique Jean describes how her intuitive, improvisational and "pleasurable" way of working was discouraged in a university environment that valued a more structured approach:

> One must still take pleasure in composing. It can't just be conceptual, at least for me. At the moment, at university, it is more the trend of conceptual art which predominates: importance is placed on the elaboration of a system, on the concept of a work which one then transmits to the computer to be translated. Boring!"[21]

Monique Jean's description of being told to construct a plan, and then give it to the computer to carry out is similar to what Turkle and Papert describe as the predominant method of teaching computer programming used within Universities. It seems: "that there is only one right way to approach the computer, a way that emphasizes control through structure and planning"[22]. When the predisposition towards planning in computer programming courses, and the historical importance of form in music composition are brought together, it seems no surprise that many courses in electroacoustic composition would emphasize a conceptual approach.

Turkle and Papert observe many of their students using an approach, which they call *bricolage*. The *bricoleurs* like "to play with the elements of the program, to move them around almost as though they were material elements—the words in a sentence, the notes in a musical composition, the elements in a collage."[23] Many, but not all, of these students are women. In the programming courses, these students had been told that their approach was wrong.[24] This *bricolage* method is similar to some of the descriptions given by some of my consultants, too. Ann Southam spoke of her enjoyment of playing and "mucking around" with sounds in the analog studio[25], and Hildegard Westerkamp said: "[I] work very interactively with these sounds. I hear them, and then make decisions." [26] [27]

Concerns about aesthetic control are not confined to an insistence on structure and planning. As Monique Jean discovered, the language of aesthetics is sometimes sexualized:

> "[my professor] who is someone very polite, very cultivated, said to me that if he really wished to become a composer (he was talking about a male student), he must learn to ejaculate. So, I said to myself, shocked, how did he perceive my music? I then understood why he always wanted me to change my music or my sounds." [28]

This is an aesthetics which insists not on structure and planning, but on a particular experience of sexuality which is specifically masculine.[29]

Carol Ann Weaver describes an approach to electronic music composition based on penetration of the ear:

> In the '70s in Indiana there was a noise, a pain level thing which the male composers and tape music people were all believing in—that when you play tape music and electronic music you have to turn it to a certain volume level that is actu-

ally painful, a penetration into the ear which is at a forceful and painful level. I don't know how many hours of sitting through that I had to do, and I was one of the few people who was really outspoken about it. The answer to this was that as you get used to this penetration, you don't mind it.... And besides, you're a bad musician, you're not very open minded if you can't take a little expansion.... It was a ridiculous argument. I remember feeling so angry, and I knew these people were just dead wrong. But they didn't believe [they were wrong]. I would just dread [those painful sound levels].[30] [31]

The professors in charge of this class were not only assaulting their students with sound, but also indicating that those who disagreed with their approach to dynamics were bad musicians, thus exerting aesthetic control, and censoring difference. Sarah Peebles says that she was not censored outright for refusing imposed aesthetic boundaries, but was ignored instead:

Being ignored had a cumulative effect, year after year. In the end, about a year after I graduated, I realized that I felt just enraged over being ignored and neglected. Also, I think it had a depressing effect on me while I was encountering the lack of interest/non-reaction. [32]

If the approaches of individual women to electroacoustic composition are discouraged by mainstream aesthetics in an institutional context, then explicitly feminist approaches are sometimes discouraged even further. Wende Bartley told me that she did not complete any pieces in her first year, because of discouragement regarding her emphasis on specifically feminist themes. One colleague was particularly upset, and walked out of a public seminar presentation when her piece, *Rising Tides of Generations Lost,* was played. This piece celebrates women's reclamation of their voices. From the fiery maelstrom of witch trials emerge syllables, then words and phrases, voices of women talking about their daily lives in the present, expressing hope for the future. Wene reports that her colleague said:

"Why do you have to write about this stuff?" He was going nuts, pacing up and down the hall. I know that this piece has provoked a lot of strong reaction. Women are often quite moved and feel a strong sense of connection to the sense of "female voice" that the piece evokes. So I've remained in contact with him, but we've had highly charged discussions all the time.[33]

The reaction to Wende Bartley's feminist work even extended to judgements about her ability to do further graduate work. According to her thesis supervisor:

Ms. Bartley has done a slow but fruitful research, with good final results. However, she has concentrated her compositional efforts in a rather narrow area. Her viewpoints should explore areas outside "feminism" as artistic expression, to justify further graduate work.

All these accounts describe teaching that prescribes and proscribes. In Wende Bartley's case, a change in viewpoint was prescribed, while in Monique Jean's, it was compositional technique. And in Carol Ann Weaver's account, a particular approach to dynamics was prescribed.

Positive Environments

Not all educational contexts are this hostile to women. The experiences of some of my consultants were more positive. For instance, Ann Southam, learning electroacoustic composition in the early days of the University of Toronto's analog studio, did not find the environment difficult. She says:

We would be told how to turn things on, what knobs and dials to do what with. Then we could work in there as many hours as we wanted, and there was a technician who was there, and we would ask him about every fifteen minutes: "How do you do this, how do you do this?" Everybody was very nice.... So there was no technical ... "you're supposed to do it this way," nothing like that. The assumption was we could make music, and so we did. It was terrific.[34]

Because the equipment was quite unfamiliar to everyone, rules for how to work with it had not yet been established. Ann Southam speaks of electroacoustic music at this time as a "wilderness of sound," and refers to it later being "paved over."[35]

Sarah Peebles says that she liked her relationship with her first composition professor, who "didn't ever make any judgements. If I made a piece that reminded him of anything, he would go and get it and show me."[36] [37] In both of these cases, the freedom from aesthetic prescriptions is important.

Claire Piché enjoyed learning from a female professor, Marcelles Deschênes, and says that this relationship was quite different from others she had encountered:

> I had a woman as professor (for a private course) and I liked that experience very much. We had really interesting arguments, and the dynamic between us was good. The main reason is that we spoke as equals. I was close to Marcelle even if we argued with each other many times. This was something that I had never experienced with male professors in private courses, because something happened which meant that there had to be a winner. I don't play that game. Even if the other thinks that he is right and that the match is won, without a worthwhile argument I keep my idea and I believe that is hard for the egos of some. With Marcelle, it was an exchange rather than a competition. What a pleasure to meet each week and to exchange about a subject which is dear to us, electroacoustic composition. [38]

In these three accounts, the power relations allow for a variety of compositional approaches and professor-student dynamics.

Feminist Pedagogy

Several of my consultants have been in a position to affect classroom dynamics and compositional processes as teachers. They discuss pedagogical techniques that they have devised as a result of watching gender interaction in the electroacoustic classroom. I have already mentioned one of Helen Hall's techniques, which is to work with students individually, outside of the group atmosphere, and away from its pressures. Then, students are able to develop skills with the equipment and confidence in their own approaches without interference. When teaching groups, she noticed that "there was a competition amongst the male students: 'I'll handle it—I can do it. I already know how to do this, watch me.' So I have to say: 'Okay, you already know how to do it, then someone else should do it.'" [39] thus shifting attention from competitive demonstration to active learning.

Susan Frykberg points out that crossing disciplines and changing terminology can free students from limiting associations, allowing them to find their own voices:

I'm teaching electroacoustic communications which is an introduction to electroacoustic sound, a cross-disciplinary course. People learn the technology... they can use it for music, radio works, multi-media, or to make sound tracks and videos. So it's a very general introduction, which is good, because it frees it up aesthetically. They have a lot of choices. And quite often people come from different [artistic or technical] backgrounds but still they do very aesthetic pieces. I like that—they come and then the technology becomes their tool. Then they use it to find their own voice.

The other course I teach is called "Acoustic Communication" and it's an introduction to sound in general. There's creativity but it's not necessarily about making musical pieces, just different kinds of sound pieces. They need the perspective that it can never fail. They make a sound document on tape [as opposed to a musical piece]. I think that just having that wording frees people up, especially people who have had a bit of training in music—harmony and rhythm—they [start to say] "Oh I can't do this, because I haven't studied long enough." It's seemed to free them up and I get really good work—and also work that's quite political, if I try to encourage them to find their own voices...To express yourself—but it's more than that. It's like stripping away all the stuff, and finding your voice inside. We've had people dealing with issues about racism for example.... There are a lot of Chinese students at S[imon] F[raser] U[niversity] and they have had a hard time in this province in terms of racist policies. Some people have dealt with being gay and some with things like cultural appropriation, or what it's like to be an Asian woman in this culture. I really encourage that kind of work.[40]

In addition, Susan Frykberg uses actively anti-sexist pedagogical approaches in her teaching work. She tries to work
against the gender boundaries that exist before students enter
the classroom, putting more emphasis on free exploration than
on technical skill by rules:

> One of the things that I think always works is an approach to
> the technology where you come in, and you say "This is a
> box" .... "This is what it does, and there are two things, if you
> do these two things" —and I'm very specific— "you will blow
> up everything. But anything else, just try it and see what hap-
> pens." And they go "Aaaaah gasp", especially the men, get
> really miffed at that approach. They say "But you can't do
> that !" I find that when I have that approach, the women are
> far happier working with the technology. They say "Well
> what do we do?" I say "Well, try it and see." I also get them to
> work in groups together, so that they support each other.
> Sometimes in these classes you get a person who's been a
> sound engineer for 20 years and they might know more tech-
> nically than I do, but creatively they might know nothing, or
> they might not know the social or political ramifications. I say
> "Well, if you do know more than this person, then share your
> ideas, pool your ideas and work together." I even run the tuto-
> rial that way. Sometimes I'll take a technical term and I'll say
> "OK. This is the term, and these are the reference texts and
> you're the facilitator.... The facilitator has to make sure, first
> of all, that we take twenty minutes to do this, that everybody
> gets to speak and that everybody understands the term by the
> time you get to twenty minutes." The emphasis is not on be-
> ing right, but on speaking. Because the path to knowledge is
> often being wrong.... I find that is a really good way to deal
> with especially technical terms.[41]

Hildegard Westerkamp acts as a role-model: she asks questions
herself, and demonstrates that she does not always remember
every technique:

> I would actually sometimes be in situations where I wouldn't
> remember how something worked [which could be] very em-
> barrassing. By that time I had enough experience in teaching
> that I could bridge that. I could say "Does anyone remember

how this works from last week?" or, "I can't remember this, where are my notes, how does this work?" and then some guy, sometimes, would come up and say "Oh, well, don't you just do this, and this, and this?" So I'd say, "Slowly, let's go through this again." Then I would use that opportunity to draw everyone in. It had the effect that no one felt stupid— maybe me, but no one else. I learned to use that to my advantage—to everyone's advantage. We would all go into the studio and say: "Today we're going to work on this, and let's see how we're going to get through this one." And it actually developed, not so much out of intent, but out of the sense that I knew I was making mistakes all the time in the studio, and that I knew I was sometimes completely forgetful about how something worked. That way the timid women felt free enough to approach me again and again about something. And the men who would sometimes—dangerously so—approach a piece of equipment without knowing anything about it and not daring to ask questions, they would sometimes come and ask questions. [42]

Also, like Susan Frykberg, Hildegard Westerkamp encourages students to work in teams, if they prefer to.

The atmosphere was such that I also said "If you don't feel good in the studio, don't go in there alone, arrange it with someone else, work together," because I know I would sometimes be in the studio for hours by myself not knowing what I was doing and not knowing how to ask someone. [43]

These techniques derive from her own experience of working in the studio, and her conviction that she can develop different ways of working in this environment:

I find I can't work with people who seem to always know what they're doing in the studio and don't explain—assume that I know certain things and assume that I'm familiar with a lot of things. It's very difficult to be with those people. If I've taught people anything, it was just to be humans and not to be afraid of asking questions, and not to get so spaced out in the studio that you actually damage the equipment and yourself—because you get into funny spaces. The studio just won't

do what you want it to do one day and you take it personally—you don't have any experience, it must be you, right? It's
terrible when that happens.[44]

Hildegard Westerkamp's teaching methods address her concern about the industry's predominant focus on technique by
encouraging students to focus on personal associations with the
music that they are creating, as well as learning how to use the
equipment itself:

> What really ended up interesting me was to see what the stu-
> dents were doing with the techniques that I taught them.
> "What are you really trying to say here with this piece, what
> is it that interests you in this?" It's not that everybody always
> has to say something concrete, but if they are deciding to
> work with a sound that they have to be conscious of, well—
> where is this coming from? It's like dreaming, you remember
> the dreams, and think about the dreams and you somehow
> incorporate them into your life. I think it's very similar. Why
> is this sound so interesting and why does it juxtapose so well
> with this sound? Or if you have this sound and that sound,
> have you thought about connecting them somehow? Why does
> this work and why doesn't this work? So you get into musical
> matters and into the nitty gritties of frequency relationships,
> rhythmical relationships, tone color, content, cultural issues,
> sound associations. Through that type of work, you get into
> all those issues that one thinks about when one is doing a
> piece. And in the end the studio itself is indeed just a tool for
> what students want to say, and they get completely involved.[45]

Desiring to alter the unhealthy, body-denying environment of the
studio, Hildegard Westerkamp decided to incorporate sonic
meditations, like those of Pauline Oliveros, into the studio
courses:

> We have a room right beside the studio, and we all lie down
> on the floor doing sonic meditations of various kinds, which
> gives you a chance to breathe, to get to know your voice and
> to experiment. The group really started experimenting with
> their voices. And the techniques that they learned about equal-
> izing and filtering in the studio, mike techniques—they heard

that they could do very similar things with their own voices. So it wasn't just the equipment that was altering their voices or their sounds, but they themselves could alter their voices so that their body became an equalizing and filtering body— changing sound quality, sound colour, rhythms. There was a very interesting interaction going on between the studio techniques, and the body as an instrument, and group work. That was something I hadn't anticipated—and it was fantastic. It changed the nature of the pieces they came up with. [We were finding] a way to work with [technology] that makes sense to incorporate it into one's life and into teaching life, so that it's not such an alien structure any more. I think I'm trying continuously to make this technology work for me because I like working with it.[46]

The effect of this work is to show composers that they do not have to give up contact with their bodies, or their subjectivities, in order to compose. Although Hildegard Westerkamp does not say that this pedagogical technique was specifically devised to contest the vision of technology as masculine, the integration of mind and body does question an implicit division between these two terms that is crucial to the gendering of technology.[47]

Concerns about the electroacoustic studio environment expressed by my consultants have thus been translated into practical strategies in the classroom. Hildegard Westerkamp's integration of sonic meditations with studio work focuses attention on the body in an environment that often denies it. She demonstrates her own humanity, her occasional forgetfulness and ability to make mistakes that define her as someone approachable, as well as technically competent. She encourages students to develop a personal investment in their work, as does Susan Frykberg, who encourages her students to find their expressive and political voices. Susan Frykberg also mentions the importance of demystifying the machine, of making it clear at the outset which actions would be destructive, then encouraging students to play with everything else. This playful approach to sound is part of what made Ann Southam's learning experience a positive one. Using phrases like "sound document" rather than "music", Susan Frykberg intends that students do not feel limited by the association of music with expertise and professionalism. Helen Hall changes classroom dynamics by putting emphasis on learning rather than technical skill, and by working with students individually to allow them release from group pressures. These pedagogical techniques have the potential of altering the gender structure of electroacoustic studio courses.[48]

Access to Equipment: stores and public studios

Outside of the university environment, electroacoustic composers can be less directly involved with institutions on a regular basis. However, composers need to purchase and maintain equipment,. This brings them into contact with music stores, equipment maintenance services, and public studios.

Access to equipment is more of a problem for women than for men. Women generally earn less. This is coupled, in many cases, with increased, or sole-support, parental responsibilities. Many of my consultants mentioned the high cost of equipment, and their wish for the establishment of more public-access studios.[49] Inter/Access is the only public-access electroacoustic studio in Toronto, Canada's largest city. Some composers attempt to buy equipment as a group, for instance, Monique Jean, Pascale Trudel and Lucie Jasmin, who established a studio together in Montréal. They have since disbanded. Most of my consultants purchase some equipment, rent other equipment, and occasionally use public facilities such as university studios, or, in some cases, the CBC studios or the Banff Centre for the Arts. Sarah Peebles notes that she also sometimes receives equipment loans from corporations.

The high cost of electroacoustic equipment means that this is a particularly expensive area of composition to approach as a full-time job. Monique Jean and Pascale Trudel discussed their situation with me:

> It's exhausting, it costs a lot, and it's a recession [1993]. It's
> mad. Pascale works as a chambermaid, and I wait tables.
> There aren't very many guys who do that to pay for their in-
> struments. [Pascale]: But in my case, it's to keep my
> independence. I want nothing to do with the university and its
> funds. [Monique]: It's incredible for Pascale. Her pieces have

been played on the radio, heard in concerts, but each year she has to start again from zero. There is no-one, no organisation behind her to give support. [50]

Gayle Young describes how difficult it was, when she became a mother, to begin thinking of herself as a hobbyist, rather than as a full-time composer:

I finally admitted that composition can never be a [self-sufficient] profession ... especially if you do four pieces a year, working full-time. Four pieces a year earns eight thousand dollars (maybe). When I knew I was going to have a child, I realized I wouldn't be able to indulge in composition, because it didn't pay, and whatever I did with my non-kid time had to pay....This was a very big emotional issue for me. Finally I accepted that it was going to have to be a hobby. It still is an emotional issue in the sense that I wish I could spend more time at it. [51]

Such decisions are made particularly difficult by the fact that, as Marcia Citron says:

[B]eing a composer in the West may be equivalent to being a professional composer. That is, from a practical and ideological standpoint, composition as an activity carries little cultural weight beyond the frame of professionalism. To be a professional composer is to be taken seriously in one's own time and possibly in the future. It involves reputation, authority, and the circulation of a name within culture.[52]

Professionalism, in fact, as interpreted by technological music magazines, is partly reflected in the possession of high-quality equipment, and in the technical skill required to operate it. This imagery is important in the consideration of the structures of music stores, and large public studios. Equipment rentals usually take place in music stores. The sales staff (except cashiers) are male, the other customers are male. The pictures on posters are of men. Wende Bartley told me that in Montréal as well as in Toronto, the initial reaction when she enters music stores is that she does not know what she is doing. Helen Hall concurs:

I remember walking into a store that sells electronic equipment, and saying that I was interested in buying a microphone. They looked at me as if to say: "Do you know what a microphone is?" I ended up asking if I could see a spec sheet, and asking about the frequency response. I had to go over their heads to make the point that I know what I'm doing.... Another time, it must have been three years ago, I was in a music store, and I was renting a sampler for a workshop that I was doing with my class at the theatre school. I hadn't used a sampler in many years. They weren't going to provide the manual, so I asked them if I could xerox it, and there were a few snide remarks, like "Are you sure you're going to be able to figure this out?" and I said "Well I hope so, but I'm not really sure, because the last sampler I used was a Synclavier and that was five years ago." They said: "You used a Synclavier?" and I said "Yeah." I didn't realize that I was saying something that would intimidate them, but I was being honest.[53, 54]

When Carol Ann Weaver had a problem with her synthesizer:

I was never so angered by anybody in the tech world as by one of the people who insulted me abusively on the phone because I could not make one particular thing function on my synthesizer. I ended up taking my whole synthesizer in to him and he discovered that this "E function"[55] had totally killed all the other sounds. So I actually won my point from him but he was trying to make me into the stupidest fool. [56]

These experiences reflect a belief, transmitted through the language and imagery of the technological world, that women do not use technology, and would therefore not know about the equipment. It is difficult for a woman composer to avoid getting caught up in the discourse of technical excellence, because she is constantly in the position of having to prove her ability.

The situation in large public studios like the Canadian Broadcasting Corporation and the Banff Centre is somewhat different. The composer has first to prove right to access through public recognition and publishing. There are salaried technicians on staff to assist composers in their work. But as Hildegard

Westerkamp notes, at times this assistance can become more like insistence:

> My own approach is very radical: With any given piece I like limiting myself to certain techniques with which I compose and am not interested in others at that point. In fact, I get overwhelmed by the many possibilities, it becomes a delicate dance between these two approaches. I have run into situations where someone (most of the time a male technician or composer) will insist on wanting to show me all those possibilities and it takes a lot of effort and assertiveness to get them to stop and work with what I do want to do. In one case I ended up throwing the person out of the studio, because he would not leave me alone and went on and on showing me stuff that I had no use for and could no longer take in. The delicate part of this dance lies on the one hand in not wanting to reject their knowledge and enthusiasm, but on the other hand being clear that this is not the right moment to pursue these possibilities. It would distract me from the compositional process itself.[57]

These are not the only relationships that women composers have with technicians and other colleagues, however. Kathy Kennedy, for instance, describes a very positive experience that she had with members of the Canadian Electroacoustic Community (CEC):

> I did a radio show, called *son d'esprit,* with Claude Schryer, Ned Bouhalassa, Daniel Leduc, all from the CEC, and I got to know that whole gang of people. Now you could say that I'm quite plugged in. And I never ever get any discouragement. I don't sense any struggle, quite frankly. They're so generous with technology, because they themselves are really high-level, high-end electronic guys—I guess they're less concerned with machismo—how many things can you plug in so fast. They're interested in a more interrogatory kind of creative process. So they're just totally supportive of my ideas, generous in giving me information that will help me to get along.[58]

Even in this positive commentary, I note that the composers in question are still differentiated from others who *are* concerned with machismo; "how many things can you plug in so fast" is still a predominant tone in music stores and studios.

Production

After the composition is completed, the next step is performance and broadcasting. This involves contact with the concert hall and/or recording studios. Some of my consultants express their belief that it is still difficult for women to get commissions from performing ensembles, or to have electroacoustic pieces performed in concert. Of seventy eight "Grants for the Commisioning of Canadian Composers" awarded to performing ensembles by the Canada Council between Fall 1992 and summer 1993, only eight were used to commission works by women.[59] During the same period, the Ontario Arts Council gave forty three grants for commissioning of new music, of which seven went to women composers.[60]

Several of the Québec composers say that difficulty getting commissions is one of the reasons that Québec women composers are so active in multi-media work. Pascale Trudel comments "They accept my pieces for concerts, but it's very rare. They take students' pieces often ... just the guys."[61] Claire Piché showed me a publication pamphlet for the SMCQ (Société de Musique Contemporaine de Québec), and told me that in 1992, they had programmed one piece by a woman, out of a total of thirty pieces. Then, in 1993, they had not programmed any. Claire Piché asked the reason for this:

> Then they said to me, "because there aren't any." I said "There aren't any?" How absurd! Do you realize? This is the Society of Contemporary Music in Québec. I don't understand how such (supposedly) open-minded people, only offer to their audience, in two years' programming, one work composed by a woman, and say that it is because there are no women composers in the world. In the world because the 1992 season was entitled "the SMCQ opens up to the world." It's not the world but only half the world. It's false representation. Briefly, I found the situation distressing and their attitude escapes me. [62]

The excuse that "there aren't any proposals by women" was also given to Sarah Peebles by a Toronto concert venue which had at that time very few performances of work by women composers. They then refused two of her proposals, and gave her the least popular evening of the week in response to the third. In Toronto the New Music Concerts programmed an electroacoustic concert in May of 1994, which included works by four composers, all men. The Canadian Electronic Ensemble concert series in Fall of 1994 included works by six composers, all men. However, there are some series that seem more balanced: the October-November 1994 Canadian Music Centre anniversary concerts included pieces by 14 women composers, with both instrumental and electroacoustic works, as compared to 55 men composers in the same concert series.

One way to change the unbalanced concert situation is to organize series that include women composers. Wende Bartley has organized a number of electroacoustic concerts in Toronto that include women and men composers from across Canada. Through her efforts, Hildegard Westerkamp and Kathy Kennedy both visited Toronto in 1993. In addition, music by women is promoted through community radio, on shows such as Sarah Peebles' *The Audible Woman,* and in publications such as *Musicworks,* edited by Gayle Young.[63]

Production Values

Access to performance opportunities is not the only concern, however. In 1992, the Canadian Electroacoustic Community called for submissions to its *Discontact!* project. They produced two compact discs with short electroacoustic pieces by CEC members. One of the pieces recorded was by Gayle Young. But she told me that she had been unsure about submitting the piece herself, and that there were only five submissions by women out of a total of forty three:

The CEC was disappointed—they included all five submissions. There must be some reason that women don't submit. I must admit that I worried when sending my piece in because it's a very low-tech piece. I think of it as low-tech even though it was done with Soundtools, a high-end digital program. I juxtaposed the sounds, but considering what I could have done with them, it's very low-tech. Maybe I'll be embarrassed when it comes out, because it's so low-tech. I've been asked to send tapes to Tellus for release, but I didn't because all of my recordings were made on slightly older equipment. I realize in retrospect that they probably were good enough. It was just my fears that they weren't the very latest, up-to-the-minute recordings, that prevented me from sending them in.[64]

Most calls for submissions for electroacoustic competitions and recording projects ask for copies on DAT (digital audio tape), or reel-to-reel tape. Often they add that "technical quality is a consideration." Again, professionalism interpreted as use of studio-quality equipment discriminates against those whose equipment is older or of lower quality, which seems often to be the case for some of my consultants.[65]

Conferences and Professional Organizations

Even though electroacoustic composers may work alone, conferences give them a chance to meet with other composers, to share ideas, and to listen to others' work. I will discuss briefly two conferences that have taken place in Canada recently. I chose these two gatherings because both are conferences with international participation that consider questions of the nexus of technology and culture such as the relationship of technology and the body and relationships between different art-forms. Neither, however, included sessions on gender and technology. Here is a commentary on the first conference, "Virtual Seminar on the Bioapparatus," held at the Banff Centre for the Arts, October 1991:

> The exclusion of gender issues from these proceedings had several implications: the discussion was taken over by male specialists whose technological expertise appeared to exceed an understanding of the socio-cultural consequences of virtual reality; virtual reality became the focal point of the discussion at the expense of crucial questions such as those concerning subjectivity; and several women felt alienated from the proceedings to the point of leaving the room. In the hallway, the discussion was animated. Many of the respondents felt othered by the world of technology. [66]

At the more recent conference in Toronto in May 1994, "Culture Technologies Convergence," organized by the McLuhan Centre, I attended a concert which included Canadian and European artists and composers. There was one woman composer (Wende Bartley), and six men. Their presentations included music, video, and virtual environments which integrated images and sound. In Wende Bartley's piece, there were three performers: herself, performing on computer, a male guitarist, and a female vocalist. Called *No Boundaries, No Beginning, No End* (1994), it was the second of two pieces based on the work of Emily Carr. The text was derived from Carr's writings, and focused on the connection between her painting style and her intimate relationship with the forest in later life. One other piece, by David Rokeby, included a female dancer in an interactive relationship with sampled sounds.

In the other two performances, all of the active agents (composers, performers, technicians, and artists) were men. Women occurred only as representations: between presentations, the screen behind the stage showed three images: the Art Gallery of Ontario logo, a Mario Brothers cartoon, and a Classical sculpture of a naked woman. One of the virtual environments consisted of Renaissance paintings of naked women, including Venus de Milo. As he voyaged through this landscape, the virtual traveller heard ethereal synthesized music. In another performance, fractal readings of the topography of a mountain were used to determine the pitches of music. As the virtual viewer's perspective on the mountain changed, the order of pitches and the rhythm of the piece also changed. Timbre and amplitude appeared to be unaffected by the viewer's perspective.

In his concluding statements, two days later, Derrick de Kerkhove of the McLuhan Program in Culture and Technology discussed how virtual reality, through its three-dimensionality and its insistence on proprioception[67] and touch, holds out the possibility of reintegrating head and body. Yet the dualistic division of head and body, culture and nature, and man and woman seemed to be enacted within the latter two virtual worlds that I saw and heard. In one, the terrain of the mountain was read and abstracted into discrete pitches by the mind of the composer, as given in instructions to a computer program; in the other, there was a division between the active cultural subject on his virtual trek, and the naked and inert objects of his vision. The virtual traveller in both of these landscapes seemed to be like the mythical [male] hero moving through a [female] landscape. As described by Teresa de Lauretis,

> the hero, the mythical subject, is constructed as human being and as male; he is the active principle of culture, the establisher of distinction, the creator of differences. Female is what is not susceptible to transformation, to life or death; she (it) is an element of plot-space, a topos, a resistance, matrix and matter.[68]

I think that both Wende Bartley and David Rokeby were attempting to represent quite different social relations in their work, in which the subject could be female as well as active (as performer in Rokeby's work, and as both performer and composer in Bartley's). In addition, Wende Bartley's work highlighted the musical interaction of acoustic instruments and the human voice with electronically-processed sound. However, I never heard any speaker at the conference discuss the differences among these approaches. Had either conference included a session on gender and technology, perhaps some of these issues of subjectivity and agency could have been publicly aired.

Professional organizations, as well as conferences, allow composers to maintain contact with others in their field, and to gather information about competitions, gatherings, and publications. The Canadian Electroacoustic Community (CEC) was established relatively recently (in 1986) to facilitate this type of contact for electroacoustic composers in Canada, and provides a welcoming forum for them. No references or qualifications are required for entry. Students as well as working composers are welcomed. Members include those who describe themselves as sound artists or radio artists as well as those who speak of themselves as composers. In addition, some members are not composers, but supporters of the organization through their roles as university professors, or through other associations (Trudi Le Caine, the widow of Canadian electronic music pioneer

Hugh Le Caine, is a patron). The editors of CEC's quarterly magazine, *Contact!*, encourage discussion of a variety of issues, including gender. Their recent recordings, *Discontact!*, (1992), and *Discontact II* (1995) provided recording opportunities for many of the members.

The openness and encouragement for women in Canada's largest organization of electroacoustic composers is important. Yet, as of August 1994, they had only eighteen per cent female membership,[69] perhaps because to join, a composer needs to imagine herself as a member of this community, an electroacoustic musician, which can only happen after struggling through the gates of gendered discourse and institutions.

Opening Up the Gates

In order for the institutional world of electroacoustic music to "adjust its structures to admit [women] and to allow them to live fully to the same extent as artists of the other sex" (Micheline Coulombe Saint-Marcoux, from article head), there is a need for change in educational practices and institutional policies. While programming the work of more women composers at concerts and conferences would provide more role models for student composers, the transformation needs to go much deeper. Feminist pedagogical practices, as used by my consultants, would do much to open up the educational environment of the university studio to a variety of learning styles and compositional approaches. Their teaching shifts attention from an emphasis on technical competence to a conversation of competence and subjectivity, where technical skill is a means of expression, and the body is not ignored. The adoption of studio practices that focus on technology and knowledge sharing would alter the dynamics of electroacoustic culture at the outset of composers' careers.

In order for composers to achieve success in their professional lives, granting agencies, recording studios, and concert organizers will also need to interrogate their assumptions about the meaning of competence in electroacoustic music, the relative importance of production values, and their openness to a variety of approaches to composition. When cultural policies and practices recognize diversity of compositional strategies and working styles as well as the divergent political and economic positions of different men and women, women may then be able to live fully in the world of electroacoustic music.

Appendix A: Student Registration by Gender in Ontario University Electroacoustic Courses 1989-94[70]

University		93-94 W-M[71]	92-93 W-M	91-92 W-M	90-91 W-M	89-90 W-M
Guelph[72] Fall		1-6	2-5	—	—	—
Win.		0-2	0-2	—	—	—
Wilfrid Laurier		1-3	2-6	3-4	—	
Queen's		4-13	1-16	—		—
Toronto		0-7	0-2	—	2-2	1-2
Waterloo		2-9	1-12	3-9	—	—
Western		—	5-2	2-6	—	—
York[73]	2140	7-10	—	1-15	2-16	6-13
	3140	0-6	—	0-7	2-10	0-7
	3120/3450	9-14	7-10			

Andra McCartney gratefully acknowledges the support of the Social Sciences and Humanities Research Council of Canada.

Notes

1. The phrase "Outside in the teaching machine" is one coined by Gayatri Chakravorty Spivak to describe the (im)possible positions of women and people of colour in the educational system (Gayatri Chakravorty Spivak. *Outside in the Teaching Machine*. New York: Routledge, 1993). The term refers to the position of women as both marginalized by the workings of the machine, and privileged within it. I am using it here to refer to the educational system as well as the system of electroacoustic institutions.
2. Marie Thérèse Lefebvre, *La Création Musicale des Femmes au Québec*. (Montréal, Les Editions des Remue-Ménage, 1991), p. 80.

3. Marcia Citron, "Gender, Professionalism and the Musical Canon," *Journal of Musicology* 8.1 (1990), 105-6.
4. The Canadian University Music Society lists 127 composition professors in Canada; nine (or 7 per cent) are women. I counted professors of both instrumental and electroacoustic composition to reach this total.
5. Liz Whitelegg, "Girls in Science Education: Of Rice and Fruit Trees," *Inventing Women: Science, Technology and Gender,* ed. Gill Kirkup and Laurie Smith Keller, (Cambridge: Polity, 1992), pp. 179-80.
6. Pascale Trudel, interview by author, tape recording, Montréal, Québec, November 3, 1993, York University Graduate Programme in Music.
7. This is my translation. For the sake of brevity in this article I have translated all of the quotes from francophone composers. These quotes appear in both English and French in the text of my Master's thesis, "Creating Worlds For My Music to Exist: How Women Composers of Electroacoustic Music Make Place For Their Voices," (York University, Toronto, 1994).
8. Wende Bartley, interview by author, tape recording, Toronto Ontario, February 11, 1993, York University Graduate Programme in Music.
9. This is a small sample, so further research would be needed to ascertain whether the result are part of a wider trend. However, they are consistent with findings in other electronic fields, such as engineering. Although efforts to induce women to consider engineering as a field began with endeavouring to increase the number of female entrants to engineering courses, more recent research has found that registration in upper-level courses, and employment levels, are still low, prompting more efforts to change the way engineering is taught and conceptualized. See Nuala Swords-Isherwood,"Women in British Engineering." *Smothered by Invention,* ed. Wendy Faulkner and Erik Arnold, (London: Pluto, 1985) 72-86; N. Nevitte, R. Gibbins, and P.W. Codding, "The Career Goals of Female Science Students in Canada." *Canadian Journal of Higher Education* 18.1 (1988), 31-48, which found that it was the most able and gifted students who dropped out of the field; for more general commentary on women and education in science and technology, see Status of Women in Canada. *Participation of Girls and Women in Math, Science and Technology.* (Toronto: Authors, 1989); Judy Wajcman. *Feminism Confronts Technology.* (University Park: Pennsylvania State University Press, 1991), especially pages 150-153; Andra McCartney, "The Science and Technology Careers Workshop: Integrating Feminist Approaches in Residential Science Education." *Resources for Feminist Research* 20 nos 1-2 (1991): 50-51; Liz Whitelegg, "Girls in Science Education: Of Rice and Fruit Trees.", 178-187.
10. Pascale Trudel, interview by author.
11. Sherry Turkle and Seymour Papert, "Epistemological Pluralism: Styles and Voices Within the Computer Culture." *Signs* (autumn 1990), 132.
12. Susan Frykberg, interview by author, tape recording, Vancouver, British Columbia, July 1, 1993, York University Graduate Programme in Music.
13. The metaphorical language and imagery of the electroacoustic industry position the electroacoustic composer as an active dominator of sound technology, which is feminized. See, for instance, Andra McCartney "Inventing metaphors and metaphors for invention: women composers' voices in the discourse of

electroacoustic music" *Canadian Music: Issues of Hegemony and Identity,* edited by Beverley Diamond and Robert Witmer (Toronto: Canadian Scholars Press, 1994): 491-502. Phrases such as master controller and slave, kill a track, virgin tape, punch in and punch out, are commonly used. Also, the computer in popular culture is often given a voice that is feminine (as in *Star Trek: The Next Generation*), or feminized (as in the film *2001*).

14. Susan Frykberg, interview by the author.

15. Hildegard Westerkamp, interview by author, tape recording, Toronto, Ontario, April 20, 1993, York University Graduate Programme in Music.

16. Helen Hall, interview by author, tape recording, Montréal Québec, September 17, 1993, York University Graduate Programme in Music.

17. Carol Ann Weaver, interview by author, tape recording, Waterloo, Ontario, November 10, 1993, York University Graduate Programme in Music.

18. Monique Jean, interview by author, tape recording, Montréal Québec, November 3, 1993, York University Graduate Programme in Music.

19. Monique Jean, interview by author.

20. Clair Piché, interview by author, tape recording, Montréal Québec, September 18, 1993, York University Graduate Programme in Music.

21. Monique Jean, interview by author.

22. Sherry Turkle and Seympour Papert, "Epistemological Pluralism", p. 134.

23. Sherry Turkle and Seympour Papert, "Epistemological Pluralism", p. 136.

24. Turkle and Papert's article is an interesting exploration of different styles of programming, drawing on the work of Carol Gilligan and Evelyn Fox Keller, among others. My only concern about it is that, as in Turkle's previous work *The Second Self,* (New York: Simon and Schuster, 1984), they set up a binary distinction. This time it is between *bricoleurs* and planners; the earlier distinction was between hackers and mainstream programmers. In the 1990 article, "Epistemological Pluralism", Turkle and Papert note similarities between the hackers and the *bricoleurs,* without commenting on their differences (approaches to control, for instance). It would seem to me that there may be more than two (or three) styles and voices, and that the differences may be more complex than a rigid distinction between planning and *bricolage.* Another analysis of difference, this time in mathematics education, is provided by Valerie Walkerdine ("Difference, Cognition, and Mathematics Education." *For the Learning of Mathematics* 10.3, (1990): 51-55). She comments that the difference between "abstract" and "concrete" approaches may also be thought of as the difference between symbolic control and practical, material necessity, depending on how privileged the subject is. This more political analysis of difference, however, still depends on a binary distinction. At the same time, although I am wary of the essentializing tendencies of these binary distinctions, I also realize that essentialism sometimes seems politically necessary. Ellen Rooney, in an introduction to an interview with Gayatri Spivak (*Outside in the Teaching Machine.* New York: Routledge, 1993, p. 2) says: "Feminisms return to the problem of essentialism—despite their shared distaste for the mystifications of Woman—because it remains difficult to engage in feminist analysis and politics if not 'as a woman'"). Spivak suggests a *strategic* essentialism (aware as she says it that this is battle terminology), strategic in the sense that it is a consciously chosen

approach rather than a belief.

25. Ann Southam, interview by author, tape recording, Toronto, Ontario; January 5, 1993, York University Graduate Programme in Music.

26. Hildegard Westerkamp, interview by author.

27. Also, Roxanne Turcotte: "I like that 'bricolage' aspect of this music. When I find myself in the studio with all that equipment, all those work tools, I feel somewhat like a painter with all the brushes and the colours that he wants to put on the canvas.... Like the painter, in the studio I feel I touch the music, sculpt it with my hands, my hearing, and my sensations." (Roxanne Turcotte, "La Musique: ou l'éternel conflit entre l'art de s'exprimer et l'art de répondre à un besoin." *Questions de Culture, IQRC* 8, (1985), 86).

28. Monique Jean, interview by author.

29. This sexualized language is not confined to electroacoustic music. Isabelle Panneton, in a general article about composition, relates some remarks that she has heard: "A composer about the work of a colleague: 'that lacks balls'; a male composer to a female composer: 'your work is magnificent, virile, masculine and well-executed!'"(Panneton, Isabelle. "Y-a-t-il une musique virile?" Les Batisseuses de la Cité. Congrès de l'ACFAS. *Les Cahiers Scientifiques* 79 (1993): 241-3). Also, Sarah Peebles remembers hearing similar terminology at university and since. I would argue that when *both* technology and music are sexualized in this way, the effect is intensified.

30. Carol Ann Weaver, interview by author.

31. This approach to electroacoustic music is not confined to Indiana in the 1970s. At a recent conference of the Canadian Electroacoustic Community (Banff, *Convergence,* 1989), a performance of Paul Dolden's *Below the Walls of Jericho* resulted in many of the audience members leaving the auditorium because of the excessive volume levels. One of my consultants told me that she felt her internal organs reacting. In a letter to the editor of *Contact!* magazine regarding this event, Dolden says: "I purposefully try to create an excessive music in which all the sounds, pitches and rhythms implode on themselves, creating a massive musical black hole of non-identity and the potential for what is currently referred to as white beginnings. These ideas are influenced by particle physics and post-modern social theorists.... By contrast, points of aesthetics and social criticism are rarely discussed by the [Canadian Electroacoustic] community because discussions at CEC events tend to be oriented toward pedestrian political issues" (Dolden, Paul. "Echoes," *Contact!* 4.5 (1991), 13).

32. Sarah Peebles, conversation with author, September 1994.

33. Wende Bartley, interview by author.

34. Ann Southam, interview by author.

35. Ibid.

36. Sarah Peebles, interview by author, tape recording, Toronto, Ontario, Februrary 24, 1993, York University Graduate Programme in Music.

37. She later told me that unfortunately none of her subsequent composition professors had this quality (Sarah Peebles: conversation with author, September 1994).

38. Claire Piché, interview with author.
39. Helen Hall, interview by author.
40. Susan Frykberg, interview by author.
41. Ibid.
42. Hildegard Westerkamp, interview by author.
43. Ibid.
44. Ibid.
45. Ibid.
46. Ibid.
47. For a discussion of the mind/body split in electroacoustic music, see Susan McClary, "This Is Not A Story My People Tell: Musical Time and Space According to Laurie Anderson" (Minneapolis: University of Minnesota, 1991), 132-147.
48. A larger study might be able to explore the ways in which these techniques would actually change the educational experience for students. Here, they are offered only as indicators of how women composer/professors work inside the university environment to attempt to bring about change. However, many of the pedagogical techniques mentioned in the last few pages are consistent with feminist pedagogy in other scientific and technological courses. See, for instance, Jean Michel, "Women in Engineering Education." *Studies in Engineering Education* 12, (Paris: UNESCO 1988): 129-132; Valerie Walkerdine. "Difference, Cognition, and Mathematics Education.": 51-55; *Women's Education des Femmes*, 9 (1 & 2), 1991—special issues on women and girls in science; P.K. Jamison, "No Eden Under Glass: A Discussion with Donna Haraway." *Feminist Teacher* 6:2, (1992), 10-15.
49. Location is also a factor in access: almost all of the current members of the Canadian Electroacoustic Community (CEC) live in, or near to, major cities.
50. Monique Jean and Pascale Trudel, interview by author.
51. Gayle Young interview by author, tape recording, Toronto, Ontario, January 13, 1993. York University Graduate Programme in Music.
52. Marcia Citron, *Gender and the Musical Canon.* (Cambridge: Cambridge University Press, 1993.) p. 80.
53. Wende Bartley, interview with author.
54. Recently, in a music store, my gender was questioned directly. According to my journal:
I walk into the rental department, past a small group of customers who are chatting. I catch the phrase "hanging around waiting for the chorus girls" before the speaker stops mid-sentence. Suddenly I become profoundly aware that I am the only woman in the store. I walk over to the manager and ask to rent the Tascam 464 recorder. He gives me a long form to fill out, which asks questions regarding my employment status, among other things. A few minutes later, the manager returns and starts to check over the form. When he gets to "York University" he asks "Are you a teacher or a student?" "Yes," I say, smiling. Another employee looks over and chuckles. "Are you a boy or a girl?" the manager shoots back at me. I stare at him until he squirms. "I am a graduate student," I reply. "And I teach." I am sure that he asked the second question without thinking. But it made me aware that to him, I have to make a choice, teacher/student, boy/girl. And obviously being a girl, I shouldn't be in that place, renting a piece of technical equipment to make music.

55. E! GRey MAttER RespONSE: a computer chip installed in the Yamaha DX7 keyboard to enable it to produce microtones and change sound properties.

56. Carol Ann Weaver, interview by author.

57. Hildegard Westerkamp, conversation with author, August 1994.

58. Kathy Kennedy, interview by author, tape recording, Montréal, Québec, September 17, 1993, York University Graduate Programme in Music.

59. Compare these statistics with those for "B" grants (for junior composers) in Music: fifteen to women, of a total of sixty three in the same period; Short Term grants: twenty eight to women, of a total of seventy one, and Travel grants: five to women, of a total of nineteen. Although these statistics do not represent an even distribution by gender, they are less skewed than the commissioning grants, which performing groups (rather than composers) must apply for. There were only two "A" grants (for senior artists) in Music during this period, both to men (Canada Council Bulletins 39-41, (Ottawa, Ontario: Canada Council, 1992-3)).

60. Ontario Arts Council Grants Listing, (Toronto, Ontario: 1992-93).

61. Pascale Trudel, interview by author.

62. Claire Piché, conversation with author, September 1994.63. See bibliography for a list of electroacoustic works by women recorded by *Musicworks*.

64. Gayle Young, interview by author.

65. There may also be aesthetic censoring in these cases, as described earlier in the section on university courses. Gayle Young hints at this when she says "considering what I could have done, it's very low-tech." Is there an emphasis in electroacoustic competitions on how processed the sound is, on virtuosity with the equipment more than with other considerations? This would be the focus of a further study. Ann Southam also commented that she has felt pressure regarding technical quality "I've worried about that, too. And in the same vein I've worried about "low-tech" compositional techniques in my own work—as if complex processing of musical material by technology or compositional tricks makes good music—or music at all, for that matter!" (conversation with author, August 1994).

66. Francine Dagenais, "Irrationalist Perspectives on Machines of Rational Thought." In *Virtual Seminar on the Bioapparatus,* edited by Catherine Richards and Nell Tenhaaf (Banff: Banff Centre for the Arts, 1991), 115.

67. The reception, by the brain, of signals from muscular movements.

68. Teresa de Lauretis,"Desire in Narrative." *Alice Doesn't:Feminism, Semiotics, Cinema.* (Bloomington: Indiana University Press, 1984), 119.

69. I included in my calculation only working and student composers (twenty eight women, one hundred and twenty eight men).

70. As of spring 1994, I found electroacoustic courses listed in the catalogues of seven Ontario Universities: Guelph, Laurier, Queen's, Waterloo, Western, York, and Toronto. The Guelph courses were cancelled at the end of the 93-94 year due to lack of funding for the area of composition as a whole.

71. Student gender Women-Men.

72. Guelph had two levels of electroacoustic music. The introductory course was held in the Fall term, and the advanced course in the Winter term.

73. York University has an Electronic Media Workshop (classic studio techniques) with two levels: an introductory course, 2140; and advanced, 3140; Songwriting and Repertoire/Creative Applications of MIDI technology is course 3120/3450.

Women Artists' Careers: Public Policy and the Market

Annette Van Den Bosch

The Relationship between Status and Income

The situation of women as artists in a period in which there is significant structural change in career and income possibilities in the arts requires closer examination. Most of the equal opportunity policies of the Australia Council and state art ministries of the 1980s were designed to 'level the playing field'.[1] This concept of equal opportunity can be found in Germaine Greer's *The Obstacle Race*.[2] Analyses of women's art practice and art history that have been written since 1975 have emphasized the ways in which art practice, criticism and art history are structured by sexual difference.[3] Because the concept of equal opportunity has been dominant there has been insufficient examination in arts policy and administration of the relationship between the way in which artistic importance is determined in the artworld, and the income of women artists. The intellectual and legislative structures that have been put in place in the last fifteen years have defined artists as a professional group in contemporary society and these definitions have rarely addressed the question of gender or difference.[4] It needs to be emphasised that if the status of a professional group and average income are directly related, why is the income of women artists less than that of men artists? Furthermore, why are the incomes of artists as a group not commensurable with their educational and professional standing?[5]

All the evidence shows that the art market does not operate as a free market delivering returns to artist-producers but that the art market functions as a financial investment market for collectors of art, of which only a small proportion is by living artists. Art collections also confer social status, and their investment function is established through both social and financial transactions. A recent Australia Council research report on artists has emphasised that the art market price does not reflect the true value of their artwork.

"It follows that the production of art has a social value, whether through initial creation or performance, that will extend beyond the immediate consumers of that art. It also follows that in an economic exchange system based on voluntary exchange markets, the social value of art will not be fully reflected in private transactions. The problem for individual artists is that, since they have to sell their output on the free market, they will finish up being underpaid."[6]

The processes for conferring financial value in the art market are determined by the function of art as investment. The network of relationships that link the artworld and the market now plays a significant part inpublic policy which determines artist education in the university and technical and further education sectors; awards Australia and Canada Council grants to artists, artist-run organizations and art institutions; determines taxation regulations for artists, collectors and donors of works of art, and the financial regulation of dealers' galleries and auction houses; and supports the legislation of contractual relationships between artists, dealers and collectors, including artists' copywright and moral rights. It is also important to recognise that cultural policy now includes the Australian Department of Foreign Affairs and Trade as much as national and local policy objectives. The number of women artists, particularly visual artists, has grown from 37 per cent to 50 per cent of the artist population in Australia over the last ten years.[7] The median income of all artists in 1992-93, (the last year that national figures were available,) was $A20,000 with only about $A5,000 of this derived from the sale of artwork.[8] On average artists work 47 hours a week, of which 25 hours are spent on creative work. Women artists spend about the same amount of time at their primary creative activity as men but they contribute more time to arts-related work such as artists' organisations.[9]

What is most striking about these statistics is thathe income of all Australian artists has dropped 21 percent in the ten year period in which the proportion of women artists in the population has increased.[10] That is, the feminization of the visual arts practice has resulted in a change in status and income for artists' similar to that in other employment sectors where women predominate.

In this chapter I will examine how the relationships in the artworld and the market are structured to devalue women artists practices and why public policy measures have failed to take these relationships into account. In particular, if women artists represent the majority of visual arts and craft practitioners, why do they earn significantly less from both the sale of their art, and their arts-related work, than male artists do?[11] The explanation I will develop is that economic rewards in our society are regarded as a measure of social status, but in the art market they are also identified with the reputation of the artist, and the investment potential of the work. If women's art is not accorded the same artistic value as the dominant masculine practices then the financial value of the work and thus the artists' income must be diminished. Women's art history and feminist art criticism have foregrounded the question of difference in the lives and careers of women and men, and in the subject matter and media of their art. The evidence suggests that these differences still remain the bases of inequity for women artists.

Women Artists Career Patterns

In the last twenty-five years feminist critiques of art history and women's art history have rephrased the question: "Why have there been no great women artists?" to ask what were the conditions under which women made art and craft in different historical periods and under different social constraints.[12] More fundamentally, feminist critics have asked why the hierarchy of genres, and media, in art and craft, have functioned to devalue the practices of women, and to exclude women from the areas of art that have been dominant in art institutions. There have been significant analyses of how collections, attributions and exhibitions in art museums reiify the concept of the 'old master' and

structure sexual difference in the presentation of art to audiences.[13] Despite the increasing numbers of women artists
practicising, the popular ideological conception of the artist,
both historical and contemporary, is male.

Women's involvement in the history of modern art was often
oblique to the male relationships that constituted a group or
movement. Women were involved through their relationships
with male artists and through their pursuit of similar aesthetic
tendencies-although their work was sometimes in other media,
or at a later period, or even in a different cities or countries.[14]
While womens' different forms of participation have often
determined their exclusion from the dominant historical account, there is a significant body of practice by women artists
that is now receiving attention.[15] Women are often recognised by
their peers as significant or serious artists, as participants in
important exhibitions or events, as contributors to debates
about art, but their reputation as artists does not result in the
same level of critical acclaim, private investment or historical
record as their male counterparts. Joan Kerr in *Heritage: the
National Womens' Art Book* has shown that there were always
women artists, but as they always existed in the present as it
were, their work never became the subject of serious collection
or historical study.[16]

> Women are never lost, they are never invisible. Every genera-
> tion says, 'Oh look, we've got some really good women
> [artists] now. At last. Aren't they good, isn't that interesting,
> isn't it lovely that women are doing this?' [But they have] no
> predecessors, no future. Therefore they are always in the
> present. And through that you get the argument that this is
> because their work doesn't last. Well it's because it's not col-
> lected and if it was collected it's in the basement, not put in
> the history books. How do you make something last when it's
> said for one moment "oh how lovely" in newspapers or maga-
> zines of the time but in no way treated as if it belongs to a
> tradition that's worth respecting.[17]

The historical context described by Joan Kerr has been
repeated in the current career pattern of women artists. The

growth in art schools since the 1960s has resulted in unprecedented numbers of women art graduates. Few of those who graduate will become practising artists, fewer still will acquire the reputation that ensures continuous purchase and collection of their work. There is historical evidence of the devaluation of art practices and genres after the entry of large numbers of women which is relevant to the contemporary context.[18] The current situation also reflects the failure of public policy measures put into place since 1984 to redress the inequity between men and women as artists, and as wage earners. I wish to focus on women's unequal returns as artists, but the inequities in women's incomes are similiar in the wider labour market in Australia.

Trends in the international art market that have led to the current situation can be identified. The re-emergence of painting in the early 1980s was intensified by the market emphasis on a small number of artists, or superstars, in order to maximize their investment potential.[19] The speculative art market of the 1980s pushed up prices for blue-chip market leaders and created a situation in which selected contemporary art in the New York and London markets was re-sold at auction for profit, in the year of its purchase from a dealer's gallery.[20] International trends are closely followed by the competetive local market in Australia, and Sydney and Melbourne auction houses began sales of contemporary artists with major reputations. The creation of superstars within the contemporary art market has exacerbated the discrepancies between prices for art, the income of those artists whose work is collected for investment, and the income of the mass of practicing artists.

Visual artists and craftspeople have been more specialized than other artists. Visual artists are predominantly painters, sculptors or printmakers and craftspeople work in ceramics, fibre or jewellery.[21] The specialization that has been characteristic of the visual arts and craft career provides an important insight into the nexus between women's careers and the market.[22] In art, the blue chip market is largely confined to painting. Printmaking and drawing, that is, works on paper, never develop the same price range as painting. Sculpture depends more on commissions. The narrower range of practice by visual artists and craftspeople limits the viability of their income from the open market, especially as the market tends to discriminate on the basis of a masculine model of reputation in order to use art and craft for investment.

The specialisation that is characteristic of the visual artist leads to the necessity to hold multiple jobs. An Australia Council survey found that visual artists and composers were the artists who were most likely to work in arts related jobs in order to make up an income.[23] On average visual artists and crafts artists spend only 50 to 59 per cent of their total working time, respectively, at creative work in their desired occupation, although they would like to spend more of their time.[24] Only 11 per cent of artists spend all of their time at their primary creative activity, and this corresponds directly to the market tendency to concentrate on a restricted number of artists in order to maximise the investment potential of their work.

Women artists are further disadvantaged by the fact that they still assume the principal role in child care in Australian families. In the 1993 study of artists, *But What Do You For a Living?* 52 per cent of women compared with 32 per cent of men were shown to be seriously affected by child care and domestic responsibilities. A larger proportion of women 16 per cent, compared to 4 per cent of men identified domestic factors as the single most important limitation on their careers.[25] In a career structure in which multiple jobs have become a necessity for survival women must be disadvantaged by the value, time and energy that they devote to family relationships.

The same study shows that, despite the time some women artists at particular stages of their lives devote to child care and domestic chores, the time spent on their art work is, on average, the same as that of male artists.[26] The difference is that women artists earn less for both their artworks and other income producing jobs, and there are more women artists at the bottom end of the income scale than men.[27] The empirical data about income provided by Throsby and Thompson re-inforces my study of the price discrepancies in the art market for the work of male and female artists. Further, in their study 36 percent of women artists responded affirmatively to the question of whether they experienced gender bias 'very frequently' or 'some of the time' during their careers.[28] It is important to realize that these findings are significant because due to inexperience or denial it is often difficult for young women, to acknowledge discrimination. Discrimination on the basis of gender is still the main impediment to women artists achieving career success.

Another aspects of the discrepancy between the financial success and career achievement of men and women as artists that demonstrates discrimination are the educational qualifications and achievement levels of women artists. Artists are among the best educated sectors of the population and women artists are better educated than their male counterparts.[29] Women artists' educational levels reverse the profile for the labour market in which men tend to be better educated than women. Yet women artists' higher qualifications are not reflected in their income or career profiles.

The criteria of career achievement defined in the study by Throsby and Thompson was a one-person show at a major gallery and/or a work purchased or commissioned by a major gallery. Although there were more female high achievers, more male artists were acknowledged as achievers than non-achievers, and the highest proportion of female artists were classed as non-achievers.[30] This may have been because of the age of the cohort, that is there were more younger women artists who had not yet reached the definition of career success. It may also be that the late age of professional entry for artists corresponds to the average age for Australian women to have children. Nevertheless, this evidence suggests that the achievements of a small number of high profile women artists which characterised the 1980s and 1990s was used by artistic gatekeepers to disguise discrimination against the majority of women artists. By artistic gatekeepers I mean, dealers, critics, curators and collectors who link the artworld and its market.

Another way to conceptualize the question of differential status and income is from a woman artists' point of view. There is historical and biographical evidence to show that women artists do not have the same benchmarks and definitions of career success as men.[31] Many artists, but particularly women artists, have emphasized their involvement in art, in the work itself, and placed far less emphasis on the process of building a reputation. Women artists have played an important role as catalysts for change in arts practice and in arts organizations over the last twenty years. The consistency of their involvement suggests that they regard innovation and organization as part of their career achievement.[32]

Another difference is that women's art practice often involves diverse media rather than concentrating on the development of one mode such as painting on canvas. For example, the challenge to the dominance of painting in the use of domestic and craft materials was central to the Feminist aesthetic of the 1970s and became influential in post-modernist art practice. Another distinct tendency is for women artists' practice and reputation to be located at the local and regional level and not receive acknowledgement in metropolitan art market centres where artists' reputations are made. Before 1960 Australia had a number of state based art markets in which modernist women artists were quite successful, and there is some evidence, that women are still able to make a living at the regional level.[33]

The evidence of continued gendered discrepancy in income levels for artists, and the question of the definition of reputation and career achievement should be explored much more thoroughly in research and policy analyses in order to develop more equitable processes for women. The model of artistic career currently in use for research and analysis is not complex enough to take into account the inter-relationships between value-laden judgements and practices in the artworld, and the financial rewards and career recognition available to artists.

The complexity of the situation is most apparent in countries such as Australia and Canada because of their inter-relationships with the international art market. The situation for women artists in the nineties should be a particular focus for a number of reasons. First, there is no evidence of significant income gains by women since 1981, despite the fact women artists have been entering the market in large numbers from the end of the 1970s. There is considerable historical evidence to show that they were not represented in dealers galleries and national and state exhibitions, and left out of serious accounts of Australian art in the prior period, the 1950s and 1960s.[34] As the most recent entrants to a market that is characterised by a masculine concept of reputation and career, they have been the most effected by the decline in the market and artists incomes since 1988. The numbers of women earning their whole income from their art and art-related work is far fewer than men. While the group of artists with prominent national and international reputations now includes women, there are still proportionally fewer women than men drawn from a greatly increased number of women in practice. To put it in another way, fewer women are recognised as major artists in Australia at a time when the marjority of artists practicing in the visual arts and crafts are women.

The Value of Women's Art Practice

The reasons for women's lack of financial and career success is the value assigned to their art. Women are far less likely than men to be represented by a dealer, and if they do exhibit with a dealer's gallery, they have fewer one-person shows.[35] Women's work does not have have the same prominence in the National Gallery of Australia or the state art galleries. There are important collections of women artists in many regional galleries but these are often Modernist collections and the acquisition of contemporary women's art is extremely limited in focus.[36] Art criticism written in the major daily newspapers tends to concentrate on major dealer and state gallery exhibitions in which women feature less prominently and less often. Although there are a greater number of specialized art magazines and newspapers in which the coverage of art practice is lively and relevant, reputations are still determined in the nexus of relationships between key dealers, curators, critics, and artists who constitute the artworld and market relationships in Sydney and Melbourne.

Historically, dealers and collectors saw women artists as child-bearers and child-rearers whose years of productive output would be curtailed or disrupted to such an extent that the serious evolution of a body of work would not take place. The concept of continuous production of art in a recognisable style which could be promoted by a dealer and through which the artist could acquire a national/international reputation was essentially a marketing concept. Since artists whose career spans a fifty year period have been predominantly men, the investment potential of their art could be marketed to the collector on the basis of a guarantee derived solely from the sex of the artist. This distinction is too rigid as a considerable number of artists have produced an importantbody of work in a ten year period, (of these Vincent van Gogh is only one of the more obvious examples). At the same time a considerable number of women artists in the twentieth century, such as Georgia O'Keefe, Alice Neel, Meret Oppenheim and Eleanor Fini have had careers which spanned half a century.

Important women artists received recognition in the 1970s as a result of the worldwide women's art movement. Many of these women had a long history of practice for which they had never been given a retrospective in a public gallery. The Grace Cossington Smith Retrospective at the Art Gallery of New South Wales in 1974, for example, was one of the exhibitions held in the 1970s to redress the balance. There are deeply rooted ideologies operating in the perception of the value of women's art and in recognizing the older woman artist, in particular. Women artists rarely receive consistent critical attention and market exposure. An artists' practice that is characterised by diverse media and activities, as many women's careers are, does not fit the modernist concept of innovation in the development of a style or aesthetic tendency that still dominates institutional and critical perceptions.

Critiques of modernism have emphasized the ways in which a dominant European and North American culture appropriated non-European indigenous and colonized cultures as sources of imagery and formal innovation. Women artists',including indigenous women artists' representations of different social experiences and perceptions on the other hand were assigned to a feminine aesthetic that conferred less value and were often minimised or ignored. Women's art practice in the 1970s was one of the most important discourses in the emergence of a postmodern aesthetic. Through performance and conceptual art forms women artists questioned the representation of the nude and gender stereotypes in art, and consciously sought to construct a new aesthetic. Identity and sexuality were repositioned as representations of living bodies marked by sex, class, and race.

A new understanding that the construction of difference through cultural representation had social effects and meanings began to influence many artists. In the 1970s and 1980s new forms and media were introduced to allow new modes of perception. Women artists, supported by increased historical research, reintroduced domestic materials and imagery, appropriated and reinterpreted conventional representations and used sources and practices from artistic movements as diverse as still life, Surrealism and Fluxus to find forms appropriate to their own experience. Women artists were more active in artists organisations, such as the Art Workers' Union and in artist run spaces, and in teaching, than in any previous period, and these activities contributed to their art practices. New demands were addressed to art schools, dealers and public galleries to recognise their work andto remove impediments to the development of women artists' careers. The initial impulse of the 1970s and early 1980s had a momentum that produced some changes but that moment has now passed and new initiatives are necessary if the careers of the marjority of women artists are going to continue to improve.

Young women artists need to know that there is a considerable body of art by women artists, since theory and practice in art schools and universities do not provide role models. young artists need to identify the different concerns and attitudes of artists' who are women. Aesthetic concerns have been debated by women for over twenty-five years; strategies for intervention in the dominant culture and ways of resisting appropriation of women's art have been discussed, tried, and shed, yet many younger artists are not familiar with them.[37] One of the reasons for the lack of any sustained teaching of women's history and theory is that the senior staff in art schools are predominantly older men. Far removed from their own education, and from the current state of the arts, they place less value on the importance of the curricula than younger artists do. Their attitudes were formed prior to the 1970s and they pay lip service to the need for change. Incidentally, one reason that women earn far less art-related income than men is that they are far less likely to have full-time teaching employment than men. This does mean that they have less influence on the education of artists and the development of their careers.

Can women's art practice be given a greater aesthetic and cultural value than it currently has? This depends on more focused critical reception, a wider tolerance of women's interest in the personal and in relationships rather than in formal stylistic concerns, and an acceptance of their representation of social/ political subjects from a gendered perspective. It involves a recognition that women's interest in the repetitious craft of making the object, or recording the experience, is part of a way of knowing and seeing that is different. Women understand the pose, the role-play, and the masquerade, and incorporate these aspects of their experience as much as their perceptions of bodies and bodily processes. Contemporary writing on women as subjects who represent their desires, emphasizes their use of multiplicity rather than unity, and questions the binary opposition between mind and body, that separates the experience of living in the body from its representation. Women's practice can be read as, and often, as critical of dominant masculine representations. Women in the arts have often been a catalyst for community relationships and social change developing their creativity in relation to others through community arts. Women's art sometimes employs aesthetic modes and practices that draw on women's culture rather than contemporary artworld concerns, and should not be de-valued or excluded as a result.

The Challenge for Policy-Makers

The visual and community arts are the major areas where women experience gender discrimination in the arts, often as a bias against their professional work which is never clearly articulated.[38] This discrimination has not changed despite greater awareness and increased equity provisions. It is time to debate openly not only equity issues in relation to women but the values assigned to women's art practice and arts-related work, and the need for more effective career support mechanisms.

The rethinking of arts policy in relation to gender has never been a more pressing requirement. Cultural policy in Australia is changing more significantly than in any period since the formation of the Australia Council for the Arts in 1967. The formation of a public sector national arts organisation responsible for policy and funding of the arts was a logical development of the growth in private art investment and audiences in the 1960s. It represented the final phase of a concept of a public culture that was synonmous with the modern nation state. Two foundational principles of the Australia Council articulated in 1972, were arms-length funding and peer assessment of grants. The 1994 Australian Labor government policy document *Creative Nation* marked another significant shift in arts policy, although the full recommendations of this document may not be implemented due to a change in the Federal Government at the 1996 elections.[39] One recommendation that was put into effect was the replacement of the specialised arts boards ofpractitioners who previously assessed grants, making policy in the process of establishing criteria and priorities, by arts funds assessed by peer assessors detached from the policy process. This will have an impact on women who form the marjority of individual artists, especially as the Australia Council has had a major budget reduction.

The other change introduced by *Creative Nation*, the establishment of major arts organisations board, (MOB,) for predominantly performing arts organisations, has been reinforced by the incoming federal Liberal-National Party Coalition Government who have separated the funding of major national companies from the Australia Council. At the same time, the Australia Foundation, modeled on the National Endowment for the Humanities in the United States has been established to develop cultural policy and funding in relation to the private sector, and to separate this aspect of policy from the Australia Council. The effects of changes by both federal governments have been intensified by a 12 per cent cut in funding to the Australia Council in the 1996 federal budget.

Creative Nation emphasized the potential of the new technologies and multi-media industries for generating income and especially, export income in the arts. For example:

> A major impediment to the development of a successful multi-media industry is insufficient dialogue and interaction between the creative and software communities. For too long these communities have been travelling along parallel paths not exploiting obvious synergies. It is imperative therefore, that we accelerate integration between them and foster links between industry and the cultural community, including film-makers, broadcasters, galleries, museums and educational institutions. Through these links, we will better develop and commercialise interactive multi-media products and services.[40]

However, there is ample evidence that women do not partici-pate in the computer and multi-media industries to the same extent as men. Since the focus of both *Creative Nation* and many of the multi-media production industries is global rather than local or community based, there is cause for concern that the practices and locations that characterize the work of women artists will be further devalued.

The new policy direction was not supported by adequate Federal funds for the retraining of older artists. Since the mid 1980s there has been a strong tendency to shift the emphasis from studio-based courses in the fine arts to design courses, including computer and digital forms of graphic design which are conceived as more vocational that is, industry oriented-than fine arts practice. However, there is still a role for the visual artist as a self-employed entrepreneur, and the evidence for this is that during a period of economic downturn enrolment in art schools has increased.

Current arts policy of both major Australian political parties emphasizes technological delivery systems, especially broadband services and digitalisation, and the marketing of the arts and media. Patricia Gilliard and Andra McCartney have written chapters in this book which show the ways in which women have attempted to negotiate their position in relation to the new technologies. However, the assumption that the arts can become self supporting and that the private sector or market will fund the arts does not take into account the need for a critical creative culture for local, or even national, audiences. The models of creative arts practice in *Creative Nation* and the associated report, *Mapping the Visual Arts and Crafts* suggest that the policy agenda for the export of the visual arts has not been thought through in relation to current models of an artists' career, and that this agenda does not take gender and cultural difference into account. [41] The second report acknowledged that the industry model may not be appropriate for visual artists and craftspersons for whom philosophic, social and critical motives are often more important than economic outcomes.[42]

Mapping the Visual Arts and Crafts is most useful in its analysis of vocational education and training needs and it would be hoped that the Coalition Government would implement some of its recommendations. The report recommended that vocational education and training in new technologies, including computer aided design (CAD), interactive media, and CD-ROM, should be determined by questions of access and equity. Women as a group, Aboriginal and Torres Strait Islander people, and regionally-based artists should be given priority in more flexible training programs that are matched by access to new technologies for artists working outside institutions and the major metropolitan centres. [43]

Arts Training Australia recognised a major pattern in the career of visual artists resulting from the nexus between education, arts policy and the market, is that many encounter problems in mid-career. As the art market tends to promote emerging artists, and artists whose reputation and work will attract collectors' buying for investment, this militates against the majority of artists halfway through their career. The report identified the need for specialist skill training for mid-career practitioners to enable them to work collaboratively in design or new hybrid art forms.[44] It recommended project management training for artists in the public art field, resulting from the one per cent for art requirement for public buildings. Most importantly, it identified the need for small business skills, including finance, marketing, law, and industrial relations for artists. This is particularly relevant as many women responded to the structural unemployment of the 1980s and 1990s by becoming self-employed and by establishing small businesses.

Gender is a Policy Issue

What is distinctive about the new policy agendas is that the politics of difference that characterised the 1970s and early 1980s have been eclipsed. The questions of gender, ethnic, and cultural difference have been replaced by the old agenda of national identity. The visual arts and crafts are a significant and growing sector of cultural activity in Australia.[45] The majority of artists and the audience are women.[46] The question of gender should be a structuring principle for any arts policy in the 1990s. Instead, its exclusion from the policy agendas of both major parties represents a denial of the questions of equity and difference which masks the recognition that equity has not been achieved, and shifts the concept of culture into a largely masculinised domain.

> "What seems clear is that there is a continuing economic disadvantage suffered by women artists as a group compared with their male counterparts. The principle of equal pay for equal work regardless of gender does not appear to operate in arts markets, notwithstanding difficulties of comparison in terms of types or quality of work and other considerations."[47]
> *NAVA Newsletter*

New cultural policies and administrative programs will not be successful unless they incorporate women artists into new media and arts practices on a more equitable basis. If clear policies are not put in place to reposition women through education, training, grants and marketing of their work then the new technologies in the cultural industries will exacerbate current inequities in career recognition and financial returns for women artists.

Notes

1. Australia Council, *Women in the Arts: a strategy for action*, (Sydney: 1984) and *Women in the Arts Further Strategies for Action* (Sydney: 1988).

2. G. Greer, *The Obstacle Race: the fortunes of women artists and their work* (New York: Farrar, Straus, Giraux, 1979)

3. G. Pollock, *Vision and Difference; Femininity, Feminism and the Histories of Art* (London: Routledge 1988) especially chapters 1, 2 and 3.

4. Canadian Advisory Committee on the Status of the Artist, A Proposed Act on the Professional Status of the Artist later called the Canadian Artists' Code, (Ottawa, 1988).

5. D. Throsby, and B. Thompson, *But What Do You Do For A Living? A New Economic Study of Australian Artists,* frontispiece, (Sydney: Australia Council 1994)

6. Ibid, p.54.

7. Ibid, p.10 table 3 figure 1; and p.13 table 7.

8. Ibid, p.46 table 27.

9. Ibid, p.45.

10. Ibid, p.30 table 20 and p.31 table 21.

11. Ibid, p.46 table 27.

12. L. Nochlin, "Why Have There Been No Great Women Artists?" in *Women, Art and Power and Other Essays* (New York: Harper & Row, 1988) and R. Parker, and G. Pollock, *Old Mistresses: Women, Art and Ideology* (London: Routledge and Kegan Paul, 1981) chapters 1 and 5.

13. T. Gouma-Peterson, and P. Mathews, "The Feminist Critique of Art History," *Art Bulletin* 69 (September, 1987): 326-57; and L. Nead, "Feminism, Art History and Cultural Politics," in A.L. Rees, and Borzello, *The New Art History* (London: Camden Press: 1987), N. Broude, M. Garrard, T. Gouma-Petersen, and P. Mathews, "An Exchange on the Feminist Critique of Art History," *Art Bulletin* 71 (March 1989), 124-7.

14. W. Chadwick, *Women Artists and the Surrealist Movement* (London: Thames and Hudson, 1985) and W. Chadwick, and I. Cortivron, (eds.) *Significant Others: Creativity and Intimate Partnership* (London: Thames and Hudson, 1993).

15. P. Charmonte, *Women Artists in the United States: A Selective Bibliography and Resource Guide on the Fine and Decorative Arts 1750-1986* (Boston Mass.: G.K. Hall, 1990) and P. Dunford, *A Biographical Dictionary of Women Artists in Europe and America Since 1850* (New York and London: Harvester Wheatsheaf, 1990).

16. Kerr, J. (ed.) *Heritage: the National Women's Art Book* (Sydney: Allen and Unwin, 1994).

17. Joan Kerr quoted by Anne Loxley, "' Girls' Night Out," *Sydney Morning Herald* February 18, 1995.

18. R. Parker and G. Pollock, *Old Mistresses,* chapters 1 and 2. The best examples are the embroiderers' guilds in the fourteenth and fifteenth century and still life painting in the nineteenth century.

19. Van den Bosch, A.Y., "What is a good reputation worth? Changing Definitions of the Artist in Australia" *Art and Australia* 30 no. 3 March 1993, 355-63

20. Unpublished research by the author.

21. D. Throsby, and B. Thompson, *The Artist At Work: some further results from the 1988 survey of individual artists* (Sydney: Australia Council, 1995).

22. Ibid pp 5-6 tables 3 and 4,

23. Ibid p.4 table 2

24. D. Throsby, and B. Thompson, *But What Do You Do For a Living?* p.21, table 13

25. Ibid, p.47

26. Ibid, p.45

27. Ibid, appendix 1 tables 9.2 and 9.3

28. Ibid, appendix 1 table 9.4

29. Ibid, p.13 table 7

30. D. Throsby, and B. Thompson, *The Artist At Work* p.18 table 9

31. W. Chadwick, and I. Cortivron, (eds.) *Significant Others,* and in Australia through catalogue essays for retrospective exhibitions and monographs on women artists such as: J. Burke, *Joy Hester* (Melbourne: Greenhouse, 1983) , S. Kirby, *Sightlines: Womens' Art and Feminist Perspectives in Australia* (Roseville: Craftsman House, 1992); and H. Kolenberg, *Edith Holmes and Dorothy Stoner: Two Retrospectives* (Hobart: Tasmanian Museum and Art Gallery, 1983)

32. For example, K. Brown,and J. Aquino, *Review of Visual Arts Boards Programs of Assistance for Contemporary Art Spaces*, (Sydney: Australia Council ,1985); and K. Brown, *Artist-Run-Spaces Research Report,* (Sydney: Visual Arts Board Australia Council, 1987) also women have had leadership positions in the Artworkers' Union, the National Association of Visual Artists (NAVA), in film-makers' co-operatives and numerous other arts organizations.

33. G. Swanson and P. Wise 'Industry Profiling for Cultural Development," Paper delivered at the conference *Cultural Policy: State of the Art* (Brisbane: Griffith University, 1995)

34. K. Vernon, "The Impact of the Womens' Movement in the Commercial Galleries in Sydney,"*New South Wales Women and Arts Festival Visual Arts Seminar Papers*, (Sydney: 1982), pp.54-87; which also included: A.Y. Van den Bosch, "Production and Reproduction: Women, Work and Art in the 1970s and 1980s," pp. 33-46. My research indicated that the representation of women artists in national and international exhibitions in the 1950s, 1960s and early 1970s was the lowest for the period since 1901.

35. C. Nemser, *Art Talk: Interviews with Twelve Women Artists,* (New York: Scribner, 1975); for Australian sources see footnote 31.

36. Kerr, J. *Heritage: the National Womens' Art Book* (Sydney: Allen and Unwin 1994); and Burke, J. *Australian Women Artists 1850-1950* (Melbourne: Green-house, 1975) have documented the earlier period. The forthcoming publication, Kerr, J. (ed.) *Past, Present* (Roseville: Art and Australia Press, 1997) discusses exhibitions of womens' art held in 1994-1995 to commemorate the two decades since International Women's Year.

37. *Lip* and *Artnetwork* were influential journals in the 1970s and early 1980s. Exhibitions which have been central to the development of a feminist aesthetic

such as *The Lovely Motherhood Show*, 1977, the *NSW Women and Arts Festival Exhibitions, 1982, Heartland,* 1986, and *Dissonance,* 1991, have not been included in mainstream accounts of Australian art history.

38. D. Throsby, and B. Thompson, *But What Do You Do For a Living?* pp. 46-47 and appendix 1 table 7.5.

39. Department of Communication and the Arts, *Creative Nation: Commonwealth Cultural Policy,* (Canberra: 1994).

40. Ibid, p. 60

41. Arts Training Australia, *Mapping the Visual Arts and Crafts* (Sydney: Arts Training Australia and the Australian National Training Authority, 1995).

42. Ibid, p.32

43. Ibid, p.62

44. Ibid, pp.60-63

45. Ibid p.11 and section 3 which deals with both the Monash Model on which economic growth indicators are based and critical analyses of the model by Hans Hoegh Guldberg, pp.81-100; also see Guldberg, H.H. *Artburst! Growth in arts demand and supply over two decades,* (Sydney: Australia Council for the Arts 1992), p.5 and pp.37-41.

46. *Artburst!* p.2 Participation Rates in art gallery visits by gender 1990-1991 Australian Bureau of Statistics also see; Cultural Ministers' Council Statistical Advisory Group, *The National Culture Leisure Industry Statistical Framework, 1990,* Canberra: Australian Government Publishing Service 1990.

47. *National Association for the Visual Arts Newsletter* (Sydney: NAVA, March 1995) p.1.

Cultural Policy as a Technology of Gender

Alison Beale

Cultural policy in Canada, as in Australia, can be seen as having multiple objectives. These have evolved over time within our histories as settler colonies of France and Britain and as economic satellites of greater powers. Cultural policy in Canada has addressed first and foremost the *relationships* between the peoples of Canada and their governments. Firstly, it has taken the form of legislation regarding human rights, linguistic and religious rights, freedom of expression, censorship, and immigration and social policies. In the case of Quebec within Canada, and in the recent recognition of Aboriginal territorial sovereignty in Nunavut (North West Territories) the divisions of power in these matters between federal and provincial governments are an important part of the picture. Secondly, cultural policy has been concerned with education, the media, and the arts. While the interest of government in influencing the ongoing process of cultural self-definition is part of the rationale for attention to these areas, private economic interests, demands on the welfare state and state developmentalism have all created pressure for the development of policy instruments in these fields since the beginning of this century. Finally, in the last fifteen years, cultural policy has become closely linked to the imperatives of foreign trade and economic competitiveness. As we suggested in the introduction, this is not so much a new departure as one for which the historic congruence of discourses about the role of government, citizenship, economic development and the political economy of culture has been preparing us for some time.

To explore the ways in which policy has acted to recognize, shape, resist, and generally interact with the meanings of culture that are formulated in everyday life, as well as to perform its more generally understood job of setting some of the legal, economic and institutional boundaries in which these meanings will be made, this book, and this essay in particular, make use of a concept of gender.

Technologies of Gender

One of the contributions of feminist theory over the last twenty years has been to foreground the class and gender status of the "universal" bourgeois European citizen, he who is the subject of the social and natural forces studied in the various disciplines of the post-Enlightenment, academy and who is the enfranchised sovereign subject in liberal democracy. This challenge has meant more than pressing for the inclusion of women as political subhjects, and as bodies, in philosophy, science and politics, and more even than drawing attention to the invisible private sphere of reproduction, and the un-or underwaged labour of women in the economic and political structures of capitalist democracy. A concept of gender has made it possible to see how women and men are disciplined into their social roles, including their sexuality, by an array of practices that range from the most intimate relationships to the structures of government and the international economy.

Because the concept recognizes the mutual influences of all these facets of our social lives, gender therefore brings up the issue of the distinctions between the public and private spheres that are used both colloquially and in research. For example, a concept of gender can help us deconstruct the role that Victorian middle class femininity played in making women of this class so desirable to authorities in socially and sexually transgressive settler societies where public/private distinctions were weakened, and we can imagine why immigration and education measures may have reasserted certain features of the gender system such as the gentility and "civilizing" influence of middle class women in relation to children and the lower classes. With such examples in mind, the question for each of us becomes how well we can understand the practices that we study—the economy, politics, cultural policy, regulation—if we fail to question the artificial boundaries of these activities and the silences around gender in relation to them. And finally, for feminists, gender is about power, since it operates not as a binary scheme of classification into opposites, but as a hierarchy, depending on the presence or absence of authority, legitimacy, and personhood.

Gender works not only through men and women but also through the classification of our activities and the attribution of worth and significance to those activities. In a discussion of cultural policy issues it is important to keep in mind the gender hierarchy which operates when, for example, the cultural productions of women or their contributions to knowledge are less valued according to the various measures of status and economic recognition our societies use. In some areas of the arts, in service industries, in teaching, and in health care, to take only the most obvious examples, both men and women may find themselves in "female" spheres, with an accompanying set of economic and symbolic consequences. The gendering of such spheres varies from culture to culture even within the framework of patriarchy and the capitalist economy, and it is in part from cross-cultural comparisons that a concept of gender has developed.

There is a dimension to gender which is especially important for cultural policy, and which makes cultural policy significant to the gender system. Gender is artifice; it is socially produced, and it is constantly constructed and reconstructed in all of our symbolic systems-from economic value and its representations, to the meanings of bodies, to our languages, and to the specialist discourses and forms of the arts and knowledge. Cultural policy, therefore, must be seen as doing much more than *reflecting* a gender hierarchy. Cultural policy is an important case because it concerns the explicit enunciation of relations between groups in society and thus in turn affects the kinds of support and recognition that discourses and symbolic constructions *of gender* will receive. Policy is an agent of gender, not merely its reflection.

The feminist cultural theorist Teresa De Lauretis introduced the concept of the technology of gender ten years ago in a book of the same name. In studies of literature, film and semiotics, she looked at how gender "both as representation and as self-representation, is the product of various social technologies, such as cinema, and of institutionalized discourses, epistemologies, and critical practices, as well as practices of daily life."[1] Her work, she explained, expanded on earlier feminist theorizing in order to break down the archetypes of "female" and "male," and pushed for an understanding of how the social subject understands herself, subjectively and socially, as a gendered being. Along with other cultural theorists, especially those like herself who have studied the reception of Hollywood cinema by women, she was interested in how we internalize, resist, and take pleasure in the dominant cultural messages about sex and gender. An important theoretical starting point was the divided and self-surveying female subject, who is placed in a literally impossible position by the universalist discourses of science, which deny the female, and a visual culture in which bourgeois spectatorship (especially of the female body) is dominant. This position *is* impossible but it is also the position that women occupy: it is not a mirror or opposite of men's experience. In the everyday cultural experiences of watching television or filling in a form, the gendered subject also experiences differences *within* herself in relation to her race, class and her sexual relationships and again is "not so much divided as contradicted."[2] For feminist theory and for the analysis of policy it is important that De Lauretis takes the contradictions within the subject as an opportunity for critics, creative artists and audiences to bring contradictions to consciousness and to create new ways of seeing, new knowledge, and new experience.

"A feminist theory of the state has barely been imagined..." [3]

Contemporary feminists from a wide range of political practices and academic interests have attempted to create some ground for intervention in "technologies of gender" by treating them as public policy issues. That is, they have sought responses from the state and the justice system, and have tried to achieve cultural changes,which may also require state support at some level. This confronts feminists with the difficult tasks of avoiding cross-cultural and transhistorical assumptions about the meaning of given social practices, and of dealing with political and juridical systems which according to some feminist analyses embody male power.

Interestingly, one set of practices which is recognized, or at least treated by some feminists as both a technology of gender and a public policy issue is transgressive sexual practice (most commonly any mercenary sex) and the commerce in certain sexual representations, that is, prostitution and pornography, and the related question of censorship. Prostitution has long been understood to have an important role in traditional societies where romantic marriage was not the norm, and where "free" women were part of social worlds (courts, salons, taverns) in which the domestic relations of the sexes did not dominate their interaction. But a functionalist analysis of prostitution in relation to class, marriage and property does not deal with what Laurie Shrage, for example, typically defines as the real issue underlying cultural convictions about the power relations between men and women that are reinforced by this practice. The ideology of women's inferiority, rather than prostitution itself, is the object of her ethical critique. She believes that "feminists have legitimate reasons to politically oppose prostitution," because it is supported by "pernicious gender asymmetries in many domains of our social life."[4] But, "prostitution needs no unique remedy, legal or otherwise; it will be remedied as feminists make progress in altering patterns of belief and practice that oppress women in all aspects of their lives."[5]

It may be difficult to reconcile such a critical but non-interventionist position with the many efforts to use the justice system instead of legislation as a way of dealing with commercial sex and its communication. Some feminists have joined with activists in communities affected by prostitution to use the police and courts to make prostitution, which is legal in Canada, more difficult for its consumers. They have fought for changes to the rules of evidence to permit the domestic prosecution of Canadian or Australian sex tourists to Thailand; they argue that "dates" be as harassed as prostitutes have been through the application of existing anti-solicitation laws; and they ask for more police time to be spent on building prosecution cases against pimps and men who have sex with minors. For Catharine MacKinnon, these strategies, and others directed at the control and censorship of pornography, are an important challenge to the law itself. Since pornography and prostitution do not merely reflect or represent ideas about inequality, but are among the agents of this ideology and are themselves practices structured in gender inequality, the law reinforces a natural injustice when it claims to treat all persons, or categories of persons, as equals in adjudicating their rights to trade in or communicate about sex. Since these persons are not equals before transactions begin, even-handedness (were it practiced by the police and courts) would not be sufficient to rebalance the situation. MacKinnon makes the strong case that this confrontation with the law is not about a "unique remedy" for prostitution, but is about the law as a gendered practice.[6]

I have chosen to start with a difficult and divisive area of concern for feminists, one frequently raised as a set of public policy issues, and recognizable in mainstream society as gendered issues, in other words, as connected to technologies of gender. I have made this choice because there is no clear consensus among either feminists or in society at large in either Canada or Australia that prostitution is itself immoral or harmful when engaged in by consenting adults, or that pornography should be censored. What I believe is important to note about these practices is that they have never been lodged within the public policy apparatuses of the welfare state as securely as have other areas of gender relations. They have been managed by the law and the market. As the welfare state is unravelled, a situation I discuss below, more and more issues of concern to women will be left to the market, as well as to the law. Before going on to look at the state, I will therefore briefly consider the law and the market.

Both Shrage and MacKinnon identify underlying attitudes and the gender hierarchy as the problem and both identify cultural change as desirable and necessary in changing these practices. They insist that we see the law itself as a cultural artefact influenced by gender inequalities, but MacKinnon goes further with this analysis:

...the place of gender in state power is not limited to government, nor is the rule of law limited to the police and courts...State power, embodied in law, exists throughout society as male power at the same time as the power of men over women throughout society is organized as the power of the state.[7]

One might argue that this totalising cross-identification of state power with male power denies the possibility of instances where the reach of the gender hierarchy is incomplete, and where a "feminist jurispridence," for example, might be attempted. More problematically, such an analysis forgoes a substantive assessment of the law in relation to women's inequality, for an assessment that is a-historical. This issue important here, because of the role that the law has come to play in the modern state.

The growth of both the public administrative functions of the state, and the law in the second half of this century, has not merely been parallel, but interconnected and transformative of both systems. Their growth can be measured on the one hand in terms of the numbers of departments and agencies of government, or government spending as a percentage of gross national expenditure;[8] and on the other in terms of the number of legal cases required in a federal system in which not only laws, but the jurisdiction of regulatory agencies and of the provinces versus the federal government must be adjudicated by the courts.[9] In fact there has been an exponential growth in the use of the law to govern Canadian society. The high water mark of this growth may have been the Canadian Charter of Rights and Freedoms (1988) which limits the sovereignty of Parliament, guaranteeing "specified rights and freedoms [to individuals] against interference by either level of government."[10] The Charter has been controversial, since it can be used to challenge equity measures. It has also been called upon to resolve conflicts between the many forms of collective rights in Canada—an important foundation of our cultural policies—and individual and property rights.[11]

This growth of the law, and particularly of the law in relation to the state can be considered in two ways. Legal historians, and political theorists such as Claus Offe, observe that the law in

Western societies has fulfilled an increasing role in the administration of proliferating public corporations and agencies. In
Canada, as I have noted, this burden is added to by the role of
superior courts in determining jurisdiction. The net result is that
law itself is less concerned with justice than administration.

There has therefore been controversy as to whether, in taking
on a public administrative function, the law has lost its independence from politics, or whether, as is the debate in Canada,
Parliament has lost powers to the Supreme Court. A third
possibility, that the law becomes more powerful alongside the
state, while the sovereignty of the citizen is diminished, is one we
must consider when the recent history of Canada, as of most
capitalist democracies, shows a growth of the welfare state and
state apparatuses to the 1970s, followed by a period in which the
welfare state is dismantled, and responsibilities, without any
reciprocal return of political authority, are handed back to the
citizenry, especially women.

In order to account for both tendencies-a move towards state
developmentalism and a law increasingly concerned with administration, and towards a diminution of the sovereignty of Parliament in favour of a Supreme Court with the authority to distribute differential rights-we need to look at the relationship of the
state to the international economy after World War II. As Janine
Brodie explains, since the 1970s nation-states such as Canada
have turned away from promoting domestic welfare and securing the national economy against exterior economic fluctua-
tions, to searching for a "new logic of development and complementary political forms."[12] This restructuring process is driven
by the centralization and concentration of capital, the globalization of markets and the internationalization of the division of
labour. The economic impacts of this process on women, direct
and indirect, have been disproportionate, and have involved not
only job losses, but the reduction of social welfare measures,
thereby adding to women's work:

> [There is]a fundamental redrawing of the familiar boundaries
> between the national and international, the state and the
> economy, and the so-called 'public' and 'private.' This realign-
> ment in turn undermines both the assumptions and sites of

contemporary feminist politics and invites new thinking about the boundaries of the political.[13]

We may begin to "imagine" here a feminist theory of the state. Using an historical analysis of capital accumulation and the Fordist mode of regulation, in order to account for the introduction by Western states of welfare and protectionist measures, work such as Brodie's considers the gendered consequences of these measures and of their recent dismantling. There are two implications in particular that are significant to a consideration of women and cultural policies.

Within classic liberalism, as Brodie notes, women's political struggle consisted of attempting to gain full citizenship, to become members of the public rather than of the private domestic sphere. As other feminist theorists have observed, the separation of these spheres had been not incidental, but fundamental to the concept of the (male) citizen as an agent freed from domestic ties and labour in order to take part in the deliberative forums of bourgeois society.[14] The Welfare State was itself in part a consequence of the struggle to shift the gender-linked boundaries of public and private, and through welfare and legislation affecting the right of women to participate in paid labour and in politics, it shifted these boundaries even further. Interpretations of these shifts are at the heart of feminist ambivalence about the welfare state, however. As Brodie says, "There is a strong body of feminist thought...which interprets the development of the welfare state as merely a transition from 'private' to 'public' or state patriarchy."[15] An alternative perspective is that the politicization of the private sphere, a focus of the women's movement since the 1960s, was aided by the welfare state through the provision of mechanisms to which women could address their demands. This view acknowledges that the representative structures and resources of the women's movement (such as legal reform and academic research) were supported by the welfare state, but argues that since they have been able to transform politics and to build alliances on issues beyond the welfare system they have transcended its patriarchal limitations.[16]

Under global restructuring, "reprivatization discourse" concentrates on economic efficiencies and the self-reliance of the individual and the family. Any attempt to reassert the nineteenth century boundaries of public and private in terms of the family, with the woman in the home, is hampered because economic conditions have undermined the "family wage" of the male breadwinner. However, the model of the citizen or family as a self-reliant consuming unit is more difficult to combat. The very significant burden of reproduction and the related feminization of poverty were acknowledged in patriarchal form in both liberal and welfare regimes, but are now absent from the discourse of "restructuring."

This situation exacerbates divisions, especially economic divisions both *among* women, who have experienced liberal and welfare reforms and opportunities differently from each other according to their class and race, and, as De Lauretis and others have argued, *within* women, who, as individuals, experience contradictions as wage-earners of very varing kinds, care-givers, consumers, and members of ethnic and racial groups. Cultural policy issues are a group of issues which are institutionalised bythe state in more than one dimension, and this fact structures these contradictions. A white "femocrat" in a a national arts institution, a potter in rural Nova Scotia, a Vietnamese immigrant piece-worker, and a graduating multi-media artist from a university or art college, will all experience the withdrawal of the state from arts funding, the linkage of entertainment options to the ability of communities to attract advertisers, the effect of the shrinkage of state bureaucracy on equity for women and ethnic and racial minorities, increased consumption taxes, changes to unemployment insurance regulations, and reduced funding for all types of education. For each woman the hierarchies of gender, race, class, language and region will affect the way she experiences these elements of the current politics and economics of culture.[17]

In other publications I have traced the emergence of the consumer model as the dominant model of citizenship in Canada today, and linked this to the increasingly market-driven cultural policies we experience.[18] It is not only the withdrawal of (however problematic) opportunities for women to experience citizenship under liberal and welfare regimes that is the issue, it is the shrinking of citizenship itself to a narrow focus concerned only with a rhetoric of consumer choice and the market viability of cultural industries.

Public Policy in an Era of Restructuring

In public policy analysis, the dominance of the consumer model is reflected in what analysts call public choice theory. As Stephen Brooks explains it, this theory has achieved ascendance in Canada as the theory of public behaviour used by legislators, and takes precedence over liberal pluralist models (in which the state is the object of competition between various interests in society) and neo-marxist models (in which the evolution of policy instruments corresponds to a stage in the development of capital, the relations of classes within nation-states to capital and to each other). Brooks observes: "Those working within [the public choice model] attempt to explain political behaviours, including the policy decisions of governments, in terms of a theory of individual choice developed in microeconomics."[19] The rhetoric of public choice theory is of concern to women for two reasons. First, it denies the existence of collective interests, and it makes the universal consumer (*homo economicus* risen again) the focal point, thereby reducing discussion of all our multiple identifications and interests, including gender, to spending and efficiency theorized from a purely individual-interest perspective. Secondly, it wears the cloak of science, and treats policy outcomes and political deals as the result of power transactions, and zero-sum games in which input equals output. As any student of critical theory knows, this pseudo-scientism is immensely durable because of the status of science as a discourse, one which claims disinterest in the process being studied. However, like much of the science it emulates, the public choice model is transformative of the institutions and the society it is concerned with. It makes assumptions about the behaviour not only of citizen-consumers, but of politicians and bureaucrats whose only motivation, too, is apparently rational self-interest, which accounts for their desire for power or to protect turf. This same common-sense view of state bureaucracies goes a step further when its *leitmotif* of cutting government waste becomes the familiar excuse for eliminating government jobs, selling off Crown Corporations, and contracting out work previously done in-house. All of these "efficiencies" have already affected the major public cultural institutions and some of the cultural programs in Canada. Proof of the power of the discourse of public choice can be found in its infiltration of the language used by the ministries, councils and public institutions reponsible for broadcasting, the arts, and education.

Nowhere among the analyses of the state and public policy reviewed so far is there any suggestion that the state is actually withering away, public-sector job losses notwithstanding. What has shifted, through the years of restructuring, is the relationships of citizens to the state. As we have seen, at least part of this shift can be attributed to international changes in modes of production and consumption, and the pressure on countries like Canada to "harmonize" their tariffs, social programs, and so on.

If this is the big picture, what are the opportunities for women and other citizens to achieve the cultural goals they want to achieve, and what opportunities are there within the policy forums presently available to engage in the identification of these goals? In the following section I look first at the remaining pertinence, if any, of the state to these goals, and secondly at the the policy process itself.

Women, Cultural Policy and Restructuring

The rhetoric of globalization can be overwhelming, and globalization can become a meaningless miasma of cultural uniformity. The power relations between states can be ignored as we concentrate on their relationships to international capital. Commodity fetishism can lead critics of U.S.-based corporations to ignore the effective difference between weapons of destruction and Disney products.[20] Yet the question remains: what evidence is there of meaningful opportunities to influence outcomes within the state and its agencies? And to what extent does the state represent or speak for a national culture?

One common response is that the state is the mediator between global forces and local cultures, or nations. A far more substantial and accurate answer is given, however, in an analysis of "neocorporatism": competitive advantage is sought by states (on behalf of their most powerful corporations) using both deregulation and the mechanisms of sectoral regulation (such as in telecommunications) to create powerful nationally-based industry competitors in these fields. In our introduction we pointed out the technological nationalism manifest in Australian policy statements such as *Creative Nation* and in Canadian statements such as *Vital Links*. One reason for the success of this rhetoric in Canada is its familiarity. Public investment in transportation and communications is an old, indeed nation-buiding practice in Canada, and has been brought forward into our current policy of encouraging the formation of telecommunications and information highway competitors. But to show that states encourage the competitive advantage of their industries does not immediately suggest a strengthening or resistance on the part of these states vis-a-vis global forces. All it illustrates is that the job of the state has become the promotion of domestic or domestically-based industry in international competition. The concentration on high-technology, internationally competitive industries has not been neutral for other parts of the cultural sector. The "market failure" argument for state support for "culture", which advocates a role for the state in Canada where markets were too small or too geographically scattered to sustain cultural producers, has lost currency. Those aspects of cultural production which are not competitive internationally are second class citizens; they are not part of the forward looking, expansive and economically sustainable future.

For Canadians and Australians who have regarded the state and the nation as the same thing, or who have believed, as many Canadians seem to, that the nation is the creature of the state, the experience of abandonment and all-encompassing economic discipline that is our present relationship to the state can be bewildering. What we find hard to absorb is that "the political gap between economic and cultural nationalism [is] widening."[21] As recent history bears out, the role of the state has been to prepare the way for intense international economic competition. In response to this in the case of NAFTA, a concept of a political sovereignty based in the citizenry rather than the state has re-emerged in alliances formed among disparate groups within Canada, and between women's, labour, environmental, and other organizations in Canada, the United States, and Mexico. Says Marjorie Griffin Cohen, "The true task for people within nations is to continue to work for ways to democratize their own countries so that the main function of nations is not to discipline their populations for international trading regimes, as it appears to be now."[22]

Of the remaining opportunities for democratic action in Canada, the fact that there are so many points at which cultural relations and cultural production are affected by government and by the actions of public and quasi-public institutions, in our relatively decentralized nation, represents both a problem and an opportunity. Marc Raboy's recent study of the making of Canadian broadcasting policy observes that "Canada is exceptional in the extent to which broadcasting policy making takes place partly in the public sphere,"[23] and he provides a few examples of the successful use of consultative forums on broadcasting, usually dominated by government and broadcasters, by public interest lobbies such as consumer groups, and women's organizations.

Of the women's organizations and other groups Raboy's study notes that they had to learn to lobby and to prepare the ground for the hearing process; they could not simply rely on the formal hearings themselves. In order, for example, to have a reference to multiracial as well as to multicultural obligations in the broadcasting system included in the revised Broadcasting Act (1991), representatives of an anti-racism organization had to use connections with a former Opposition multiculturalism critic to secure an invitation to appear at hearings. A group of media professionals who wanted women included in the Broadcasting Act had to negotiate a deal with actors' union and media watchdog representatives to create the consensus, and wording, that they had been informally told by the chair of the parliamentary committee they should have in place, before ministerial support for the inclusion of women (which had been privately indicated) would be publicly declared and the recommendations seen through to legislation. This was one of the few occasions where the private broadcasters, who did not want this provision, did not prevail. Raboy warns organizations of the dangers and losses that can occur if they underestimate their own strength or their ability to learn to be "players" in such forums.

But we must also add that the obstacles to the participation of women in decision making about broadcasting and the cultural industries have been almost completely untouched by content and employment equity rules that women, minorities and the disabled have achieved. Raboy shows the extent to which broadcast industry representatives have access to senior bureaucrats and politicians, and describes the public consultation process as having only a mitigating rather than transformative effect on the business-as-usual relationship between government and broadcasters:

> ..one observes a definite historical continuity of economic and political issues, defined by industry and decision makers, as the driving force of Canadian broadcasting policy. As to social and cultural factors, these are primarily promoted by the creative sector, by organizations representing various social interests and by watchdog associations, which monitor the evolution of the system in the name of a general public interest...Without [these groups' access to public opinion through formal public consultations] broadcasting policy in Canada would be determined almost exclusively according to the economic interests of industrial parties, modified to take into account the political agenda of the Canadian state.[24]

At the time of the negotiation of the North American Free Trade Agreement (1993), arts organizations, including union representatives, industry representatives, and the Canadian Conference for the Arts (the national arts lobby organization), as well as many women's organizations were among those fighting to exempt the social safety net, direct and indirect funding measures for the arts, and Canadian content measures and other guarantees of access to Canadian markets for Canadian cultural producers. Ultimately, five areas (printed publications, films and video, music recording, music publishing, and broadcasting) were exempted from the Agreement, but under the now notorious "notwithstanding" clause in Article 2005,"a Party may take measures of equivalent commercial effect in response to actions that would have been inconsistent with this Agreement but for paragraph 1 [the paragraph providing for the exemption]." This clause has become notorious precisely because it has been used to threaten and in some cases implement retaliatory action "of equivalent commercial effect", but even more because it represents, to the cultural industries, a paper shield, "more diplomatic in nature than legal.Since the exemption does not protect a Party from retaliation for relying upon it, it proves little actual protection for a Party's cultural industries." [25]

If protection for cultural industries is a toothless paragraph in a trade agreement, what of the arts and the forms of cultural production that are not among the five exemptions? If the characteristic feature of Canada's current position on culture is to stress the industrial nature of cultural production,[26] how can we expect our national government, which has apparently failed these "industrial" clients as a business manager, to take an interest in areas which do not even meet this description? The evidence shows, of course, that this interest is diminishing daily.

Conclusion: Fantasy, Rationality, or New Visions?

Donna Scott, Chair of the Canada Council, chose the occasion of the presentation of the 1995 Governor General's literary awards to advertise the Council's availability as matchmaker between shy private sector arts patrons and those financially irresponsible artists who "sadly, are at the end of the line when it comes to monetary rewards."("I know there are other unwed couples out there!") She announced that "the Canada Council is uniquely positioned to assist, administer, select, discover—in fact develop a whole range of programs for businesses so that they can express their love of the arts and their unique role in validating our fragile country." [27]

In other words: *The welfare mums of the arts community don't need hand-outs, they need husbands. They need them very much, since welfare is on its way out. They are very good at stretching a pound of hamburger, they'll bring up the little artists for you, and hey, they'll even help out the community, what with all their volunteering and consuming and job-*

creating. And when the business day is done, just sit back and enjoy those symbolic values! Feel the fragile nation growing stronger! P.S. Worried that your spouse might bite the hand that feeds her? Relax. Auntie Donna is here to make sure you don't throw your love away.

Not surprisingly the writers present at the awards ceremony, women and men, were offended at being lined up like mail-order brides. Yet this speech, with the subtext of (spousal) tax breaks for acquiescent businesses, represents the current direction of federal government policies for the arts.

In this chapter I have expanded on the concept of gender and have suggested that the "technology of gender" is one useful way of describing cultural policy. The relationship of women to the post-welfare or restructured state has been identified as an important factor in understanding how policies for cultural relations, the media, and the arts, become technologies of gender in the current political-economic context. As a technology of gender, cultural policy in its current forms is associated with such institutions, practices, and discourses, as management, economics, and publicity. The hegemony of economic rationalism, and the use of gender to sustain a powerful normative vision of the "natural" division of public and private spheres in public policy, can, however be challenged through creative, critical and political work.

The arts as "feminine", irrational, spiritual, and, in the romantic tradition, as the antithesis of economic values (all of which makes their public-sector support portrayable as economic and moral dependency), is an image that has persisted throughout the recent period in which the arts in Canada and Australia have been required to model themselves as cultural *industries*. This contradiction is an example of what the Australian critic Meaghan Morris describes as the "absurdities" of policy. She challenges the rationalist claims of cultural policy, insisting that "everyday life" has become, in the name of "culture" an object of bureaucratic fantasy, policy desire, and media hype.[28] Certainly, from a Canadian perspective, it can be shown that policies related to culture have had this comprehensive ambition and allure for a very long time.[29]

The rationality of policy can be deconstructed, and it can be factually countered on a claim-by-claim basis. But beyond this a whole world-view needs to be re-visioned. In our introduction we explained that one of the reasons for bringing together the contributors in this book was to demonstrate the range of forms and discourses through which women analyze and express their concerns about cultural politics and cultural policy. New visions for cultural policy can be created by advocating for alternative values, including feminist values, arguing for the legitimacy of forms of knowledge not usually brought to the policy table, and bringing to light the critical connections between public and private, and between economic policies and cultural policies that mainstream policy discourse has presented in only their most superficial dimensions.

Notes

1. Teresa De Lauretis, *Technologies of Gender: Essays on Theory, Film and Fiction* (Bloomington and Indianapolis: Indiana University Press, 1987), p.2. In her preface to the book De Lauretis acknowledges a debt to Michel Foucault, "whose critique of the technology of sex does not take into account its differential solicitation of male and female subjects," and to Louis Althusser's theory of the ideological interpellation of the subject which is likewise gender "blind"(p.ix). In her list of social technologies which also act as technologies of gender, De Lauretis includes Western art and high culture, the media, schools, courts, the family, the academy and the intellectual community, avant-garde artistic practices and radical theories, and feminism itself. See p.3.

2. Ibid., p.2.

3. Catharine A. MacKinnon, *Toward a Feminist Theory of the State* (Cambridge:Harvard University Press, 1989), p.249.

4. Laurie Shrage, "Feminists and Prostitution," in Cass R. Sunstein (ed), *Feminism and Political Theory* (Chicago: University of Chicago Press, 1990),p.199.

5. Ibid., pp.198-9.

6. MacKinnon's engagement with the law has as its goal a feminist jurisprudence, which she conceives of as involving "substantive"rights for women as opposed to the abstract (liberal) view of the law as currently practices and the empiricist left view, according to her, that " all law does or can do is reflect existing conditions." *Toward a Feminist Theory*, p.248. For a Canadian feminist anti-censorship view, see Lise Gotell, "Policing Desires: Obscenity Law, Pornography Politics, and Feminism in Canada" in Janine Brodie (ed.), *Women and Canadian Public Policy* (Toronto: Harcourt Brace, 1996): 279-317.

7. Ibid., p.170.

8. "Back in 1900, the Public Accounts for Canada listed only a couple of dozen separate departments and agencies of government. Ninety years later, the Public Accounts listed 120. At Confederation, total government expenditure in Canada accounted for little more than 5 per cent of gross national expenditure. Today, government expenditure comes to about 45 per cent of GNE." Stephen Brooks, *Public Policy in Canada: An Introduction*, 2nd Ed. (Toronto: McClelland and Stewart 1993), p.17. Brooks notes, however, that of the 45 per cent of GNE spent by governments, about half involves transfer payments such as welfare and support to organizations.

9. Ibid., pp.101-4.

10. Ibid.,p.102.

11. Ibid.,p.17 and pp.240-57.

12. Janine Brodie, "Shifting the Boundaries: Gender and the Politics of Restructuring," in Isabella Bakker (ed.) *The Strategic Silence: Gender and Economic Policy*, (London: Zed Books, 1994), p.46. My thanks to Professor Marjorie Griffin Cohen of Simon Fraser University for a discussion of these issues and for directing me to publications on the "feminization" of labour, NAFTA, and the gendered impacts of restructuring. See also Marjorie Griffin Cohen,"The Implications of Economic Restructuring for Women: The Canadian Situation," in Bakker, *The Strategic Silence*, pp. 103-16.

13. Brodie, "Shifting the Boundaries," p.46.

14. Seyla Benhabib, *Situating the Self: Gender, Community and Postmodernism in Contemporary Ethics* (London: Polity Press, 1992). See especially chapter 3, "Models of Public Space: Hannah Arendt, the Liberal Tradition, and Jurgen Habermas."

15. Brodie, p.54. See also Marjorie Griffin Cohen, "New International Trade Agreements: Their Reactionary Role in Creating Markets and Retarding Social Welfare," in Isabella Bakker (ed.), *Rethinking Restructuring* (Toronto: University of Toronto Press, 1996), pp.187-202.

16. Brodie, "Shifting the Boundaries," p.54.

17. See Fay Cromwell-Tollenaar, "Equity: Fact or Fiction," *Matriart* V.5, no.4 (1994), pp.20-22.

18. Alison Beale," Subjects, Citizens and Consumers: Changing Concepts of Citizenship in Canadian Cultural Policy," in Allen Seager, et al (eds.), *Alternative Frontiers: Voices of the Mountain West*, (Montreal: Association For Canadian Studies,1997): 51-65.

19. Brooks, *Public Policy in Canada*, p.35. Brooks' review of the various theories of public policy emphasizes their ideological influence as much as their logical consistency, and concludes that there are social factors "that enable some theories to live on in the face of mounting evidence of their flaws." p.47.

20. Marjorie Ferguson, "Media, Markets and Identities: Reflections on the Global-Local Dialectic," *Canadian Journal of Communication*, V.20, no.4, (1995): pp.439-59.

21. Ibid, p.449. "As a muscular corporatist state policy reroutes broadcast and cultural industries along a national 'information highway,' change is packaged in terms of 'sustainable competition.' The latter euphemism is one whose political

marketing gloss fails to conceal its logical inconsistency: *Sustainable competition is an oxymoron of the first order when market liberalism calls for competition, but functions by its elimination through mergers, alliances, and acquisitions.*" p.450. Italics in original.

22. Cohen, "Implications of Economic Restructuring," p.199.

23. Marc Raboy, Influencing public policy on Canadian Broadcasting," *Canadian Public Administration* V.38, no.3 (1995):411-32. [Quotation used by permission of the Institute of Public Administration of Canada].

24. Ibid., p.430.

25. Barry Appleton, *Navigating NAFTA: A Concise User's Guide to the North American Free Trade Agreement* (Toronto: Carswell, 1994), pp.190-1.

26. Rowland Lorimer and Nancy Duxbury, "Of Culture, the Economy, Cultural Production, and Cultural Producers: An Orientation," *Canadian Journal of Communication*, V.19, nos. 3/4 (1994):23.

27. "Notes for a Speech by Donna Scott, Chair of the Canada Council, at the 1995 Governor General's Literary Awards ceremony," The Canada Council/Conseil des Arts du Canada, Toronto, 14 November, 1995.

28. Meaghan Morris, *Ecstasy and Economics; American Essays for John Forbes* (Sydney: Empress Publishing, 1992), pp.127-8.

29. Beale, "Subjects, Citizens and Consumers." op.cit.

/

If you have enjoyed reading this book, you will be interested in the following recently published Garamond Press titles:

Pat and Hugh Armstrong et al
MEDICAL ALERT: New Work Organizations in Health Care

William K. Carroll ed.
ORGANIZING DISSENT: Contemporary Social Movements in Theory and Practice, (second, revised edt.)

Catherine Cavanaugh and Jeremy Mouat, eds
MAKING WESTERN CANADA: Historical Essays

Tania Das Gupta
RACISM AND PAID WORK

Robert Hackett and Yuezhi Zhao
SUSTAINING DEMOCRACY? Journalism and the Politics of Objectivity

David Livingstone and J. Marhall Mangan
RECAST DREAMS: Class and Gender Consciousness in Steeltown

John McMurtry
UNEQUAL FREEDOMS
The Global Market as an Ethical System

Sylvia O'Meara and Doug West, eds
FROM OUR EYES: Learning from Indigenous Peoples

Chris Schenk and John Anderson, eds
RE-SHAPING WORK: Union Responses to Technological Change

Dennis Thiessen, Nina Bascia and Ivor Goodson
MAKING A DIFFERENCE ABOUT DIFFERENCE:
The Lives and Careers of Racial Minority Immigrant Teachers

Garamond Press, 67 Mowat Ave., Suite 144, Toronto, On. M6K 3E3,
Phone 416-516-2709, fax 416-516-0571, e-mail Garamond@web.net

Write, phone, fax or e-mail us at the following address for more information or
if you would like to receive a catalogue. Check out our Home Page at
http//www.garamond.ca/garamond

AGMV
MARQUIS
Québec, Canada
1997

Kingdom Come

BY LAWRENCE KEARNEY

Middletown, Connecticut

WESLEYAN UNIVERSITY PRESS

Grateful acknowledgement is made to the following publications, in which some of these poems have appeared: *The Atlantic Monthly, Chicago Review, Massachusetts Review, Michigan Quarterly Review, Missouri Review, New Letters, Paris Review, Poetry Northwest,* and *Virginia Quarterly Review.*

The poems "Delight" and "K Mart" first appeared in *Poetry.*

Library of Congress Cataloging in Publication Data

Kearney, Lawrence, 1948–
   Kingdom come.

   (Wesleyan poetry program ; 98)
   I. Title.
PS 3561.E245K5   811'.5'4   79-28183
ISBN 0-8195-2098-5
ISBN 0-8195-1098-x pbk.

Distributed by Columbia University Press
136 South Broadway, Irvington, N.Y. 10533

Manufactured in the United States of America
First Edition

—Most distinguished voyager, what was your eon like?

—Comic. For terror is forgotten.
Only the ridicule is remembered by posterity.
Death from a wound, from a noose, from starvation
Is one death, but folly is uncounted and new every year.
I took part, I tied neckties
For no purpose and danced dances for no purpose.
A customer, a buyer of sweaters and pomade,
A mimicker, a shy guest,
A fop impressed by his reflection in shop windows.
My age was second-rate and my mind was second-rate.
I was overgrown by the bark of unconsciousness.
I tried hard to imagine another earth and could not.
I tried hard to imagine another heaven and could not.

—from "Visitor,"
by Czeslaw Milosz

Contents

I

Delight

After the delights of the body falter,
& the delight of the mind in invention
has dulled, there is still the delight
of failure: a hundred daily evasions,
losses so slight they could dance
on the head of a pin.

                      And occasionally,
something larger—like getting fired
or divorced or losing a child, anything
you think you can never get back.

When it happens, you stand there
staring at your hands, wanting grief
to tear at your shirt. You blame others,
but at heart take your failure
greedily to yourself.
It is yours:
the proof of your power
to ruin your own life.
It is coming home
after your second divorce
& your mother hugs you at the front door,
both of you crying & kissing, full of solace
& relief & the secret delight
that once again you have failed, *I
told you so,*   *oh darling*

I told you so.

K Mart

Mother is off to LADIES WEAR,
Father to HOME FURNISHINGS.
As usual, I'm with him.

Passing HARDWARE, he instructs me
in the merits of variable-speed
drills, the sham of saber saws,
the parable of human folly
embodied in third-rate drop-forged
hammers. I nod. I'm twelve. He's
teaching me to shop like a man.

AUTOMOTIVE; SPORTING GOODS;
a foray into COSMETICS
for deodorant & shave cream—
the lights droning overhead
their rheumy, incessant gossip,
here, in the one place we talk.

When it's time to go, his lessons
lapse. He wanders off by himself,
whistling his special call for Mother:
two notes
so high & clear they rise
above the whole store—
that tired, adult head, the jowls
rich with ridicule, with affection, Father
floating there like some exotic bird—
calling again & again for his unseen lover
across the abyss of goods between them.

Mother, Alone in the Attic

1.   What I want is to open the trunk
& lay out the winter clothes.
To dust the moth crystals off.
To put on the muskrat coat,
my mother's, & be the Mama Bear
of the fairy tales.
                My husband
at work, doing whatever it is he does.
And the children at school. Though soon
they'll be home for lunch, carrying
some small grief or accomplishment,
& I will crouch by the window
& pretend I'm not here
& wait for them to leave.
                    And when they've gone
I will go downstairs, still in mother's
muskrat coat, & the bread,
the peanut butter & jelly, all the food
the children have left on the table
will tremble as I begin to dance—
thumping at first,
making the linoleum groan,
but then I'll whirl & whirl
till I lift off the floor,
till I let loose in the house forever
the fur-coated beast
from the cave of my heart!

2.   Exhausted, I flop back
on a pile of mother's quilts . . .
that antiseptic, almost sexual smell
of moth crystals. A few feet

13

above me, the dark shaggy beams
lean into each other, holding
everything up. I can almost touch them.
When I was a girl, I'd sit in the attic
for hours—I loved the slanted walls,
the child's ceiling, the one room
my parents would have to stoop to enter.
There, the world seemed closer:
I'd look out the oval window
& everything would be clean—no people
or noise, just the high-up branches
of the sycamore in our front yard,
its leaves half-yellow, half-shadow,
turning & turning in windlight.

Tomorrow, I go back to the hospital.
At first, when the cancer took,
I fell to pieces. One breast gone,
& in 6 months, the other. I'd never known
such attention: how every minute the pain,
that harsh insistent lover, stayed faithful.
Passion, they say, emaciates;
& it's true. I thinned to a girl.
And occasionally, above me
I'd see the doctors, smiling,
circling like crows,
the moon-eyed nurses, or my husband
bending to kiss me goodbye for the day
as though I were already dead.

I saw it all & said nothing.
It was my only revenge,
& a small one, at that—
to see their maneuvers so clearly,

but never let on . . .

And yet, at this moment,
how I long to talk with them!
To call my husband & children
up the rusty stairs to sit with me
here in the attic. And if they came,
how I would hold each of their faces
& kiss each of them full on the lips
& tell them how difficult & unnecessary
it has become to love them.
Say that I am not ashamed.
That I am angry nearly all the time.
That their helpfulness
is just another kind of greed.
That for the first time in my life
my life is my own, now
that it's finished.

Father Answers His Adversaries

It's early March, Eisenhower still
president, & Mother's heating up supper
for the third time tonight.
We're at the table doing homework,
& she tells us Father's next in line
for foreman, that today he'll know for sure.
He's three hours late.

Half past eight the Chevy
screeches into the carport.
For a minute, nothing.
Then the sudden slam, & the thump downstairs
to the basement. Beneath our feet
Father lays into the workbench
with a sledgehammer—the jam jars
of nails, of screws, of nuts & bolts
he'd taken years to sort out
exploding against the wall.

Later, sheepish, he comes up,
slumps in his seat & asks for supper.
And when Mother brings his plate
& he looks up at her
& she takes his head on her breast,
he blushes, turns away, & spits out
that final, weary-mouthed answer
to all of it—General Motors & the bosses
& the union pimps & the punched-out Johnnies,
every yes-man goddam ass-lick
who'd ever been jumped to foreman
over him—*ahhh, crap's like cream,*
it rises.

The Influenza Outbreak of 1958

You'd think after all our farming
there'd be no more rocks
left on earth, all of them gathered by now
into heaps or the kind of walls
they have in New Hampshire—
chinked puzzlepiece contraptions
to keep the rocks still in the ground
from wandering across the fields.
But no. You dig up a hundred
in the garden & there's a thousand
more by autumn: rocks & seeds of rocks
clear to the rock-center of the planet.
Or you heave them into space
only to have them fall back, burning
to dust, a skin of dust on everything
that's flat, dust in the air
in the yellow light from the bay window,
floating, not even seeming to fall.
How could rocks get so small or so light?
you'd wonder, lying in bed long afternoons
with the flu—when you were sick enough
to stay home from school, but not so sick
you couldn't enjoy it—piling
Grandmother's down-filled quilts
into mountains you could people with soldiers,
dozens of rubber G.I.s on one knee, their bazookas
aimed at a pair of pigeons in the eaves
above the window, who'd managed
finally, in their muddled, parental way,
to piece together a nest of twigs & string.
And soon, Mother would come up,
& she'd ask about your soldiers,

& you'd tell her their names
while she unbuttoned your pajamas
to rub your chest with Vicks,
when the afternoons were endless,
when it was just you & Mother
& the camphor eating into your chest
like a ten-year-old's idea of love.
Love that would cure what ailed you
or kill you trying.

Dead on His Feet in Lackawanna

Like weather, your father's moods
were the world. And changed.
Some mornings
it would have been so easy
for him to slide in the Chevy & go—
Texas, California, who knows
what a man is capable of
without six kids.
                    But he stayed.
Thirty years, the scourge of Lackawanna,
he fed the drill press what it wanted.
Thirty years of working-class swagger,
wearing the sweat-oiled stink of a reliable
machine, wearing cigar smoke & khakis,
his balls on his sleeve, he could give
the old "fuck you" to the foreman
or a fist in the face to Mattie
the Mafia loan shark, & no one
would mess with him—till the day
his ring caught in the drill press,
making hamburger of one hand & mangling
half the other when he tried to pull it free.

*

Now, every time you see him
he's smaller. Soon he'll have shrunk
to the size of your son.
You could carry him in your lunch box.
You could hold him in the palm of your hand:
lift him to your mouth & tell him
you learned in your own good time
to make something human out of bitterness,

to call it a job & work it
like an old excuse. And when he asks
for a story, you tell him the one
he used to lull you to sleep with,
the kind of story it doesn't matter
whether you believe or not, you tell it
the way you heard it, a thousand years
before you were born . . .

> In a certain town lived a man.
> Every day he got up in the dark
> three hours earlier than he wanted to.
> He hoisted the morning on his back
> & went to work. He was always tired
> & his hands were always dirty.
> The earth was his enemy
> & swallowed him a day at a time.
> But he wouldn't go easy.
> He'd drag the sky
> down with him if he had to.
> He was a man, dammit.
> He had hands.
> He brought home the bacon.

There Are 23 Steel Mills in Buffalo, N.Y.

1.   On summer nights
the stars won't rain,
the red dust will not rise, will not
become a man again:
we can hear it
on the other side of the bedroom wall,
gnawing the clapboard
while we sleep.

Chewed down to its knees,
South Buffalo collapses,
& we ooze through the siding
into the dark, metallic air.

How we've longed for this! —
to lift with the smoke
coiling above the roofs,
to caress one another, at last,
without shame.
                      But we are
ashamed, even in dreams.
Each of us drifts off alone.

2.   Before dawn
we float back to our beds.
The houses clumsily reassemble.
The back yards unclench
& let the moonlight seep through.
The steel mills sing our names
softly; they know who we are.

By 6 we're up

& at breakfast, reading the paper—
whispering as we read,
in wry, submissive voices:
the voice to be used at work
to apologize, to confess,
to exact penance
from every word we know . . .

Yes.
I will.
Whatever you say.
—the words coming on
in piston-strokes
as we slog to the corner
to catch the bus for work,
the words our mouths fill to
over & over, without love
for ourselves or this place
we have made with our own hands.

II

One bursts through creatures
when he lets go of things he has loved.
—Meister Eckhart

Vermont Mother's Milk

Two weeks into October & already
snow on Camelback, a grey you can see
from our valley. And a few maples
still yellow at sundown, the rest dingy
or unleaved: more desolate, somehow,
than winter. Though these beige cornstalks
make me think of blonde hair,
of somebody's blue-eyed boy
walking toward home—the stalks clacking
against his raggy tweed coat, & leaf-smoke
drifting from a neighbor's yard, drifting
as he is, closer & closer to home,
though he never arrives.

       Is this home, then?
Or merely homely? Bethel, Jericho,
Goshen, Canaan, hill towns with the names
of the Bible & an antique longing
for righteousness this side of the grave.
A stand of birch across the road,
mother's milk hardened to bark—
a notion of home, of original nourishment
the earth here has at evening. L'heure bleue,
the French call it, naming the kind of light
snow casts into a room at dusk . . .
You broke my heart, Mother
told me once, *I know you didn't mean to,
but you broke my heart just the same.*
L'heure bleue. The birches nodding
in the deep blue air. They understand,
Mother, that I meant to phone.
They too are brokenhearted
& slender as young girls, under a sky

Bruegel might have thought of—a farm scene
in which a woman calls the fields
for her son to come in for supper;
but the one she calls has his back to her,
his tractor churning the corn back to earth
& the blue exhaust-smoke chugging
past his shoulder toward home, where he lives,
where someone stands on the porch calling,
though he doesn't hear,
or hears, & will not answer.

Snow on the Sea

Out there, peninsulas of fog
ooze effortlessly in, breaking up
at the edges without sound.
And a slow-motion movie of snow
is falling, then rising, out
over the half-covered deck chairs
into the sea. . . . It's a scene
Father would appreciate, something
his lyrical sarcasm could work
for hours: a summer resort
mid-winter, all this snow
vanishing into all that ocean.

We haven't spoken in five years.
Resilient, irrevocable, a snowfall
more authentic than human love,
our heartless opinions of each other
settled on our shoulders
flake by flake till we froze.

Under snow, everything looks the same.
Even us, though we'd both deny it:
two snowmen
built by two moony brothers
who will not speak, who have lain all night
by the bedroom window watching the snow—
their breath leaving twin parabolas of steam
where they've leaned on the glass,
dreaming of Mickey Mantle, of spring,
of a sea that takes everything away
& gives nothing but water back.

Sunflower

The leaves, at best
ludicrous, too many floppy hands
& no pockets to put them in.
And the head, that stalk-toppler,
so bowed down the backside of it
has gone to soot—
hanging on till Halloween,
or God knows, Thanksgiving.

While poets praise your summer graces,
you undo them all
in October: gawking at your feet
like a schoolgirl in brown shoes.
As if, out of pity or carelessness,
death will pass you up,
& come November your broad
leprous head, still alive,
will have finally reached the ground
& in three days rotted
transcendentally away . . .

Fat chance.
That gape, that stooped
fly's eye of a face,
it's just another way
of dying—
to stare at the earth
till you've been dead a week
& one by one
your last seeds drop
into the upturned face
of the hereafter.

Water

In the morning
I find coyote tracks
circling the well,
where they've smelled the water
fifty feet below.

And later, in the arroyo—
the prickly pears with half-moons
bitten out of their milk-green leaves.

By tonight the coyotes' mouths
will have swollen from the needles,
& in a week they'll be dead
of hunger or infection, death
tasting like water:

dying just after dawn, the ground
still sweet with night-air,
the scent of a few tossed cirrus clouds
as they buff & stray
across the water-colored sky

weightless as Monet's water lilies,
his blindness fusing water, light
& lilies to a fractionless glow
he knows is his death
& drinks till he drowns.

Light on Water

In California people are easy
with each other; they slide
in & out of each other's arms
with grace & indifference.
They laugh often & leisurely,
making you feel at ease,
& you hate them for it.

And wherever you look
there's the ocean: a blue desert
the wheat of light scatters across
but will not take root,
a fine shimmer further out
where the water's skin
is light transformed to a meadow
of Queen Anne's lace & corn flowers,

& beyond it, all communion
& lack of clouds, a sky so empty
you can see the future in it,
dropping a trail of blue breadcrumbs
the crows will eat.

III

The Emperor's Old Clothes

Everyone could see them,
which made them common
& ridiculous—the cuff & sleeve,
the collar of mortal ermine,
its circular shadows on a field of snow.
And the embroidery: gold braid
teased into mille fleurs & a trellis
of vine leaves that made the young girls
who worked it blind—that it was all
too heavy. That every time he put them on
he wore the tedium that made them.

He called in tailors.
They saw that what he wanted
was to be embezzled out of that weight,
that the consummate betrayal
is the betrayal of self:
the way it is for us
when we hear news of a suicide
& are shaken—how could anyone, willingly,
enter that absence we most fear?
No, we say, we must wear our lives
till they wear us out.

Not emperors. Nor tailors.
They know what the suicides know—
the ones the emperor saw at the window
that Midsummer's Eve: their weary fish-mouths
moving up & down as they tried to speak,
to somehow shape the words that would say
It was easy. We do not repent.
We never fell from Grace,

33

we flew! . . .

           And how he felt then,
turning back to the mirror, the darkness
behind him in the mirror saying Yes.
The mahogany closet sagging in on itself
saying Yes. And the tailors nodding
as they stepped from the darkness,
holding eternity up by the seams.
How the old robe slid from his shoulders,
how he entered, ever after,
the glad-rags of the invisible.

Jacob & the Angel

1.   At first, I thought it was an angel.
I was alone & the black air
hummed with moths with the smell
of creosote & flowering aloe & I
thought it was an angel.

It was my father.
I could tell by the stink
of garlic. And the weight,
heavy as only an old man can be.
That great belly rolling down
on my back, & my arms
flailing under him. And though I heaved
to rise out of being a son,
to be alive in another body
& cast him off, being a woman
or a stalk of wheat
or an angel myself,
he threw me back,
each time I'd almost risen
he threw me back,

& I was a man again.

2.   Kneeling there, under him,
I remembered a dream
from years before:

of a ladder entering Heaven
which the heavenly hosts
went up & came down,
shimmering with an icy light,

the way the river gets
sometimes under the moon.
And I wanted to speak with them,
they seemed so free of any
human concern or delight.

But when I fell to my knees
& begged them to take me,
they laughed, & climbed back
toward Heaven & would not
let me touch them.
All but the last one —
who hesitated, then turned
around, bent close
to my ear & whispered
get up, you fool —
you can't climb a ladder
on your knees.

3.   Remembering those words,
I was ashamed, & rose up,
& threw my father to the ground.
Let me go, he cried.
It's almost dawn.
Let me go & I can bless you.
But I was his own best son,
& would not let him go.

I trampled him there
for over an hour.
Stomped him & stomped him
till I could feel his soul
moving beneath me & he no longer
cried out. And in that hour

36

all bitterness beween us
was gone. . . . In its place
there was only the music
of repudiation, a clear song
like the women sing by the well
as they haul the bucket in.
As the sun was, just then,
hauling its bucket of light
over the hills to the east
so I could see my enemy at last.

But who knows what I saw.
It could have been anyone—
the ruined face, the caved-in
chest like the body of a bird—
though it was a man's body,
I'm sure of it. A man.
Somebody's father.
A pot-bellied angel
neither the sky nor earth
would claim.

Christ at Emmaus

When He appeared on the road beside them,
the two men thought He'd caught up from behind.
Just another stranger wanting to talk.
And they talked, as men will, of weather,
of houses that had cracked in half from the heat.
The men were farmers, & complained
that their barley had already shriveled
on the stalk, & what little was left
the grasshoppers devoured.

The stranger said He was a fisherman.
But not long ago, He told them,
He'd been a Rabbi in Jerusalem,
a Rabbi so powerful thousands
of men & women would die for His sake.
The Romans will herd them into stables,
He said, & they will go: heartsick
& stupid with holiness,
only to die twitching on stakes.
And I will appear to each of them
the moment before death
& feed each a piece of orange
to ease their suffering. And all,
He said, all because the Romans
think they have killed me,
that I rose from the dead, that they
have committed the unspeakable blunder
of creating a Savior.

But Rabbi, one of the men asked Him,
how can You live with Yourself?
All those deaths for nothing . . .

He shook His head. Things happen,
He said, & then changed subjects,
gesturing effusively as He praised
the noble thighs of the barmaids
of Nazareth. He went on like that
for nearly an hour, the most ordinary
of men—sentimental, weeping with tenderness
as He spoke of His mother.

When they reached Emmaus
they stopped for wine at an inn.
Their heads were buzzing from the heat.
The Rabbi lifted His glass
& held it a moment in the light.
There were holes in His hands.
It's as if this glass of wine
were a man's heart, He said.
Look—the light passes through it,
but comes out the other side reddened;
more beautiful, but diminished.
And when the bread came, He broke it,
& gave each of them a piece.
There are some things, He said,
that even God does not forgive.
And death, my friends, is one of them.

The Death of Anastasio Somoza

When we shattered the door,
when it fell in like a face,
he was just getting his pants on.
El Presidente, of the doleful moustache
& the watery, sensitive eyes—the one
who mowed down the old women of Matagalpa
as they came home from market
with their sacks of tortillas & beans,
the one who called anyone he killed
"a terrorist."

Miguel & Jaime had the shotguns.
I don't want it messy, I told them,
I want to haul him down to the square—
if you use those
he'll be all over the walls.
So they lowered their guns,
grabbed him under the arms
& got him to his knees.

I put my pistol to his head
& he started crying, babbled
something about his son.
I bent & kissed him on the forehead
& he went quiet. His eyes glazed over
like he'd forgotten where he was,
& he looked up at me.
My boy, he said. *My boy*.

That's when I let him have it—
a single bullet to the brain.
Sometimes, that's all a man has, a single act

to prove he's alive. For a moment
everything hangs in a clear, cruel light,
like a photograph. You're at the edge
of the exact moment of annihilation.
Your finger eases back on the trigger.
You're alive or you're dead.

West Texas

Father, out back, near your grave,
the windmill throbs—
a sawed-off airplane that never leaves.
And the wind goes field to field
as it always does, grazing on dust.

I got the corn in late this year.
And for three weeks
there's been clouds but no rain,
the sky bearing down—
making the radio spit static
till I can't hear a thing, not even bad news.

Lately, I've been dreaming of Boston,
that time we visited your sister.
I was five or six, I think,
your little girl, & you took me
to see the ocean . . .
                Fifteen hundred miles away,
I'm still there, holding your hand
at the end of the world.
It's yours, you say, whispering
that you're giving me the ocean,
that if I hold it close enough
nothing can take it from my hands.
Not death. Not forgetfulness. Not even
the wind, though it shakes the roof
all night. Because I know what it wants.
Because night after night I listen through it
until I hear the Atlantic, roaring
off the coast of Amarillo.

Someone Else's Story

1.   a field of goldenrod

It's September, 1905,
& we're on the Trans-Siberian Railway—
headed for the edge of the earth,
though the plains dip & roll endlessly.

Kirilov scowls like an ape
as he punches our tickets.
He never gives correct change
because he knows the passengers fear him.

Outside the train, just out of reach,
the last light drains west,
pulling its pink skirts after it.
Thousands of moths

are rising from the dark plains:
suddenly, out of their midst, a wren appears,
beating & beating at the window.
It has Mother's face!

2.   our village: 1908

In winter, our village
greyed to a cinder: white
at the edges, but dark inside.
People kept to themselves.

Even the tinker
neglected his rounds, preferring
a bottle of cheap vodka
to haggling for potatoes.

Only the grave digger kept busy.
Once or twice a week
the bells would sound,
& cursing his wife, his luck,

the cold, Krevchenko went out
to dig another hole.
"What a waste," he'd mutter
later in the tavern,

"the ground's harder
than my old woman's kettle.
And I dig it up just to put it back.
And in between

dump in the dead.
Poor bastards. God knows
if they ever thaw out,
even in Heaven."

3.   reading *The Brothers Karamazov*

It's like looking down a well:
you see yourself far away,
living someone else's story.

There, on the other side of the water,
you've made all the right moves.
Perfected, your possibilities look back at you.

And when you leave, your life
stays behind, under the water,
& you never get it back.

IV

Ghosts

1.　where they end up

In themselves,
where they wanted to stay:
the anxious in elevators,
the bullies in machines,
the lucky ones in the vast
black energy between stars.

For most, though, death is the home
of someone they've held onto.
Lost in the wallpaper,
or roosting mournfully on the television,
they are everywhere we are.

When the weather lulls
& the dusty light
leans into the living room
you can see them
bumping sleepily at the window,
trying to get out.

2.　what they do

Without bodies, what can they do?
Float or stay put.
The newly dead, who are restless,
wander from house to house
like tourists, confused
by the lack of oblivion.

Death isn't dark, as they'd imagined.
But not light either.

47

It's a blonde vapor
they wear like skin.
If there is light, they are it.

3.   how they make love

Slowly,
like those shorebirds whose motion
they remember from an old movie
about New England, they circle
each other with longing & reticence.
And everything cloudy, as love is.
But without the body's greedy affection
for details—the way your lover's
breasts hang as she dries herself
after her bath, the shape & particular
warmth of her nipple
puckering under your kiss.
                                        No. None of that.
But slowly, with the kind of tenderness
that comes from having nothing to give,
their circles get smaller, slower,
till they are rubbing like beach grass
when the wind is down, closing
on that moment when they are neither
one nor the other—just two
old souls trying to touch,
to hold someone
without drifting through his arms.

4.   what they want

To live, of course.
Consume themselves ferociously,
unkillable as bad habits.

They want everything
they can't have: another chance;
to make the same mistakes;
to cinch around bone again,

owning their banality,
the fat, lovely middle-of-the-day—
to sing to themselves while making
the tuna fish sandwiches for lunch,
to weed the garden on the weekend,
confiding in the nasturtiums.

Mostly, they want revenge.
To complain bitterly of being cheated.
To rage, to devour the living
& be done with it, let themselves die
& yet never be dead, burning
with a love that avenges,
that softens their mouths
endlessly into ours.

Burning Out

for J. W.

"In trying to make themselves angels,
men transform themselves into beasts."
— *Montaigne*

1.　　To be young & it's Boston
in '56, down by the Charles,
the fairies gliding arm-in-arm
among the dogwood & late blossoming
cherry trees, & you are here, among them
or watching, their celebrant & victim,
back warming beneath the press
of sunlight through drowsy May air
down where the Esplanade
funnels toward the bandshell
like the rush of light
toward a lens,
　　　　　　　　never to imagine
yourself 15 years later,
kneeling toothless by the urinals
in the Greyhound men's room,
ready, at last, to love anyone.

2.　　Love took your teeth,
what was left of your hair, & you begged
for it—to be thrown on the bed
by some beef-cake & ravished.
It was the subduing, not sex,
you were after;
the emollient of feeling used . . .

Sweet man,

when we're so shoveled out
that not even hate
gets us out of bed in the morning,
when it's only our lust to submit,

shall we, like you, call it love
& praise it?
                    Love
& its relentless breakdowns
that sweeten our energies
                    toward repair,
love, to be finally
emptied out of yourself,
a conical throat of water
narrowing down the drain

to darkness,
to dreams of sleeping with angels
                    & of waking beloved
in the fine air of morning, light
in the arms of light.

Cuba

In my dream, Joey, both of us were alive
& walking in Delaware Park.
The dew glistened on our shoes.
Neither of us spoke of your death.
We talked of other mornings, in winter,
when we'd drive up Hopkins
home from Bethlehem Steel—
two washed-out Marxists, sure suckers
for the good intention & the dialectic
under every rock. The blue snow
swirled the blue streets of South Buffalo,
& the streetlights hazed into swell-bellied
moons. And to pass the time
you always had a story . . .
about the Navy, or a woman,
or the way the sea shimmered
at night off the Moroccan coast.
Next year, you'd say. Next year for sure
you were going to Cuba, leave the snow
& the mills, cut cane for a living.
Come off it, Joey, I'd say, you'll be lucky
to make it out of the county. And anyway,
I've heard it before—you change your life
more often than your underwear.

Something was always trying to get out
when you'd talk. Friday nights
at Locklin's, you'd be pouring existentialism
down some 15-year-old's throat, your hands
flapping as you talked, your cigarette
weaving a smoky trail of enthusiasm
you could never bring yourself

to believe . . .
                    Who needs it.
Who needs it, you said
that time after Michael's funeral.
Our backs to the bar, the gang of us
nodded in unison. For once
we believed you, knew what you meant,
all of us stuck with what we knew
we were—sentimental & drunk
& fattening into our thirties.

All winter, brain reamed by booze,
you wanted to die. None of us knew,
though anyone could see it:
that grand gesture of denial
hovering like a ghost just beyond
your skin . . . that it was as close
as you'd ever get to Havana.
Sundays on the West Side, weighing 260,
browsing for a coronary, how you'd hit
the bakeries for cannoli. Or mornings
after work, dreaming you were out in the cane
as we roared up Hopkins in your Olds 88
& you'd lean out the window shouting
eat dust you bourgeois creeps,
how it was one jazzy epiphany after another,
Joey, right up to the moment
you shoved the gun in your mouth
& took off.

After the Interrogation

There is the sack of skin, dark
or light, ready to give out
under small cunningly-applied pressures
its passage of blood
from the heart to the tongue.
There is firefall & gangrene,
there are forty-three days of interrogation
& a fifteen-year sentence in the works.
Plenty of time to dream in your cell
of a young woman's breasts:
the purple areolas deepening to black
at the nipples, of burying your head
between them & never coming up.
Death would be like that, you say —
something that makes you ache inside
the way a woman can make you ache.
Or a few sad fragments of speech
from *The Cherry Orchard* come back to you,
& you remember the first time you read it
how you wanted to cry, because it was true,
that sadness. Russia dying
into the twentieth century — what could have been
further from your life? — & yet Chekhov
was speaking only to you: telling you
he was once as scared as you were
of blank paper, of its stare, but just wrote
& wrote because all he wanted
was someone to talk to, that what was
writing anyway but someone talkng
to someone he couldn't see.
How it came to you later, one morning
on Hoedjes Bay, up-coast from Capetown,

54

the wind driving the sand off the dunes
into your nostrils, your hair,
a few thick-necked cumuli
skudding inward toward land & no rain,
the waves crashing four abreast,
each one a mouth
talking & talking, slab after slab of language
heaved up from the sea—
& for the first time you knew
you were born to this life to write
in the open, to read the braille
surface of things & give emptiness
a face.
                    Pigeons
scratching the cement in the cell-yard
wake you, but in your mind
you're back in Johannesburg,
that tree on State Street: the pigeons
underneath clucking like grandmothers
as they devour the pink clusters of fruit
they imagine have fallen only for them.
How they remind you of the guards—
all appetite & affability.
And yet, nothing like the guards
at all. Who are not birds, but only men
doing a job, & you
are the job.
                    And it's only now, finally
awake from this morning's beating,
that you see it: the window.
The guards have left the window open.
But not out of carelessness, & not for the air.
So.   All that blather about power
& how much of it the State can wield

55

over a person, when any child
could have told you—pain.
A ten-penny hose artfully employed,
a glass rod worked from the tip
of the penis to its root & then broken,
bending the arm past the elbow's
ability. . . . Enough pain
that they won't have to kill you, you'll
do it for them, *that* kind of power.
And that once dead, you are theirs.
Public. Molecular. Stripped of thought,
of its privacy, which terrifies them
as it once terrified you—the solitude
& particulars of moving through time.
Time, which goes only as far
as the window, which is four feet away
& is open & is seven flights down.
That everything you've written
since that morning by the ocean
is there, just past the window, saying
don't do it—though something
in your body is moving anyway, & no one,
not even you, has a right to stop it.
But your arms are too mangled to pull.
You'll have to help. You'll have to make it
on words alone this time, drag yourself
by the tongue to the window,
lean far enough out
& let go . . .
                    into a rush
of women's breasts, your wife, her breasts
sagging against her blouse as she bends
over the well in the courtyard at home
looking at her hair in the water. And in her hair

a pale-green comb of Malagasy tortoiseshell,
& you think, of all things, why that?
A comb. Something trivial & exquisite
your last thought on earth
as the cement shoves into you
so suddenly & so hard
it doesn't hurt—just the momentary
nausea, a few miserable syllables
coughed up with the blood, & then silence.
Silence by the well in Soweto. Silence
under the tree on State Street. Silence
with its boot in the door of your voice.

The Heaven of Full Employment

for my grandfather

1.   Now you are nearly nothing—
a few handfuls of ash
in a crematory vase.
Your great emphysemic hulk
powdered into anonymity,
the smoky machinery of Glasgow:

grey of the wooly overcoats
& the rooftops by the Clyde-bank
7 in the morning & can't breathe,
grey of the lungs that died
three years before you did.

2.   It's the June before you die
& we're walking down by Ardrossen,
stopping every fifty feet
so you can breathe.
The storm the night before
has laced the beach with garbage,
& the balls of black seaweed
burst under our shoes.

And while we rest against the pilings
you hawk a knot of blood
the size of a baby's fist
into the sand, & begin
your wheezy, low-pitched rant—
of the heaven of full employment,
of Celtic Destiny & the imminent
collapse of the West, the workers

58

rising from the dead on the last day
of history, good riddance
to the bourgeoisie & to Glasgow
their city, their finest creation,
Glasgow & its endless money-sucking
slaughter of the poor.

3.   The poor, like the dead,
were everywhere. In your soup,
in the denture glass on the nightstand,
in the mirror in the morning
when you shaved.
                        Your father,
a Dublin drunk, thirteen kids
& you the eldest, three sisters dead
by the time you were twenty,
you let Marx fill your brain with bread
because you saw through the slogans
to the white heat at center. Hunger.
Because Lenin had laid the eucharist
on your fat Irish tongue
& someone had to say something,
starlings lived better than people,
& that someone, goddammit, was you,

with your nimbus of rage,
& your bullying
& the old song & dance
down at the shipyards in the black
before dawn, BROTHERS,
IT'S ANOTHER DAY,
& WE CAN CHOOSE—
WE CAN THROW DOWN OUR CHAINS,
OR WE CAN WALK THROUGH THAT GATE

59

& KISS ENGLISH ASS FOR FIVE BOB A DAY,

& WHAT I'M ASKING YOU IS
HOW LONG WILL YOU SWEAT
TO FEED THE BOSSES
INSTEAD OF YOUR OWN CHILDREN,
HOW LONG WILL YOU GO DOWN
ON YOUR HANDS & KNEES
& LET THEM EAT OFF YOUR BACKS,
WHEN YOU'RE MEN, FOR CHRIST'S SAKE,
& MEN CAN RISE UP & TAKE WHAT'S THEIRS, IT'S
YOUR BACK, YOUR SWEAT,
WHAT ELSE DO YOU OWN?

4.　　And every morning they walked
through the gates. And every
morning, you followed:
the factory horns down river
scattering the dust
of the lost revolution, the sun
still not up, & what was left
of the moon flaking belly-up
into light on the river
your last days in the world.

5.　　Saltcoats, Red Clydeside,
the Gorbels, Ardrossen . . .
Your places forget everyone.

Even the fog looming off Arran
no longer contains you.
Nor the gaffers in Lonnie's,
hunched over their pints
or dragging their dusty lungs

60

home to the wife,

though one of them
must have known you, must
have seen your fumes
rise that morning
out the crematory chimney
into the blue planks of light
angling through the clouds—
where the dead,
that proletariat of last breaths,
gathered you in their vast arms
as one of them.

6.   Yes. To believe that.
To imagine your smoke fanning over the streets, lifting
to a final palavering of heroes
& fizzle of Celtic twilight, while miles below
the Clyde slides seaward
dreaming its tired dream
of the Atlantic Ocean. . . .

Though there's nothing in that dream
for either of us.
I crouch over your death
as if it were a text
from the other world:
but all I can read is smoke,
the stink of cigarettes & onions,
the breath of an old man
who wants only to crumble & blow away
without white light
or churning upwards to God
or a single moment of silence

to bear witness—

only the earth, going on
anyway—the grass,
the sparrow-choked cypresses,
the air itself, teeming.

7.   Sometimes, while shaving, I see it
moving beneath the bones of my face.
Lousy lungs & lousy politics, bad news
mailed from your life to mine,
there, in the bathroom mirror,
your face:

a durable, ordinary object
in someone's Russian novel,
& it's near the end of the story
& we've finally caught on
that all the characters
are the same person, the separate lives
braiding to a common death, a brotherhood;
that the troika riding all night
with a message from the Tzarina
summoning you to Petersburg
is a message from you,

to you—Look: how the horses' hooves
send up flowers of snow, the waxed
runners sighing under the weight
of the snotty-nosed driver
who takes another heft of vodka
as he passes the house of the village priest,
the priest tickling his wife
behind the knees as she bends over the table

with his bowl of supper, the snow
swirling at the window & the sound
of horse bells, the sound
of a troika rushing past.

8.　　This then:
a postcard you sent me
from Edinburgh of a fifteenth-century
engraving of the crucifixion. In it
the Cross has become a tree
whose branches bend low
with all manner of fruit.
On the right, two men
quarrel over the same branch,
both of them straining
to reach higher than the other.
While on the left, a monk
holds a branch down
so the woman beside him
can pick a pomegranate.
And in the middle,
two well-fed cherubim
climb toward the dead Christ,
Who hangs frowning & finally bereft
of that urge to live
His death feeds,
while further out, on the branch
He hangs from, a dark-throated bird
roosts & sings.

Grandfather,
I want to be that bird.